SOCIAL STRUCTURE
and AGING:
Psychological Processes

SOCIAL STRUCTURE and AGING:
Psychological Processes

Editors

K. Warner Schaie
The Pennsylvania State University

Carmi Schooler
National Institute of Health

Ψ Psychology Press
Taylor & Francis Group

New York London

First Published by
Lawrence Erlbaum Associates, Inc., Publishers
365 Broadway
Hillsdale, New Jersey 07642

Transferred to Digital Printing 2009 by Psychology Press
270 Madison Avenue, New York NY 10016
27 Church Road, Hove, East Sussex BN3 2FA

Library of Congress Cataloging-in-Publication Data
Social structure and aging.

Bibliography: p.
Includes index.
1. Aging—Social aspects—United States—Congresses.
2. Aging—Psychological aspects—Congresses.
3. Life cycle, Human—Social aspects—Congresses.
I. Schaie, K. Warner (Klaus Warner), 1928- .
II. Schooler, Carmi.
HQ1064. U5S598 1989   305.2′6′0973   87-33209
ISBN 0-8058-0093-X

Publisher's Note
The publisher has gone to great lengths to ensure the quality
of this reprint but points out that some imperfections in the
original may be apparent.

Contents

DISCUSSIONS OF CHAPTER 3

4

DISCUSSIONS OF CHAPTER 4

DISCUSSION OF CHAPTER 6

Contributors

Ronald P. Abeles, PhD, Behavioral and Social Research, National Institute on Aging, Building 31C, Room 4C 32, 9000 Rockville Pike, Bethesda, MD 20892

Robert C. Atchley, PhD, The Scripps Foundation, 354 Hoyt Library, Miami University of Ohio, Oxford, OH 45056

Uri Bronfenbrenner, PhD, Department of Human Development and Family Studies, Martha Van Rensselaer Hall, Cornell University, Ithaca, NY 14853

David L. Featherman, PhD, Institute on Aging, University of Wisconsin, 1180 Observatory Drive, Madison, WI 53706

Robert Glaser, PhD, Learning Research and Development Center, University of Pittsburgh, 3939 O'Hara, Pittsburgh, PA 15260

James S. House, PhD, Institute of Social Research, The University of Michigan, Ann Arbor, MI 48106

Daniel P. Keating, PhD, Department of Special Education, The Ontario Institute for Studies in Education, 252 Bloor Street West, Toronto, Ontario, M5S1V6

Melvin L. Kohn, PhD, Department of Sociology, The Johns Hopkins University, Baltimore, MA 21218

Margie E. Lachman, PhD, Department of Psychology, Brandeis University, Waltham, MA 02254

M. Powell Lawton, PhD, Philadelphia Geriatric Center, 5301 Old York Road, Philadelphia, PA 19141

George C. Myers, PhD, Department of Sociology, Duke University, Durham, NC 27703

Matilda White Riley, PhD, National Institute on Aging, Building 31, Room 5C 27, 9000 Rockville Pike, Bethesda, MD 20892

Alice S. Rossi, PhD, Department of Sociology, University of Massachusetts, Amherst, MA 01003

Timothy A. Salthouse, PhD, School of Psychology, Georgia Institute of Technology, Atlanta, GA 30332

K. Warner Schaie, PhD, Gerontology Center, S-210 Henderson Human Development Building, The Pennsylvania State University, University Park, PA 16802

Carmi Schooler, PhD, National Institute of Health, B1A14 Federal Building, 7550 Wisconsin Avenue, Bethesda, MD, 20892

Kenneth M. Weiss, PhD, Department of Anthropology, 309 Carpenter Building, The Pennsylvania State University, University Park, PA 16802

Susan Krauss Whitbourne, PhD, Department of Psychology, University of Massachusetts, Amherst, MA 01003

Sherry L. Willis, PhD, Department of Individual and Family Studies, S-110 Human Development Building, The Pennsylvania State University, University Park, PA 16802

Foreword
Why This Book?

Matilda White Riley
National Institute on Aging

A law enacted by Congress in mid-October 1986 symbolizes the changes of concern to us in this book. Congress voted that employers can no longer require workers to retire when they reach age 70 (with certain exceptions such as police officers and college professors). As Senator Heinz put it, this act does not end discrimination, but it does "guarantee freedom of choice, and sends strong messages to older workers that we do value their contributions" (*New York Times*, October 18,1986). In itself, of course, the act will affect only small numbers of people. But it may well portend a reversal of the century-long decline in labor force participation of men over 65.

Today we can look upon the act as a change in social structure made possible by psychological changes in attitudes of members of more recent cohorts. These changes precipitate ways in which some people will now spend their later years. The act illustrates the dialectical relationship implicit in the topic before us: social structure and the phychological aging processes.

On behalf of all participants in the conference on social structure and aging, from which this book results, I want to express appreciation to Pennsylania State University and to Warner Schaie in collaboration with Carmi Schooler for giving us the opportunity to discuss this topic. This book is the first in a series that will be adapted from conferences on biological as well as social and psychological aging. The conference grew out of several planning meetings of the Social Science Research Council. Those meetings were built on some 10 years of work done by the Council's Committee on Life–Course Perspectives (of which I was chairman and in which

Ronald Abeles and several of us at the conference were involved). Thus, we do not approach our topic de novo; rather, we are engaged in a scientific effort that has been and continues to be cumulative.

Our major *objective* within this series is to improve understanding of aging over the life course through:

- Integrated conceptualizations that will bring together the relevant disciplines.
- Research agenda that will lead to greater specification and clarification.
- Improved methods that will be used for conducting the needed research.
- Development of a knowledge base that will guide public policy and professional practice.

In pursuit of this objective to enhance the scientific understanding of aging, our Social Science Research Council Planning Committee called for a series of conferences that would *view life-course development as interdependent with social structure and social change*. Three sets of interrelated variables were identified:

1. Processes of *aging* (or development)—that is, aspects of the ways in which people grow older biologically, psychologically, and socially.

2. Age-related *social structures* and social changes—that include (a) *roles* (e.g., work roles, political roles) with their associated expectations, facilities, and rewards or punishments; (b) *values* that are built into these structures (i.e., standards of what is true, good, beautiful); and (c) *other people* who interact and are interrelated within these structures.

3. *Linkages*—that is, mechanisms that link aging processes with changing social structures. Such mechanisms may be (a) psychological (e.g., coping, self-esteem, sense of personal control); (b) biological (e.g., changes in neural, sensorimotor, endocrine, immunological and other physiological systems that can impact directly on the aging process); and (c) social (e.g., supportive or hostile relationships, opportunities or constraints affecting productive performance).

The planned series of books taken from these conferences thus focus on the nature of the interdependence among these three sets of variables.

For our deliberations here in this first book—with our selected focus on the relationship between psychological aging processes and social structures—I see a twofold challenge: first, to *specify* these relationships and be done with abstract and global statements; second, to recognize the relationships as one of *dialectical interdependence* — that is, to recognize that social structure is both cause and consequence of psychological aging processes.

In regard to the first challenge, *specification* of the relationship, we all look forward to reports of current research work. Many scholars who have already made early contributions are with us today. For example, Warner Schaie and Sherry Willis have taught us a great deal about *what* psychological aging processes result in optimal performance in old age. Melvin Kohn and Carmi Schooler have show *what* aspects of social structure lead to enhanced functioning. Alice Rossi has described *what* aspects of family structure relate to individual development, and so on. We need only read the table of contents to recognize the many contributions that address this first challenge of specifying *what* aspects of social structure relate to *what* aspects of psychological aging processes and of formulating testable hypotheses about the connecting *linkages*.

Even more exciting, I believe, (although this is often overlooked) is my second challenge: to recognize and clarify the *dialectical interdependence* between social structure and psychological aging processes. This requires that we examine over time the interplay between aging individuals who are influenced *by* social structure and social structures that are *constructed*, as well as changed, by aging individuals. For example, the recent legislation abolishing mandatory retirement, a structural change, might be attributed to a shift in the predominant patterns of psychological aging — that is, a shift from a passive to an active orientation, from a widespread willingness for disengagement to a growing assertion of personal control. This and similar structural changes could markedly alter patterns of aging in the future. As one instance of such change, imagine what it would mean if older people were no longer stereotyped as universally incompetent! (not a trivial suggestion).

With these challenges in mind, the work resulting in this book constitutes an important beginning toward guiding future changes. This book like those to follow, can help us formulate clearly specified hypotheses and examine them from the differing perspectives of multiple disciplines. I am proud to have participated in and opened the conference at Pennsylvania State University not only on behalf of the Social Science Research Council's Planning Committee but also for the National Institute on Aging, which supports such interdisciplinary work.

Introduction:
Social Structure and Behavior

K. Warner Schaie
Pennsylvania State University

Over the past several years, there have been increasing efforts by a small group of developmental psychologists and sociologists to conduct a series of dialogues in order to conceptualize more satisfying ways of bridging the reciprocal relationship between changes in social macro- and microstructures and the process of psychological development that concern issues of human aging (e.g., Schooler & Schaie, in press). Our purpose in this book is to see whether we can expedite these efforts by examing in some detail the various ways in which societal structures and psychological aging processes intermesh. My introductory remarks have three objectives: First, I would like to orient our reading audience to some salient issues that we discussed at the conference on social structure and psychological aging processes. Second, I would like to present a brief examplar from my own work to show how the interface of social structures and behavior becomes apparent in the work of at least one psychologist. Third, I would like at the very outset of this book to make some advance comments on the nature of new research paradigms that, I believe, will be needed to advance our efforts in testing specific propositions that will elucidate the reciprocal relationship between societal and individual development.

PRIMARY ISSUES AND GOALS
OF THE BOOK

In the series of proposed conferences, from which this is the first book

1

to result, we discuss different aspects of the relation between social structures and adult development. Our particular objective in this first book is to focus specifically on the kinds of structural variables that demographers and social psychologists believe to be important indicators of the societal dimensions that constrain individual behavior. In the past two decades, we have seen the development of a substantial body of knowledge regarding the psychological processes involved in human aging. Before this information can be applied with confidence for the purposes of primary prevention or public policy decisions, there are a number of issues that require resolution. Much of the behavioral work has been conducted in studies that used samples of convenience, which calls into question the external validity (generalizability) of the findings. Laboratory and field studies, moreover, have shown that these processes are highly individuated and that the occurrence and magnitude of behavioral age decrements may be affected by many environmental circumstances and population characteristics. In addition, there is evidence to suggest that changes in social structure occurring over time also impact behavioral consequences for the aging individual.

We now need to develop systematic approaches to apply our knowledge of those aspects of social structure likely to affect individual behavior to the design and interpretation of empirical investigations in the behavioral sciences. Such an effort would require the interaction of behavioral and social scientists for the purpose of forging interfaces between their often divergent conceptual approaches. This interaction would permit tests of explicit and generalizable propositions regarding the impact of social structures upon the human aging process. In addition to raising the level of awareness of behavioral and social scientists to these issues, we hope that the development of models for more policy-relevant behavioral science research on human aging will be a concrete outcome.

Our primary goal is to take a serious stab at conceptualizing the manner in which social structures impact upon adult psychological development. Of particular interest is the development of paradigms that operationalize structural dimensions in a manner that would permit differential outcome predictions for individual psychological development. To achieve our goal, we encourage readers to examine the particular macro- and microstructures discussed in this book with respect to their differential impact upon particular psychological processes in adulthood.

In order to contribute toward a break from the traditional static view of the role of environmental influences taken by many researchers, we encourage conceptualizations that emphasize the manner in which *changes* in social structure might impact upon psychological processes. Requisite data bases with respect to the dependent variables available over sufficiently long time spans are currently available only for fairly limited psychological domains. That is why we have commissioned some detailed analyses with respect to a few sample cases (intellectual abilities, personality, and interpersonal behavior), and we have also encouraged speculative essays that might encourage work in other domains where existant data bases are still quite limited.

At the level of microstructures, we would like to emphasize the examination of detailed analyses of the work place, the home, the school, the institution, or any other particular environment thought to impact psychological outcomes differentially by age or cohort membership. Our effort begins with a review of existing situational taxonomies that have addressed or could address age- or cohort-related developmental issues. Such taxonomies are then related to behavioral outcomes, and attempts are made to identify the nature of the dimensions underlying the categories that best predict individual behavior.

AN EXEMPLAR OF THE INTERFACE
OF STRUCTURE AND BEHAVIOR

The example I consider comes from my work on adult intellectual development and relates to the impact of the cohort flow in certain demographic characteristics upon age-related changes in cognitive performance. Later in this book, Sherry Willis examines the sample case of adult cognitive development in more detail. Here I paint a very broad picture to set the scene for our further discussions.

In recent years, we have seen extensive discussions by life-span oriented developmental psychologists devoted to the importance of context in the study of behavioral development (e.g., Baltes, Cornelius, & Nesselroade, 1979; Bronfenbrenner, 1979; Schaie, 1978, 1982a, 1986b; Willis, 1985). The initial thrust of such discussions was directed primarily to the question of how laboratory studies could be generalized to field situations, or how information gleaned from nonrepresentative convenience samples could be applied to broader populations and policy issues. More recently, however, the focus of concern was shifted to the more fundamental question of whether contextual parameters, usually defined as social structures, have direct causal impact on the direction and rate of behavioral development (cf. Gribbin, Schaie, & Parham, 1980; Stone, 1980). A related issue is whether changes in the population parameters for selected developmental processes may in turn have direct consequences for changes in social structure. There is a paucity of empirical studies in which psychologists have explicitly included social context as part of their experimental design. Perhaps the most noteworthy substantive area in which, at least, a beginning has been made is the study of age changes and age differences in adult cognitive development (cf. Schaie & Willis, 1984).

The major structural context that has been investigated by developmental psychologists is the effect of birth-cohort membership upon cognitive performance with advancing age (cf. Schaie, 1984a, 1986a; Schaie & Hertzog, 1986). In addition, differential structural attributes of successive birth cohorts with respect to the distribution of educational characteristics, income, and occupational and health status have been related to individual performance differences and to developmental trajectories for the ability domain. Some attention has in the past been given to the impact of health status, expressed also by specific disease entitities (Hertzog, Schaie, & Gribbin, 1978), and to the long-term effects of cognitive styles and family status (Gribbin et al., 1980; Schaie, 1984b).

My example comes from the Seattle Longitudinal Study (SLS), a multiwave panel study that uses as its population frame the membership of a metropolitan health maintenance organization (cf. Schaie, 1983). In this study, random samples of community-dwelling adults, ranging in age from the 20s to the 80s were sampled 7 years apart in 1956, 1963, 1970, 1977, and 1984. Study participants were assessed with measures of Thurstone's first five primary mental abilities (Schaie, 1985; Thurstone & Thurstone, 1941), and limited demographic information was also obtained. In our example, we restricted the discussion to four primary abilities:

1. *Verbal meaning*, the ability to comprehend words, a measure of recognition vocabulary.
2. *Spatial orientation*, the ability to mentally rotate objects in two-dimensional space.
3. *Inductive reasoning*, the ability to infer rules from examples that contain regular progressions of information.
4. *Number*, the ability to manipulate numerical concepts by checking simple addition problems.

What I discuss here are some broad features of the cohort progressions shown by our studies of these cognitive abilities. The design for our analyses of cohort differences represented an independent random sampling model in which each cohort at each age measured was assessed by means of a separate sample, thus being controlled for possible effects of testing, reactivity, and experimental mortality (Schaie, 1965, 1973, 1977). We obtained cohort difference estimates by taking the differences between observed means for each pair of cohorts at all common age levels then averaging across all estimates to avoid undue weighting in terms of differential sample sizes. Next we constructed cohort gradients by cumulating cohort difference estimates across the cohorts available for analysis.

Differences between successive cohorts as expressed in *T* score points (1/10 SD) were cumulated from the oldest cohort born in 1889 up to the most recently measured cohort born in 1959 for the four abilities of verbal meaning, spatial orientation, inductive reasoning, and number. These are presented in Fig. 1. Readers should focus on the differences in slope and shape of the cohort gradients for different abilities. *Inductive reasoning* comes closest to showing a linear positive cohort progression. Even here there are diversions from linearity, with relatively steep increments up to the 1931 cohort and far slower and decelerating increments thereafter. The most substantial pattern of positive increment across successive cohorts is shown by *verbal meaning*. After an initial modest dip, this ability rises until the 1924 birth cohort followed by another modest dip. This is followed by a further rise to an asymptote attained by the 1945 and 1952 cohorts, once again followed by another modest dip. *Spatial orientation* also shows a basically positive cohort progression, but with a much flatter and variable profile. This ability reaches an initial asymptote for the cohorts from 1910 to 1931. A further rise to a new peak occurs in 1938, which is followed by a drop to the earlier asymptote in 1952, but with recovery to the higher level by the most recent cohort. A very different pattern is shown for *number*. Here a peak above base is reached by the 1910 cohort at a level maintained through the 1924 cohort. Thereafter an almost linear negative slope is found that continues through the most recently observed cohort.

These data obviously suggest that previous discussions of the impact

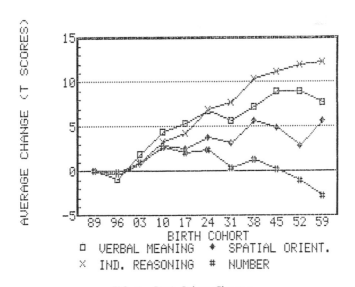

FIG. 1. PMA Cohort Changes

of cohort differences upon intellectual performance in adults have been too simplistic. It is no longer possible to hold that benign changes in health status, lifestyles, and education have a generalized positive effects that will inevitably lead each successive generation to reach an asymptote greater than that achieved by its predecessor. Instead, we note that cohort progressions occur at quite different rates for different abilities as well as display noncontinuous patterns. For some variables, positive cohort trends reverse even to the point that, over a wide range of cohorts, the most recent cohorts may perform at a level lower than that shown at equivalent ages observed for much older cohorts. It seems to follow then that changes in socialization patterns and other environmentally programmed experiences must differentially impact cohort progression as well (cf. Nesselroade, 1983; Schaie, 1984a, 1986a).

The observed differential cohort profiles now raise the question of whether we can identify contextual variables having differential impact on the abilities that we have studied and that also show differential cohort profiles. Figure 2 shows cohort patterns for several contextual variables. Those that seem most directly related to the crystallized abilities,

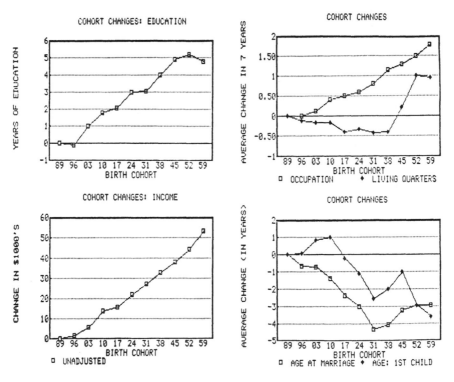

FIG. 2.

education and income, show almost linear positive cohort gradients, albeit less steep for education than for the inflation-confounded income measure. But just as for the ability measures, there are contextual variables having much more complex profiles. Frequency of occupational change, for example, actually declined slightly until the 1938 cohort but thereafter showed a steep rise; this is in contrast to our other mobility measure, change in living quarters, which showed a rising cohort trend throughout. Family status variables also show complex cohort patterns. Thus, age at first marriage steadily fell until the 1931 cohort, and has since been rising; whereas age of first child attained an initial peak for the 1910 cohort, then followed the pattern for age at first marriage but showed a steep drop for the most recent cohorts.

After considering the interrelation of ability and contextual variables, I contend that many irregularities in the cohort progression for the ability measures might be better understood if we examine shifts in contextual variables occurring over the same time periods (see also Gribbin et al., 1980) That is, some "stair-step" phenomena seen in ability cohort profiles may represent fluctuations in sampling and/or general population characteristics on contextual variables that constrain the distribution of individual differences on mental abilities. The question arises, of course, whether changes in the contextual parameters have been instrumental in leading to the observed shifts in cognitive performance levels, or whether changes in ability parameters have contributed to the shifts in contextual variables.

The data I present here suggest that there are substantial shifts in performance level for some but not all cognitive abilities across successive population cohorts. The magnitudes of such shifts are well within the range of reported age-related decline. We may conclude therefore, at least provisionally, that part of the disadvantage faced by older individuals when compared with their younger peers must be attributed to the fact that successive cohorts reached higher performance asymptotes. However, this particular disadvantage may be a temporary one, albeit of particular concern with respect to those now in the last third of their work life. That is, cohort progressions for those cognitive variables where they are most pronounced have clearly slowed, and in fact may be reversing for the late baby-boom cohorts. For some abilities, a negative cohort gradient has prevailed for several decades. Individuals reaching early old age in the next decade may therefore be at less disadvantage, or perhaps be advantaged with respect to the immediately succeeding cohorts (cf. Schaie, 1982b; Schaie & Willis, 1986a).

THE NEED FOR NEW PARADIGMS

The cohort differences in cognitive performance levels are paralleled, at least in our panels, by similar cohort differences in contextual exogenous and endogenous variables. It must now be asked whether cohort differences in demographic characteristics drive the observed cohort differences in mental abilities, or whether at least some observed demographic changes may actually have arisen as a consequence of genetic or environmentally determined shifts in ability level in the population (cf. Riegel, 1976). To the extent that such shifts are particularly prevalent at some ages but not at others, it might be argued that the cross-cohort shifts in ability may represent a population process à la Featherman (1985). Thus far our attempts at causal modeling of the relationship between contextual variables and mental abilities have resulted primarily in the fitting of models reciprocal in nature (Stone, 1980). However, there are some exceptions: Significant paths have indeed been found for the endogenous variables of cardiovascular and arthritic disease (Stone, 1980) and for the exogenous variable of work complexity (Dutta, Schulenberg, & Lair, 1986).

I would like to speculate, nevertheless, that the substantial shifts in level and rate of cognitive performance in older adults may well result in substantial shifts in demographic indicators and other contextual indicators. For example, later maintenance of cognitive ability will induce more people to seek further education past young adulthood, with resultant age by cohort shifts in educational levels. Increasing numbers of middle-aged and older people via utilization of psychotherapy and other growth experiences are likely to enhance their level of flexibility. More able and flexible older people might seek greater work complexity (cf. Schooler, 1984) and be eligible for economically more rewarding pursuits, leading to shifts in the age by cohort occupational distributions as well as the occupational change distributions (Kohn & Schooler, 1983). Even the demonstration that much of the apparent intellectual adulthood may be experiential (cf. Schaie & Willis, 1986b) will lead to increased efforts on the part of community-dwelling elderly to seek out remedial and self-help programs. Nor should we disregard the effect upon public policy and resulting changes in environmental contexts that result from the efforts of scientists who demystify prevalent stereotypes about the aging process.

Our lack of success in explicating the specific contextual variables that may be implicated in cohort differences and age changes in mental ability or other psychological variables must be attributed to the fact that we have yet to formulate sufficiently specific hypothesis that can be tested in carefully described subsets of the broader population. In addition, we have yet to understand fully the impact of the lagged occurrence of demographic shifts, their consequences for psychological development, and possibly the resultant shifts in the demographic characteristics having affected the behavioral processes in the first place.

Traditional analyses of psychological processes as outcome variables tend to emphasize the identification and quantification of the relation between structural independent variables and occurrence of individual behavior at a single point in time. By contrast, we would like to concentrate upon issues related to the differential prediction of outcomes of behavioral processes occurring from young adulthood into old age. Particular attention should, of course, be given also to linking theoretically well-grounded models of psychological variables that have either developmental implications or lend themselves more readily to build interfaces with the well-researched attributes of social structure.

As we read the detailed presentations and discussions in this book, it is my hope that we pay close attention to the design requirements, which allow us to address the questions I have posed. Indeed, I hope that this will prove instrumental in spawning the kind of interdisciplinary efforts that will provide the new research paradigms to move us forward to a more explicit study of the fascinating but frustratingly complex interface between social context and individual development.

REFERENCES

Baltes, P. B., Cornelius, S. W., & Nesselroade, J. R. (1979). Cohort effects in developmental psychology. In J. R. Nesselroade & P. B. Baltes (Eds.), *Longitudinal research in the study of behavior and development* (pp. 61–87). New York: Academic Press.

Bronfenbrenner, U. (1979). *The ecology of human development.* Cambridge, MA: Harvard University Press.

Dutta, R., Schulenberg, J. E., & Lair, T. J. (1986, April). *The effect of job characteristics on cognitive abilities and intellectual flexibility.* Paper presented at the annual meeting of the Eastern Psychological Association, New York.

Featherman, D. L. (1985). Individual development and aging as a population process. In J. R. Nesselroade & A. von Eye (Eds.), *Individual development and social change: Explanatory analysis* (pp. 213–241). New York: Academic Press.

Gribbin, K., Schaie, K. W., & Parham, I. A. (1980). Complexity of life style and maintenance of intellectual abilities. *Journal of Social Issues, 36,* 47–61.

Hertzog, C., Schaie, K. W., & Gribbin, K. (1978). Cardiovascular disease and changes in intellectual functioning from middle to old age. *Journal of Gerontology, 33,* 848–857.

Kohn, M. L., & Schooler, C. (1983). *Work and personality: An inquiry into the impact of social stratification.* Norwood, NJ: Ablex.

Nesselroade, J. R. (1983). Temporal selection and factor invariance in the study of development and change. In P. B. Baltes & O. G. Brim, Jr. (Eds.), *Life-span development and behavior* (Vol. 5, pp. 60–87). New York: Academic Press.

Riegel, K. F. (1976). *Psychology of development and history.* New York: Plenum.

Schaie, K. W. (1965). A general model for the study of developmental problems. *Psychological Bulletin, 64,* 91–107.

Schaie, K. W. (1973). Methodological problems in descriptive developmental research on adulthood and aging. In J. R. Nesselroade & H. W. Reese (Eds.), *Life-span developmental psychology: Methodological issues* (pp. 253–280). New York: Academic Press.

Schaie, K. W. (1977). Quasi-experimental designs in the psychology of aging. In J. E. Birren & K. W. Schaie (Eds.), *Handbook of the psychology of aging* (pp. 39–58). New York: Van Nostrand Reinhold.

Schaie, K. W. (1978). External validity in the assessment of intellectual development in adulthood. *Journal of Gerontology, 33,* 695–671.

Schaie, K. W. (1982a). Longitudinal data sets: Evidence for ontogenetic development or chronicles of cultural change? *Journal of Social Issues, 38,* 65–72.

Schaie, K. W. (1982b). The aging in the coming decade. In K. W. Schaie & J. Geiwitz (Eds.), *Readings in adult development* (pp. 3–11). Boston: Little, Brown.

Schaie, K. W. (1983). The Seattle Longitudinal Study: A twenty-one year exploration of psychometric intelligence in adulthood. In K. W. Schaie (Ed.), *Longitudinal studies of adult psychological development* (pp. 64–135). New York: Guilford.

Schaie, K. W. (1984a). Historical time and cohort effects. In K. A. McCloskey & H. W. Reese (Eds.), *Life-span developmental psychology: Historical and generational effects* (pp. 1–15). New York: Academic Press.

Schaie, K. W. (1984b). Midlife influences upon intellectual functioning in old age. *International Journal of Behavioral Development, 7,* 463–478.

Schaie, K. W. (1985). *Manual for the Schaie-Thurstone Test of Adult Mental Abilities (STAMAT).* Palo Alto, CA: Consulting Psychologists Press.

Schaie, K. W. (1986a). Beyond calendar definitions of age, time and cohort: The general developmental model revisited. *Developmental Review, 6,* 252–277.

Schaie, K. W. (1986b, September). *Social context and cognitive performance in old age.* Paper presented at the annual meeting of the American Sociological Association, New York.

Schaie, K. W., & Hertzog, C. (1986). Toward a comprehensive model of adult intellectual development: Contributions of the Seattle Longitudinal Study. In R. J. Sternberg (Ed.), *Advances in human intelligence* (Vol 3, pp. 79–118). New York: Academic Press.

Schaie, K. W., & Willis, S. L. (1984, September). *The role of cohort analysis in psychological research: The case of intellectual abilities, obsolescence and retraining.* Paper presented at the annual meeting of the American Sociological Association, San Antonio, TX.

Schaie, K. W., & Willis, S. L. (1986a). *Adult development and aging* (2nd ed.). Boston: Little, Brown.

Schaie, K. W., & Willis, S. L. (1986b). Can intellectual decline in the elderly be reversed? *Developmental Psychology, 22,* 223–232.

Schooler, C. (1984). Psychological effects of complex environments during the life span: A review and theory. *Intelligence, 8,* 259–281.

Schooler, C., & Schaie, K. W. (Eds.). (1987). *Social structures and cognitive processes over the life span.* Norwood, NJ: Ablex.

Stone, V. (1980). *Structural modeling of the relations among environmental variables, health status and intelligence in adulthood.* Unpublished doctoral dissertation, University of Southern California, Los Angeles.

Thurstone, L. L., & Thurstone, T. G. (1941). *Factorial studies of intelligence.* Chicago: University of Chicago Press.

Willis, S. L. (1985). Towards an educational psychology of the adult learner: Cognitive and intellectual bases. In J. E. Birren & K. W. Schaie (Eds.), *Handbook of the psychology of aging* (2nd ed., pp. 818–847). New York: Van Nostrand Reinhold.

Demographic Factors and Adult Psychological Development

Robert C. Atchley
Scripps Gerontology Center,
Miami University

In developing this chapter, I took the editors at their word. They asked me to take a conceptual, speculative look at how demographic paradigms might help us understand the social structural context within which adult development takes place and how demographic change might affect adult development. Accordingly, I do not take a highly controlled and technique-oriented approach to demography but instead use demographic and human development perspectives to paint with a broad brush.

The purpose of this chapter is not so much to answer questions as to sketch out a large arena within which creative questions can be asked. I do not attempt to address all areas of either demography or adult development. My goal is *not* to review the literature in either area but instead to provide a synthesis of my own ideas, with all due respect to the notion attributed to the late Louis Wirth: "You show me a person with a new idea and I'll show you a person with a poor memory."

The chapter is organized into three sections: (a) demographic effects on adult development, (b) demographic differentials in the group context within which adult development takes place, and (c) demographic changes that might influence adult development.

DEMOGRAPHIC INFLUENCES ON ADULT DEVELOPMENT

The *demographic perspective* deals with population size, composition (proportional distribution of individual attributes such as age, sex, occupation, or living arrangements), and geographic distribution; and how these structural aspects of a population are altered by fertility, mortality and morbidity, migration, and social mobility (change in social position). *Population Studies Perspective* is a broader area of inquiry that brings the contributions of a wide variety of disciplines to bear on our understanding of the demographic factors (Hauser & Duncan, 1959). The population studies perspective emphasizes that demographic factors are best understood in a context that includes the social, political, and economic evolution of the society whose population we are investigating. This chapter is based entirely on the situation in the United States, and I have serious reservations about the extent to which any of my ideas apply to other cultures.

The *adult development perspective* concerns the psychological evolution of the individual from the time he or she reaches the socially defined beginning of adulthood to the end of the human life span. As used here, the word *development* implies neither contraction nor expansion but merely the cumulative response to one's life history. Individual development involves the acquisition and accumulation of *ideas*, which we often differentiate into knowledge, attitudes, values, beliefs and ideologies, and *psychological skills*, to which we apply labels such as intelligence, learning, memory, creativity, thinking, problem solving, and coping. Further, the developmental perspective looks at the mind and its various dimensions as an evolving whole. This evolutionary perspective is useful for us to gain insights into the effects of aging on the interaction between the individual's mental processes, subjective experiences, and adaptive strategies on the one hand and his or her social environment on the other (Atchley, 1983).

Demographic effects on adult development can be both direct and indirect. For example, the size of one's birth cohort directly influences the social context within which adult development takes place. Because peer groups are age graded and limited to a size that will allow face-to-face communication, as the size of an age cohort increases the larger the number of peer groups to be found within it, the greater the diversity of behavioral norms across peer groups, and the lower the sense of identity with the entire cohort (Mott, 1965). All these factors can influence which skills are reinforced and which are not. On the other hand, cohort size indirectly influences occupational development through its effect on the amount of competition within an occupational area. The degree of job competition in turn may influence the priorities given to various developmental issues. This topic needs further research.

I discuss demographic effects on the development of cognitive skills, cognitive content, and personality throughout adulthood. Again, I provide a mere sampling of the *types* of ideas that can come from bringing demographic perspectives to bear rather than an exhaustive (and probably exhaust*ing*) compilation.

Cognitive Skills

Cognitive skills must be learned, and much of what we refer to as "higher cognitive processes" are learned in adulthood, particularly the judicious application of cognitive abilities in practical arenas. Population size, diversity, and distribution all affect the *quality* of the environment within which cognitive skills are acquired. For example, Coleman (1966) noted that the absence of middle-class, achievement-oriented children in inner-city schools was the major factor accounting for the poor performance of inner-city students, much more important than the preparation of their teachers or the amount of funds spent on school buildings or supplies. Thus, the size of urban communities fosters the development of class-homogeneous residential enclaves in such a way that middle-class students, already advantaged by the richness of their home environments, gain greater advantage in school; whereas school has much less capacity to alter the life chances of the children from inner-city ghettos. By contrast, in communities of 50,000 people or less, residential segregation is much less likely to result in class isolation by school. When everyone in a community goes to the same schools, then there is greater opportunity for working-class children to use middle-class children as role models, which in turn can have a dramatic effect on the cognitive skills they *aspire* to develop. Too little study has been made of the influence of class-based differential aspirations on eventual attainment of cognitive skills.

Demographic variables can also affect cognitive skills indirectly because of their effects on the educational system itself and because of communication through mass media. Basic skills such as reading, writing, speaking, arithmetic and mathematical reasoning, and critical thinking are lacking in many adults today. Although I do not minimize other influences, I believe that demographic factors played an important part in creating this situation. Easterlin (1980) has argued that the large numbers of children per household during the baby boom meant that families were able to provide less transmission of cognitive skills and information per child, compared to what was possible in earlier, smaller families. When the baby-boom cohorts entered the education system, their large numbers stretched and then broke down the capacity of schools to deliver effective basic education.

The explosion in demand for educators to teach the baby-boom cohorts occurred when the small birth cohorts of the depression years were entering the labor market. In the rapidly expanding economy of the 1960s, schools fared even more poorly than usual in competition for the "best and the brightest." Many who were hired by public school systems in the 1960s would have been rejected had it been a buyer's market. Colleges and universities had similar problems. The resulting dilution of quality in teaching was directly caused by rapidly fluctuating student cohort sizes.

If this line of reasoning is carried one step further, pressure from the baby-boom cohorts' need for formal education also retarded the development of formal educational programs to meet the needs of adults over age 25 who had to revitalize their skills to adapt to a changing society. Education for adults has generally been bypassed by public educational institutions, and most adult programs in public shools today emphasize adult basic education rather than an upgrading of job skills or a leisure education. Part of the reason for this goes back to the enormous resources required to attempt the education of the baby-boom cohorts. Likewise, the steady influx of newly trained baby boomers delayed employers' recognition of the need for periodic training of personnel to reinforce existing knowledge and skills or to provide new knowledge and skills. For example, most of my colleagues who have taken workshops on effective teaching agree that we probably need a refresher course about every 5 years, yet opportunities for such training are scarce. No doubt some part of our reluctance to provide adult education also stems from the widely held stereotype that mature adults are less able to learn.

Because many adults lack basic cognitive skills, we can expect pressures on public remedial programs in basic education to increase. In these programs, teachers need training in how best to teach these skills to people who are at varying levels of individual development.

Ironically, when the cohorts born in the 1930s and 1940s reach retirement age, retirement income prospects will probably be rosey, but employers may not be anxious to see these employees go if their verbal communication skills are perceived to be superior to those of the baby-boom cohorts who will replace them. If this perception occurs, we may see more employer incentives to retain employees beyond normal retirement age. Incidentally, if the baby boomers do not catch up to the cognitive skill level of the cohorts just preceding them, then the cross-sectional age data on cognition, expecially in areas such as vocabulary, should yield some interesting surprises.

The rapid growth and urbanization of the population which occurred after 1950 promoted the centralization of communication in America— national broadcast networks, wire services, magazines, and newspaper chains. Ironically the new forms of communication, although technologically superior to the old in terms of the volume and variety of information that they could pass, were short on a crucial quality: credibility. In a small community, most communications take place within a familiar

frame of reference and come from people we know, so we can confident-
ly assess their credibility. In the mass society, information bombards us
from all directions, and much of the time we do not have the intellectual
background necessary to understand it. How this affects cognitive skills
can be illustrated by the following metaphor.

> Imagine yourself in a room seated at a large table piled with pieces of a
> gigantic jigsaw puzzle. A funnel above your head is pouring more pieces
> on the table faster than you can sort them, let alone fit them. You note that
> the pieces are of different colors and textures, and do not belong to the
> same jigsaw puzzle. You feel that you haven't time—perhaps never will have
> time—to "get it together." Getting it all together is a different kind of deci-
> sion than merely deciding what to do with a piece. Suppose that the puzzle
> you are trying to fit is the pattern, the very meaning of your life. Then too
> many bits pouring in faster than one could make sense of them would mean
> being endlessly suspended in judgement and restricted to superficial facts,
> unable to develop a coherent and profound life philosophy—cheated of
> meaning. (Klapp, 1978, p.55)

Therefore, all American adults, especially those who are part of a highly
mobile urban society, must develop skill in dealing with information overload and communication "noise"—messages they haven't the tools to de-
code. Research is needed on the mechanisms people use. The task of
dealing with information chaos gets more difficult as the population density of the locality where one lives increases because as population increases, the number of subgroups within the population increases, the
norms vary more widely across subgroups, and the deviations from norms
become more common (Mott, 1965). As a result, widely shared norms
decline as a basis for "getting it together."

Cognitive Content

In this section, we look first at demographic effects on ideas in general
then turn to the life course. Demographic factors influence not only our
mental skills but also the substantive content of our minds: our ideas. Ideas
can be classified in numerous ways. Attitudes are our predispositions to
like or dislike particular things. Values are our abstract conceptions of
relative desirability (Rosenberg, 1965). Beliefs are our notions of what is
true. Ideologies are systems of "interdependent ideas (beliefs, traditions,
principles, and myths) held by a social group or society, which reflects,
rationalizes, and defends its particular social, moral, political, and economic interests" (Theodorson & Theodorson, 1969, p. 195). The content
of these various kinds of ideas for a particular adult is in part determined

by the size of the population in the locality where the person lives, the socioeconomic attributes of the person and his or her family, and his or her region of residence and migration history—all demographic factors.

In American society, as the *size* of the community increases so does the degree of cultural pluralism. Urban centers have large diversified economies, numerous religions and ethnic groups, multiple political jurisdictions, varied social status of neighborhoods, and cosmopolitan population. Pluralism is tolerated, and social control through conformity to community opinion is reduced. As a result, adults in large urban areas have opportunity for exposure to a wider range of ideas compared to their small town counterparts. The downside of this freedom is that the anonymity of the city can also be alienating. One may be freer in the city, but the cost may be the sacrifice of a security that comes from identification with a group. Identity with a group means that the individual member can adopt the group's ideas, which relieves the individual from much of the burden of choice. In a metropolis, the adult may not find a single group with which to identify. Instead, city people tend to compartmentalize their ideas and use one set at work, another at home, another at play, and yet another out in the community. The potential for internal conflict among ideas is increased when individuals have few relationships that cross multiple environmental boundaries. Compartmentalization is much less common in small towns. Much of our research in adult development seems to imply that the specific situation does not affect mental ability, but our everyday observations do not support this assumption (Salthouse, 1982). Environments vary enormously in the demands they place on our cognitive capacities, and access to a variety of environments is related to population size and density.

Region of residence (related to population distribution) also affects the content of one's mind. Contrary to the myth that television has homogenized American culture, regional subcultures are alive and well. For example, if we look at ideology with respect to life course, family, work, and politics, there are vast differences among South Carolina, California, Minnesota, Texas, and Massachusetts. Yet we know little of the effects of these regional variations on adult development.

Migration history can also have a profound impact on the content of ideas. Most adults live out their adulthood within a relatively small geographic area. This means, of course, that their pool of ideas used to structure everyday life remains relatively consistent compared to people who move often. Nonmigrants also have the opportunity to develop relationships of extended duration, which tends to reinforce and encourage a consistent framework of ideas over the life span.

Migration tends to be quite common in young adulthood, and relationships outside the family tend to be of relatively short duration. Because the pool of ideas differs across metropolitan areas, migrant young adults are often presented with conflicting and confusing ideas. Having an adequate definition of the situation upon which to make choices is important to psychological security, and people who change localities often may have more difficulty forming an adequate definition of the situation compared with others. Developmental implications of this sort of amgibuity are largely unexplored.

Migration is strongly related to the life course. In young adulthood, migration rates tend to be high, with about 66% of the population making a residential move during their 20s. About 20% of young adults are chronic movers, making moves every few years throughout their young adulthood, often over great distances. The psychological demands of high geographic mobility are reduced somewhat by the development of a "culture of moving" that is shared by chronic movers. They tend to seek each other out and to provide social support to one another. However, the social support one can get from relative strangers may be qualitatively different from the support possible within a long-standing social network. Thus, we would expect chronic migrants to have difficulty in identifying a body of ideas connected with their "roots." This idea needs to be tested.

The lower migration rates associated with middle age provide much more opportunity for solidifying one's personal structure of ideas. Having children and community ties accounts for much of this residential stability (Sandefur, 1985). The cultural milieu remains relatively consistent (at least compared to the multiple environments migrants face); and relationships that reinforce and support one's personal constructs (Kelley, 1955) tend to be more personalized, less connected to stereotyped roles, of longer duration, and therefore of greater depth, all of which support stability of idea structures (Atchley, 1983).

The empty nest and retirement free people to move. A relatively small proportion of people actually move in response to retirement, and those who voluntarily move tend to be people looking for new ideas or for areas where they feel sure the climate of ideas will be compatible with theirs (Bultena & Wood, 1969; Longino, 1981). On the other hand, increased dependency needs can produce involuntary moves that challenge individuals to cope with a vastly different environment of ideas than they are accustomed to. Although most adult offspring willingly care for their parents, the dependency relationship requires a dramatic shift in one's social ideology of living arrangements. Even when older parents are relatively independent, they often have to move to an unfamiliar community in order to be near the family on which they rely for support. Coping with a new and complex environment of ideas and people is invigorating to some but taxing to most. As long as the individual is predominately independent, selective interaction can minimize psychological discontinuities.

However, moving to an institution is a substantial change that usually strains the individual's capacity to assimilate new ideas. Thus, adjusting to an institution could be expected to take much longer than adjusting to a new community, which could be expected to take longer than adjusting to a new neighborhood within a familiar community. Here we are talking just about changes required in the individual's content and organization of ideas.

Thus, migration over the life span for many people produces opening and closing of the environment of ideas. Living in a nurturing family (notice that I did not say a "stable" family) provides the individual with a base of relatively durable ideas; gaining education and job experience opens the individual to a much larger body of ideas but also exposes her or him to more contradictions and conflicts; having residential stability typical of middle age promotes the consolidation and simplification of the individuals structure of ideas; acquiring the freedom of retirement opens opportunities to expand horizons; and entering into dependency and institutional residence imposes new, external idea structures and demands that the individual must assimilate and conform to.

Orrin Klapp (1978) provided an excellent heuristic framework for understanding and diagnosing the effects of migration on cognitive content. Of course, his framework can be used to understand psychological results of other types of change, too. Challenging the conventional wisdom that expansion is better than contraction, Klapp developed the idea that the healthy person sometimes needs to expand but at other times needs to contract. He used the terms *opening* and *closing*. Good opening, on the one hand, is exciting because it represents variety and new ideas that build on existing ones in seemingly innovative ways. Bad opening, on the other hand, results in information overload, confusion, inner conflict, and indecisiveness. Good closing is comfortable familiarity. It involves remembering and reinforcing idea structures that produce feelings of safety, security, rootedness, and belonging. Bad closing is redundancy of ideas to the point that they become banal and boring. To Klapp, the healthy individual responds to environmental conditions, such as migration, by opening or closing his or her idea structure to achieve a satisfying balance between the two. People also can be expected to avoid both bad closing and bad opening—both boredom and confusion. What may be most disconcerting about migration is that opening is uncontrolled and the individual does not yet know enough about the new area to perform good closing. This is another promising topic for research.

CONCEPTS OF LIFE COURSE

The term *life course* refers to an idealized and age-related progression or sequence of social roles and group memberships that individuals are expected to follow as they mature and move through life. In order to know *which* idealized schedule a particular individual is most likely to use in developing his or her projected life history, we must know the gender, social class, ethnicity, race, and other social characteristics of the person because there are hundreds of possible combinations, contingent on demographic characteristics (Atchley, 1975; Neugarten & Datan, 1973). In addition to the fact that the life-course definition used by the individual is his or her crude road map for finding a successful way through the maze of life's opportunities and constraints, the life-course perspective adopted by the individual will in turn have dramatic influence on choices and opportunities concerning specific roles, groups, and environments. Thus, life-course definitions and decisions can vary considerably, which potentially could have a profound influence on adult development; yet we have practically no descriptive research on these variations and their effects. The diverse demographic composition of the population translates into enormous diversity of life-course concepts and, therefore, life histories. Indeed, the multiplicity of possible routes makes the prediction of specific roles and relationships that we could expect healthy aged individuals to experience a practical impossibility. Instead of looking at specific roles, we might do better to look at decision points in the age structure.

PERSONALITY DEVELOPMENT

Healthy adult personality development requires that the individual be able to reconcile conflicts between his or her temperament, mental habits, and preferences, on the one hand, and external pressures from others that require the individual to behave and think in particular ways, on the other. Population size, cohort size, family situation, and labor force participation are all examples of demographic factors that can affect personality development in adulthood.

Population Size

As the population in one's immediate environment increases, norms become less clear cut, deviations from norms become more common, and feedback becomes less consistent. In order for a young adult to develop a healthy personality, he or she must have reasonably consistent feedback from others concerning the effectiveness of her or his performance. This feedback can then be used as a basis for adjustment. Lacking consistent feedback, the individual can be left confused and alienated. Most people resolve this problem by developing a peer group made up of persons who share values and provide support for one's performance.

In young adulthood, the composition of support groups often changes rapidly, both because a great deal of geographic mobility occurs during this life stage and because each individual is evolving and changing. In middle adulthood, support groups tend to be more stable, therefore feedback tends to reinforce and crystallize the external aspects of personality (Neugarten, 1977). In later adulthood, mortality causes attrition in the support group. Fortunately, a healthy personality, once developed, does not require as much social support so long as the environment remains familiar and predictable. But migration in later life to a new community or to an institution can cause the need for new feedback, and difficulty in forming new friendships may hamper the person's capacity to use a support group to get the needed feedback. Much overconformity that has been observed in older adults may stem from these factors combined with a densely populated, heterogenous, and unfamiliar environment. All these topics deserve research.

On the other hand, the lack of clear-cut behavioral norms in large, densely populated areas can be an advantage to adults who have mastered the basic activities of daily living to the point that they are fully functional, independent adults. They can then use their routine satisfactory performance as a secure platform from which to explore more personalized areas of development. For example, reaching a comfortable job plateau in middle age can free a person to devote time and energy to more artistic or expressive aspects of his or her personality. We expect that tolerance of such a change would be greater in a large urban area than in a small town where continuity and conformity are more expected and more noticeable. Again, these ideas need to be tested.

Cohort Size

The size of one's birth cohort, compared to those preceding or following it, can have a marked influence on the age at which full adulthood is attained. When the cohort is large compared to the job market, then leaving home and becoming an independent adult tends to be delayed. If, as Kohlberg (1973) contended, the moral development of young people requires principled thinking that arises from their experience of sustained responsibility for others' welfare and their experience of having to make irreversible choices, then delayed entry into full adulthood can postpone important aspects of personality development. Since 1975, young adults have been leaving home at later ages. What effect, if any, this has had on personality development is unknown.

Family Formation and Disolution

Marriage, natality, and divorce are all demographic factors that can dramatically change the individual's social situation and therefore be a stimulus for personality development. We look at each of these factors in turn.
Again, remember that development means evolution, not necessarily expansion.

Marriage. Late marriage is typical of higher socioeconomic classes, and
in recent times the proportion of young adults electing to never marry
has increased compared to cohorts who were coming of age in the 1950s.
Pampel (1983) found that part of the increase in people's propensity to
live alone that occured between 1960 and 1976 was due to an increase
in the desire to live alone, whereas part was due to divorce or later marriage. Marriage can be a stimulus for the development of a less self-
centered personality. In strong marriages, the partners are relatively secure adults who are willing to make whatever compromises necessary in
order to support the goals and self-esteem of the other (Atchley & Miller,
1983). Successful marriage thus broadens the context within which personal desires and fears are evaluated.

One the one hand, delaying marriage can be an advantage if it enhances
the probability that the partners will have secure and independent adult
identities. On the other hand, if delayed marriage is simply an artifact
of later entry into adulthood, then little might be gained. This is another
excellent research topic.

Cohort size influences the "marriage market" because, although the
number of men and women within a birth cohort is usually about equal
by marriage age, on average, husbands are 2.5 years older than their wives.
For example, in the late 1960s a "marriage squeeze" resulted from the fact
that the number of women at marriage age exceeded the number of men
by about 10%. In the 1980s the number of men of marriage age has been
higher than the number of women (Kammayer & Ginn, 1986). These fluctuations were the result of rapid changes in fertility connected with the
beginning and end of the baby boom. Marriage squeezes result in mis-
matches and inability to find a partner, both difficult situations for people who want to marry. A marriage squeeze may either enhance the
person's capacity for dealing with uncertainty or produce serious levels
of anxiety. We do not know which response is most common.

Natality. Increasing numbers of American young adults are choosing not
to be parents. Perhaps as much as 30% of the baby-boom cohorts will have
no children (Bloom, 1982). Apart from the obvious implications for such
individuals' capacity to meet dependency needs outside an institution in

later life, childlessness also removes an important stimulus for human development. Being a parent challenges one's conception of self, taxes coping ability, and alters just about every aspect of the structure of everyday life. Being a parent can be quite a humbling experience. By the time child rearing is complete, those parents who see it through usually have relatively few illusions about the perfectibility of humankind. They may be more likely than others to be nurturing and sympathetic to younger generations. On the other hand, those who never have children may be more able to preserve their illusions. Whether confronting the realities of another's development is beneficial for one's own personality is another unanswered question.

Those who have children are having them later on the average, but this average masks enormous class differences that are discussed later. Late child rearing potentially allows parents to approach parenthood from a more secure adult personality, which may minimize the negative effects that parenthood can have on self-esteem. For example, people who become parents late in life are much less likely to be abusive compared to those who become parents early.

Marital Dissolution and Reformation. Divorce rates are no longer increasing, but they still remain at very high levels compared to earlier eras. To some extent, these higher rates reflect a shift in ideas about how much aggravation one ought to be willing to tolerate in marriage coupled with a more romantic cultural ideal of marriage. Most divorces occur in early adulthood, during what is already an unsettled life stage. Divorce can call one's self-concept into serious question.

In addition, most people want to remarry, and the process of selecting a second or third marriage partner can be complicated by the need to meet not only one's own needs but also the needs of one's children. Those who succesfully endure this process may be more flexible to begin with and later may be even more open to negotiation.

The common assumption is that divorce has negative effects on both spouses and children, but the truth is not that simple. If divorce and remarriage result in better matches of spouses with one another and of parents with children, then effects can be positive. Children with abusive parents are probably better off without them. And there is increasing evidence that single parents can be quite effective. On the other hand, there is some evidence that patterns of abuse are likely to recur in later marriages (Kalmuss & Seltzer, 1986). The point here is that the demographic facts about divorce rates should not lead us to uninformed conclusions about the impact of divorce on human development. Our challenge is to construct theories that will be flexible enough to allow for a variety of inputs and outcomes (Riegel, 1976).

Number of Generations in the Family. Families with three, four, or even five generations have been part of the human experience for a long time. What is new is the growing proportion of families with four, five, and even more generations. This has resulted from greater survival both *to* later life and *in* later life. A large number of family generations has developmental effects through the individuals' perceptions of generational structure, which may affect the span of generations over which his or her own life history is projected. Responsibilities to generations on either side of one's own seem to be clear to most people, but beyond that the guidance people can get from the culture is minimal with regard to what priority should be given to family members two or more generations removed. We look at this issue again in the context of future trends.

Labor Force Decisions

Previoulsy we reviewed some developmental effects of cohort size that occur in the realm of employment of young adults. There are also important gender and social class effects on development in young adults related to jobs and/or careers. In this section, we look at a different stage of the employment cycle: retirement.

We must understand that retirement would probably not exist as a widespread social pattern if the advent of high-energy technology had not taken place during a time of rapid population increase. Technology was destroying jobs rapidly, while at the same time natural increase and immigration were adding to the labor force rapidly. The wear-and-tear theory of biological aging (which has since been discredited) led to the assumption that aging rendered people unfit for employment. To cope with the increasing labor surplus and the high unemployment rates caused by it, we first removed children from the labor market through child labor legislation; then we took out older people through the institutionalization of retirement (Atchley, 1982). The point here is that retirement was created to meet society's needs, not the needs of individuals.

It was not until retirement income systems matured to the point of being able to approximately replace earnings that the concept of retirement began to have mass appeal to the public. Now, the existence of retirement signifies to people within the working population that they need to be concerned with more than just their jobs, for someday they will probably retire. At that point, they will need goals other than employment to provide structure for their lives. Thus, according to functionalist logic, the *existence* of retirement as a life stage *causes* people to take actions designed to smooth the transition to retirement and to prepare them for a more autonomous lifestyle. Retirement encourages people to think to a future beyond child rearing and employment.

For many, retirement represents little significant life change. They live in the same place, interact mostly with the same people, and engage in familiar activities. They may even still be employed, but part time. For others, retirement is a time of great psychological expansion. For example, the growth of Elderhostel programs attests to the interest of retirees in formally organized personal growth. Indeed, most adult education geared to retirees is for growth rather than for acquisition of basic cognitive skills. This should say something about the validity of some decremental models of adult development that focus only on the "losses" connected with retirement.

As the upper age categories within the older population have increased in size, today's middle generations have many more potential role models to look to than was true in the past. This will increase the potential for individuation in retirement. Concepts of life in retirement are already becoming more complex, with people beginning to realize that retirement may be punctuated by periods of having to care for older parents and require more expense and assistance toward the end of life. Thus, the demographics of retirement influence our concepts and ideas about retirement.

In addition to these four direct and indirect influences on adult personality development, demographic selectivity can have important effects on the group context of development, which is the subject for the next section of this chapter.

DEMOGRAPHIC SELECTIVITY AND THE GROUP CONTEXT OF ADULT DEVELOPMENT

In large and complex societies, demographic processes change the relative size of various population components. We briefly look at some differentials in fertility, mortality, and migration and how these differentials might influence research and theory about adult development.

Differential Fertility

In the United States, total fertility rates (TFRs) in both the Black and Hispanic populations are a good bit higher than those in the general population. The overall TFR is at the replacement level, which means that the proportion of Blacks and proportion of Hispanics are increasing within the population, whereas the proportion of White non-Hispanic population is declining. For example, in 1980 the Hispanic population was 6%

of the total and is expected to increase to 15% by the year 2000 due to high fertility and immigration (Kammeyer & Ginn, 1986).

Differential Mortality

The biggest mortality differential is by gender. For example, in the United States in 1980 life expectancy at age 25 was 47.4 more years for men and 54.2 more years for women — a difference of 6.8 years. Add to this the age difference of 2.5 years between husbands and wives, and the average wife at the age of 25 can anticipate outliving her husband by 9.3 years. The implications are obvious. Women's conceptions of later life include a high probability of widowhood. What impact does the expectation of widowhood have? Do women prepare for widowhood? If widowed, women over 45 are much less likely to remarry than are men in similar age categories. Given the preference for living independently of other generations in the family, many more women must learn to live alone and like it. Studies have shown that most of them succeed, but exactly how they accomplish this needs more study.

In 1980 more than two-thirds of the population age 85 and over were women. If, as some have speculated, people become more androgenous with age, then perhaps this large imbalance has no implications for adult development. However, research support for the androgeny hypothesis has been mixed; therefore, we would expect that some older women might want to develop in order to get sufficient satisfaction of their socioemotional needs purely from other women. Some environments for older people, such as government rent-subsidized housing, are totally without men. I am not making a judgment about which gender is better at what. I am merely pointing out that for women who are used to looking to men for the satisfaction of some of their psychological needs, living in a female world can require substantial adjustment.

Migration Differentials

We have already discussed how age patterns in migration might affect development. This section deals with the impact of social class differentials in migration. Retirement migration is heavily concentrated in the upper middle class. Thus, upper income people are more vulnerable to attrition in their social networks from migration compared to older people lower on the socioeconomic scale. Indeed, a recent television report on very rich older people in Palm Beach, Florida, depicted a group of very old, very isolated women whose most frequent contacts and interactions were with people being paid to minister to their needs. A life spent traveling in exclusive circles may well be a considerable liability in old age, another area in need of research.

EFFECTS OF DEMOGRAPHIC CHANGES ON ADULT DEVELOPMENT

Most demographic changes influence social structure and, in turn, the social context of human development. In this section, I concentrate on what seems to me the most important changes and their implications. I first discuss how demographic change relates to changes in social institutions and to changes in technology. Then I look at adult development in relation to the dramatic growth expected in the older population, the aging of the baby-boom cohorts, the maturing of the work force, and the potential for explosive growth in the population of elderly minority-group poor.

To put demographic change into the proper perspective, we must recognize that the pulse of demographic expansions and contractions does not necessarily occur in synchrony with the pulse of expansions and contractions in society's social institutions. Because we as a society are not long-range planners, there is usually considerable lag time between the actual occurrence of problems and the steps to correct them. For example, age discrimination in employment produced large numbers of older people forced to live in poverty without retirement pensions for over 20 years before we finally enacted Social Security. It took another 50 years for retirement income systems to mature to the point at which the average worker could retire without economic hardship. Even now we have problems delivering adequate retirement income to some categories within the older population, such as single older women.

Demographic change must also be seen in the context of changes in technology. For example, in our society today, less than 1% of the physical energy required to produce all goods manufactured by American industry comes from human beings. The work is done by machines using electricity, steam, or internal combustion. The simple fact of the matter is that if every able-bodied retired man in the United States were in the labor force, our unemployment rate would nearly double. Technology frees society from the need to employ all adults; but at the same time, we need equitable and rational ways to allocate available jobs, to circulate a large population through a small array of jobs, to reduce the size of the labor market, and to provide financial support to those whose labor is not needed. Given a stabilizing population size and rapidly increasing automation, for instance, it does not seem sensible to talk seriously about dealing with Social Security's problems by forcing older people to continue to work. Who are we going to push or keep out of the work force in the process? How will those being pushed or kept out survive economically?

Thus, the implications of demographic changes become clearer when we look at them alongside other important societal trends. Now let's look at some specific demographic changes that we can expect over the next two decades.

Rapid Growth in the Older Population

We all know the familiar numbers. The population age 65 and older is growing much faster than the rest of the population, largely due to improved survival in large birth cohorts. Those age 95 and older are the fastest growing category within the older population.

Ranging from age 65 to age 105 and over, the older population spans over 40 birth cohorts and is extremely diverse in terms of life history, social characteristics, health characteristics, economic resources, and social resources. This diversity also can be expected to increase, expecially along economic lines as income inequality increases within the older population. One implication of this increased diversity is the further breakdown of the traditional three-stage life-span model of the life span — childhood, adulthood, and old age. More and more I expect that age will tell people little of what they can expect to find in an older individual. With increasing numbers, there may well be increasing dispersion within older age categories on various psychological functions. Older people are recognizing the fact that their identification with others on the basis of age makes little sense except under limited circumstances.

If this prediction holds, over the next 20 years we should see a liberation from stereotypes formed about those over 80 on par with the loosening of stereotypes formed about the young old that has occured over the preceding 20 years. Of course, this means that those over 80 will have more freedom to take an expansionist view of their own development. With diversity within the older population increasing, age consciousness is less likely to develop. This has potential implications for those who use age-stratification theory to focus their research. As the number and size of actual cohorts in the older population increases, we will have an opportunity to observe how long it takes our culture to deal with the fact that treating *old age* as a single age stratum is unrealistic in the extreme.

The large age range and diversity within the older population may also lead us to conceive of new life stages within later life. Theories of adult development have tended to deal with age 65 to 105 as a single life stage. New ideas are needed that capture the independence and growth often accompanying retirement; the challenges to coping ability caused by caring for older parents when the children themselves are living on retirement income; and the development occurring when a person must cope with no longer being self-reliant. For example, Gadow (1983) challenged us to think of the frailty of extreme old age not as a limit but as a challenge to development. Mental energy and physical frailty can combine, she said, to produce a fierce inner life that must remain inner because there is no physical capacity to act upon it. Gadow argued that this can produce a new life form in which the energy and passion formerly spent on external matters are focused on an inner transcendence. This provocative idea deserves examination. We will be aided in the process of developing new ideas by being able to observe large numbers of people as they deal with these experiences. But to take advantage of this opportunity, we must be willing to reward descriptive, theory-building research.

The future of mortality and morbidity within the older population is uncertain. In the past, our population projections have tended to underestimate gains in life expectancy (Crimmins, 1984). Thus far it appears that adding years to life expectancy in later life has not resulted in lengthier periods of disability (Olshansky, 1985). Instead, the mortality gradient at the end of the life span has simply been pushed upward. Nor does it appear that the mortality curve is squaring off at around age 85 as Fries (1980) predicted (Myers & Manton, 1984). How much further upward the mortality gradient can be pushed is questionnable. The population over age 95 is rapidly increasing, which indicates that we have not yet reached the limit. What are the developmental implications of reaching one's 100th birthday? This could one day be a common occurrence.

Aging of the Baby-Boom Cohorts

The adult development of the baby boomers will be challenged by the politics of retirement income and health care financing long before they reach old age. They are already being led not to expect much from federal programs. What has been their response? Are they more insecure about their retirement and old age? Have they taken more steps than cohorts before them to prepare financially to meet their own needs? The reserves planned for the Social Security retirement trust fund should be sufficient to finance Social Security retirement pensions for the baby-boom cohorts without raising taxes for those who are employed. However, these large reserves must be left untouched by Congress. I think we can count on hearing much rhetoric about all the "better" uses to which those funds could be put. The issue here is that our policial process does not appear to be capable of the integrity necessary to provide a solid sense of security. Thus, members of the baby-boom cohorts are likely to have to live with a greater sense of insecurity about Social Security than the cohorts preceding them.

On the other hand, a large proportion of the baby boomers will probably enter retirement with adequate economic resources. They will have spent their working lives in mature pension systems. They will have the educational and economic capital needed to provide a stable platform for psychological development in retirement. Their larger numbers will mean that forming groups around leisure interests may be easier than it is now. Fewer of them will have children, which means that if they need assistance in the home, they will probably have to yield their privacy to strangers more often than is the case now. This also may have developmental implications.

A big question mark concerns what the health care financing picture will look like when the baby-boom cohorts begin to need personal care and health care in large numbers. Right now we are in a crisis of long-term care. Medicare is being cut back annually. Medicaid is not reimbursing providers for the full cost of care. Private long-term care insurance is hard to find and tends to be inadequate. Health care cost inflation is double the rate of inflation in general. The causes of the current problems are far from clear. Suffice it to say that so long as we remain in our current muddle, insecurity about being able to afford needed health care in later life for one's family and for oneself will remain part of the context of adult development. As the baby-boom cohorts approach old age these problems will be exacerbated.

Maturing of the Work Force

As our median age increases from 30 in 1980 to around 40 in 2020, employers can be expected to make more investment in the adult development of their employees of all ages. With small birth cohorts entering the labor force, new jobs will need to be filled partly by retrained middle-aged and older workers. This trend may challenge our current negative stereotypes about the poor potential for cognitive development among mature adults. Developmental research may also play an important part in the evolution of effective training programs for mature adults. Workers of retirement age will probably be given more incentives to remain on, and perhaps more part-time employment options will appear. Developmental research may be important in helping us to identify those adults who are our best prospects of continued employment. However, it would be a mistake to assume that, if given the chance, most older people would remain in the labor force. The best evidence we have now indicates that even substantial economic incentives are not enough to keep most workers from retiring when they become eligible for full retirement pensions.

Adding Generations to the Family

In 20 years, five-generation families will be common. In ethnic groups with early childbearing, as many as seven generations may occur. The adult development impact of numerous generations will probably come from increased *complexity* and *ambiguity* in family relationships. For example, suppose we focus on a 55-year-old person who has a living parent age 77, a living grandparent age 99, an adult offspring age 33, and a grandchild age 11. What responsibility, if any, does the focal person have for the care of the 99 year old? Does the 33 year old share any responsibility? Because the 77 year old is also "old," does that reduce his or her reponsibility for care of the 99 year old? These questions have no clear answers right now. We will be working them out over the coming decades.

Thus, later life family dynamics and expectations in the future may be based more on *negotiated* relationships and less on traditions than is now the case, which means that negotiation skills will assume greater importance. What a higher reliance on negotiated order would do to the currently high sense of filial duty among younger generations is unclear and would make an excellent topic for longitudinal research. Right now people tend to care for their older parents even if they do not feel especially close to them. But if family responsibilities become more voluntaristic, then what? We also do not know how the high divorce and remarriage rates since the 1960s will affect perceptions of family structure and responsibility in later life. Guilt related to caring for a family member is an important, but uninvestigated, part of adult development now. How will changes in family culture influence this?

Certainly the quality of family interactions in the future will depend on the extent to which income security and health care financing are handled by government. Solid financial support from government leaves families free of many financial worries and allows them to concentrate on what families can best provide — personalized care and social support. If the cost of care in both time and money is shifted too much on families (which in the future will contain fewer numbers per generation), then families will break apart. In the past, when relative responsibility laws were enforced, many older people left to avoid pauperizing their families, and many younger families left to avoid being economically destroyed. These actions, though perhaps practical, probably had significant negative psychological effects on all generations of the family. Again, developmental psychologists have been slow to investigate these types of effects.

Explosive Growth in Population of Elderly Minority Poor

Currently, population growth is the highest at the bottom of the socioeconomic structure. Racial and ethnic discrimination in employment translate into unemployment and poverty, which in turn drastically reduce the chances that children will grow up in family environments capable of providing them with adequate resources for development. Educational systems exist in at least two tiers: inner-city schools and suburban schools. Resources do not flow equally to these two tiers. Thus, the poor are also given the poorest educational opportunities for development. Many minority poor thus physically and legally reach adulthood without having developed the cognitive and social skills necessary to find a place in society's economic system. They do not have the economic disincentives to having children that occur among the upwardly mobile, therefore the cycle of poverty continues. Our theories of adult development have focused mainly on the middle class, and we have much to learn about the developmental challenges in the working class. Rubin's (1976) pioneering work on family, growth, marriage, and work in the working class provides a rich starting point for researchers in adult development.

The war on poverty was declared "won" by Ronald Reagan at a time when 35 million Americans were living below the Census-defined poverty level. Support for poor children has eroded, but not because more resources are going to older people as Preston (1984) has argued. Indeed, when resources were looked at longitudinally from 1968 to 1982, the elderly lost ground whereas children overall gained economic ground (Duncan, Hill, & Rodgers, 1986). Support for poor children eroded because our national commitment to income security for all Americans disappeared as soon as the economic going got tough. Prospects for children of the poor are not improving. Dooley and Gottschalk (1985) found considerable stagnation at the lower tail of the earnings distribution, which could not be explained simply by lower education, less experience, or entrance of the baby boom into the labor market. They suggested that the structure of labor demand may be important to look at here. We simply are not being effective in finding a place in our economic system and labor force for those at the bottom of the socioeconomic structure. Despite many studies and demonstration programs, we have yet to identify ways to provide the needed cognitive knowledge and skills effectively to this segment of the population.

If we do nothing to bring the underclass into the economic system, we will have a rapidly growing population of poor entering later life with no economic resources at all. And worse, they will have lived their entire adult lives knowing that their opportunities for development were vastly inferior to those offered the middle class.

CONCLUSION

In conclusion, the size, composition, and distribution of the population are important dimensions of the sociocultural *context* within which adult development takes place. These factors directly and indirectly affect cognitive skills, cognitive content, and personality development.

Demographic events such as birth, illness, death, and migration can be strong stimuli for psychological development. These factors also strongly influence development indirectly by altering the size and composition of subgroups within communities.

In the future, demographic factors such as the rapidly growing number and density of older population, the uneven cohort flow resulting from aging of the baby-boom cohorts and the smaller cohorts to follow them, the maturing of the work force, the expansion in the number of family generations, and the greater growth in the population of older minority group poor represent substantial changes that will require the development of new skills and ideas.

It should be obvious that the study of adult development can benefit enormously if we consider the effects of the demographic components of social structure. Indeed, I would argue that only when our knowledge of development is coupled with demographic concepts of proportionality will we be able to bring our knowledge of development to bear successfully on social policy.

The field is wide open to join demography and adult development, and I wish those who enter it good fortune.

REFERENCES

Atchley, R. C. (1975). The life course, age grading, and age-linked demands for decision making. In N. Datan & L. H. Ginsberg (Eds.), *Life-span developmental psychology: Normative life crises* (pp. 261–278). New York: Academic Press.

Atchley, R. C. (1982). Retirement as a social institution. *Annual Review of Sociology, 8*, 263–287.

Atchley, R. C. (1983). *Aging: Continuity and change*. Belmont, CA: Wadsworth.

Atchley, R. C., & Miller, S. J. (1983). Types of elderly couples. In T. H. Brubaker (Ed.), *Family relationships in later life*. (pp. 77–90). Beverly Hills, CA. Sage.

Bloom, D. E. (1982). What's happening to the age at first birth in the U.S.? A study of recent cohorts. *Demography, 19,* 351–370.

Bultena, G. L., & Wood, V. (1969). The American retirement community: Bane or blessing? *Journal of Gerontology, 24,* 209–217.

Coleman, J. S. (1966). *Equal schools or equal students?* Washington, DC: U.S. Government Printing Office.

Crimmin, E. M. (1984). Life expectancy of the older population: Implications of recent and prospective trends. *Research on Aging, 6,* 490–514.

Dooley, M. & Gottschalk, P. (1985). The increasing proportion of men with low earnings in the United States. *Demography, 22,* 25–34.

Duncan, G. J., Hill, M., & Rodgers, W. (1986, August). The changing fortunes of young and old. *American Demographics,* pp. 26–33.

Easterlin, R. A. (1980). *Birth and fortune.* New York: Basic Books.

Fries, J. F. (1980). Aging, natural death, and the compression of morbidity. *New England Journal of Medicine, 300,* 130–135.

Gadow, S. (1983). Frailty and strength: The dialectics in aging. *Gerontologist, 23,* 144–47.

Hauser, P. M., & Duncan, O. D. (1959). *The study of population.* Glencoe, IL: Free Press.

Kalmuss, D. & Seltzer, J. A. (1986). Continuity of marital behavior in remarriage: The case of spouse abuse. *Journal of Marriage and the Family, 48,* 113–120.

Kammeyer, K. C. W., & Ginn, H. (1986). *An introduction to population.* Chicago: Dorsey.

Klapp, O. E. (1978). *Opening and closing: Strategies of information adaptation in society.* New York: Cambridge University Press.

Kelley, G. A. (1955). *The psychology of personal constructs.* New York: Norton.

Kohlberg. L. (1973). Continuities in childhood and adult moral development revisited. In P. B. Baltes & K. W. Schaie (Eds.), *Life-span developmental psychology: Personality and socialization* (pp. 179–204). New York: Academic Press.

Longino, C. F., Jr. (1981). Retirement communities. In F. J. Berghorn & D. E. Schafer (Eds.), *The dynamics of aging,* (pp. 391–418). Boulder, CO: Westview Press.

Mott, P. E. (1965). *The organization of society.* Englewood Cliffs, NJ: Prentice-Hall.

Myers, G. C., & Manton, K. G. (1984). Compression of mortality: Myth or reality? *Gerontologist, 24,* 346–353.

Neugarten, B. L. (1977). Personality and aging. In J. E. Birren & K. W. Schaie (Eds.), *Handbook of the psychology of aging.* (pp. 626–649). New York: Van Nostrand Reinhold.

Neugarten, B. L., & Datan, N. (1973). Sociological perspectives on the life cycle. In P. B. Baltes & K. W. Schaie (Eds.), *Life span developmental psychology: Personality and socialization* (pp. 53–69). New York: Academic Press.

Olshansky, S. J. (1985, Aug.). *Pursuing longevity: Delay vs. elimination of degenerative diseases.* Paper presented at the annual meeting of the American Sociological Association, Washington, DC.

Pampel, F. C. (1983). Changes in the propensity to live alone: Evidence from consecutive cross-sectional surveys, 1960–1976. *Demography, 20,* 433–447.

Preston, S. H. (1984). Children and the elderly: Divergent paths for America's dependents. *Demography, 21,* 435–457.

Riegel, K. F. (1976). The dialectics of human development *American Psychologist, 31,* 689–700.

Rosenberg, M. (1965). *Society and the adolescent self-image.* Princeton, NJ: Princeton University Press.

Rubin, L. B. (1976). *Worlds of pain: Life in the working-class family.* New York: Basic Books.

Salthouse, T. A. (1982). *Adult cognition: An experimental psychology of human aging.* New York: Springer-Verlag.

Sandefur, G. D. (1985). Variations in interstate migration of men across the early stages of the life cycle. *Demography, 22,* 353–366.

Theodorson, G., & Theodorson, A. (1969). *A modern dictionary of sociology.* New York: T. Y. Crowell.

Discussion of "Demographic Factors and Adult Psychological Development"

George C. Myers
Center for Demographic Studies
Duke University

In his chapter, Atchley uses the metaphor "painting with a broad brush" to describe his effort to relate demographic structures and changes and their effect on adult development. The expression is apt, although the execution is less than perfect. Like the impressionists, he paints with a broad, but short stroke, hoping by imagination, passion, and the use of tone to produce a canvas that *in its entirety* depicts an integrated and meaningful overview of the nexus between demographic and psychosocial developments — in short, a whole that is greater than the sum of its parts.

It is common among demographers, as Atchley notes, to distinguish two main perspectives in their field: demographic analysis and population studies. The former focuses primarily on key elements of the demographic system (size, growth, density, distribution, and composition) and relationships between these factors as affected by fertility, mortality, and migration. Atchley's chapter devotes little attention to demographic analysis per se. The second perspective, population studies, focuses on the social, economic, and political determinants and consequences of population structure and trends. For the most part, Atchley ignores the former and concentrates on the consequences of demographic factors. There is a rich tradition, extending back at least two centuries, of examining the implications of demographic trends. Recently, there has been a flurry of interest in what has come to be called demographics, that is, relating demographic factors to specific applied concerns of industry, marketing, government programs, and the like. However, there has been far less concern for the subject that Atchley's chapter examines — the impact on adult psychological development.

Thus, he has taken on a daunting task for which we should be grateful. The intent is to stimulate social psychologists to consider how demographic factors influence the social context in which cognitive development takes place throughout the life course. Furthermore, it is clear from his remarks that raising some interesting questions could lead to fruitful research efforts.

Now that I have presented the general framework within which he is operating, let me examine how he goes about relating macroelements to microelements. In the first place, Atchley outlines an impressive list of nearly all the major demographic factors, both static and dynamic, that might be viewed as important—population size, density, growth, distribution, composition, fertility, mortality, migration, family structure, marriage, divorce, and so on. The list can hardly be faulted for its comprehensiveness. He then relates these, either directly or indirectly, to aspects of psychological development, in particular, to cognitive skills, cognitive content, and personality. Viewed broadly, these appear to be meaningful outcomes to examine. However, virtually all these relationships involve intervening factors that pertain generally to social or environmental contexts chosen on a rather ad hoc basis.

The relationships, therefore, move rather complexly from macro- to microlevels. The important questions that can be raised about such relationships are whether they fulfill criteria such as conceptual adequacy, operational adequacy, empirical adequacy, and generalizability. In general, we need to examine whether the facts pertaining to the demographic, contextual, and development factors are correct and the linkages appropriate. In this regard, I examine three major issues around which Atchley has organized his chapter: (a) the broad scale macrodemographic changes that have operated in the past to affect psychological development, particularly at younger ages, (b) demographic composition and selectivity as they influence development throughout the life course, and (c) demographic factors relating to population aging and its implications.

MACRODEMOGRAPHIC
AND SOCIETAL EVOLUTION

A good deal of Atchley's formulation owes its inspiration to Émile Durkheim's notion of *morphologie sociale*, a concept extensively examined by one of his followers Maurice Halbwachs (1960) in his book *Population and Society: Introduction to Social Morphology* (originally written in 1938). As Durkheim (1895/1938) earlier noted: "The facts of social morphology [i.e., the volume (population) and density of population] ... play a preponderant role in collective life" (p. 111). Thus, the population factors embodied in social morphology play a key role in the evolution of societies, altering the well-known forms of societal solidarity from mechanic to organic and increasing differentiation (e.g., the division of labor) and the adherence to norms. These are key themes that run throughout Atchley's chapter. Population increases in size, becomes more dense, distributes more widely (geographic mobility rises), and so forth. At the same time, fertility and mortality decline, marriage declines, and divorce increases. To be sure, many of these developments have occurred over the long term, but the emphasis on unilinear change and the determinism that it implies stretches our notions of credibility.

There are indications that underreplacement fertility may lead to population declines in some Western societies: Mortality levels have increased in some countries; the "baby bust" has replaced the "baby boom"; mobility and divorce rates have declined in recent years in the United States; average age at first marriage has recently increased after declining for some time; central cities have become less dense; and new immigrants have changed the ethnic composition of this country in fundamental ways. In short, many major demographic trends are subject to more variation than Atchley is willing to accept. It is not so much that what he has noted is incorrect, but that many trends are not unilinear and, therefore, are more problematic.

This has an important bearing on the posited relationships. If the increased size of age cohorts and the number of children in the family lead to less cognitive skill reinforcement, lower sense of identity, cognitive overload, and restricted occupational development, what happens when the size of the age cohorts declines as it has in the past two decades? If geographic mobility declines, as it has recently, will that mean an enrichment in cognitive content toward conformity and reduced deviation from norms?

As the presentation unfolds, Atchley moves increasingly away from a strict determinism, at least insofar as any necessary relationships between demographic and psychological factors are concerned. In fact, the prevailing view seems more psychologistic. For example, he uses Klapp's notion of opening and closing when he states that "the healthy individual responds to environmental conditions, such as migration, by opening or closing his or her idea structure to achieve a satisfying balance between the two." Later he notes that "a marriage squeeze may either enhance the person's capacity for dealing with uncertainty or produce serious levels of anxiety. We do not know which response is most commmon."

In short, although it is an interesting exercise to trace out the broad implications of macrodemographic trends on development outcomes, greater care must be used in describing the nature of the independent, intervening, and dependent variables. Moreover, the linkages between these variables may be far more complex than even those proposed.

DEMOGRAPHIC COMPOSITION
AND SELECTIVITY

Atchley's treatment of demographic composition and selectivity is far less problematic, and his conclusions are less sweeping. Examining such demographic factors in the life course would seem to offer important insights into the study of developmental changes. The size of age cohorts (variable as they are over time), age-related patterns in geographic mobility, family formation and dissolution, and age-related employment patterns are all meaningful dimensions for consideration, especially as they interact among themselves. A considerable amount of demographic analysis has been conducted in this regard, but with a lack of systematic attention to psychological development outcomes. Atchley quite rightly points out several research areas in need of further attention.

POPULATION AGING

The final section of Atchley's chapter focuses on the nature of population aging and its implications. Clearly, in this arena he is on much more familiar ground. Growth in the number of older persons, improved survival, and increasing diversity of the older population have important implications on how we conceptualize old age and the physiological functioning of older persons. Although not a revolutionary notion, a revision of the traditional three-stage life-span model certainly is in order. Questions of the relative identification of older persons with others simply on the basis of age and the existing degree of age consciousness will be central concerns confronting researchers for some time.

For baby-boom cohorts, the issue interfaces most dramatically in terms of their economic and health expectations and society's view of how future government programs should be structured. Careful monitoring of these cohorts' expectations (and feelings of security and insecurity) and how they shape current and future behavior (in such domains as retirement, saving, leisure, and the like) are of considerable importance. Finally, the implications of demographic changes on family structure and relationships, especially as they relate to personalized care and social support, are sure to be high on the research agenda of gerontologists.

It is noteworthy that Atchley closes his chapter by discussing the ethnic and racial diversity of tomorrow's older persons. This has particular importance when we consider how the adult development of less advantaged persons in future older populations may differ from that of more advantaged, middle-class older persons.

CONCLUSIONS

It has been pointed out by one wit that there are two ways to get to the top of an oak tree. One is to be aggressive and climb up. The other is to sit on an acorn and wait for it to grow. To his credit, Atchley has chosen the former approach. Although I have reservations about some of the sweeping generalizations contained in his chapter, the demographic paradigms he suggests could have far-reaching research implications. I find the macrodemographic formulations presented initially to be somewhat problematic, but as he comes to focus on demographic considerations pertaining to stages in the life course, especially at the older ages, the relationships become more grounded, and the research possibilities enhanced.

Atchley's contribution to this book calls attention to the fact that our current knowledge of how larger social structural transformations, in this case mainly demographic, relate to adult development is limited at best. The challenge is to develop a meaningful dialogue that will lead to interdisciplinary research. Atchley provides a rich agenda for attaining the top of our oak tree.

REFERENCES

Durkheim, E. (1938). *The rules of sociological method* (2nd ed.). Chicago: University of Chicago Press. (Originally published 1895).

Halbwachs, M. (1960). *Population and society: Introduction to social morphology*, (O. D. Duncan & H. W. Pfautz, trans.). Glencoe, IL: Free Press.

"What Develops in Adulthood?": A Developmentalist's Response to Atchley's Demographic View

David L. Featherman
University of Wisconsin-Madison

Professor Atchley's survey of points of articulation between American population dynamics and topics about adult psychological development is insightful and informative. The canvas on which he paints is big; the brush strokes are bold and sweeping; the detail work unfinished. From a distance the composition is pleasing, perhaps compelling. But to this friendly critic, the artfulness of Atchley's creation fails to satisfy a more searching penetration of the surface features.

My latent dissatisfaction arises from the genre of this art. True, it is one that has served social science well. But to my thinking, it no longer proffers a helpful vision or a working perspective that motivates deeper, expanded understandings about the fusion of structure and process—about society and lifelong human development in this case.

Professor Atchley's genre is the social structure and personality approach of social psychology, which has guided sociological thinking about socialization and adult development for several decades (see House, 1977, for a review). It is a view, linked to role and social learning theories, that portrays human ontogeny as a relatively passive bearer of the social forces thrust upon the individual as he or she passes through an age-graded, age-stratified society (see Dannefer, 1984, for a strong version of this view). Where the approach does take individual mind and action into consideration, it describes a radically abiological actor whose action intentions are wholly woven from the sociocultural fabric (see Wells & Stryker, 1988, for a "structural symbolic interactionist" version of the social structure and personality genre).

Perhaps most importantly concerning my remarks, Professor Atchley's canvas offers a view that has no particular answer to the question—"What

develops in adulthood?"—because it has no precise definition of development. That is, his "social structure and personality" does not distinguish
adult development from the entire range of changes in mind and behavior
that might take place in the age stratum or grade called adulthood. (See
Featherman, 1986; Featherman & Lerner, 1985, for a critical elaboration
of this point, found within the life-span human development approach,
and for a new operational definition of development.) So, for example,
Atchley's definition of adult development implies "neither contraction nor
expansion, but merely the cumulative response to one's life history" and
denotes "the acquisition and accumulation of *ideas*, which we often
differentiate into knowledge, attitudes, values, beliefs and ideologies, and
psychological skills, to which we apply labels such as intelligence, learning,
memory, creativity, thinking, problem solving and coping."

    Thus, adult development in Professor Atchley's terms encompasses cu-
mulative responses in mind and behavior to life history. In effect, adult
development is no different from child development except that the cu-
mulation of sociocultural effects is of longer duration.

    My second point of generic dissatisfaction with Professor Atchley's art
is his deployment of the population perspective. I quite agree that a demographic analysis of society in terms of the "demographic equation" (involving additions to the size and composition of the population through
fertility, deletions through mortality, and both geographic and social redis-
tribution via mobility and migration) is different from a population analysis (Hauser & Duncan, 1959). The former is an accounting scheme and
focuses on a limited set of vital processes connecting population size and
structure to cohort (but not necessarily individual) behavior in particular historical moments (see Ryder, 1965, for this fine-textured distinction).
The population analysis I suggest subsequently is a frame of reference
that links demographic structure to individual adult development and the
latter back to demographic structure and its development.

    Based on these two sources of dissatisfaction with the deep structure
of Professor Atchley's bold strokes on the big canvas, let me address the
remainder of my necessarily brief remarks to three questions: What develops in adulthood? What can we learn from a population analysis about
adult development? And what major changes in the developmental agenda of adults are underway in contemporary America? I, too, paint on the
big canvas, and with no greater precision than my predecessor. Perhaps
in the end, you might see no major differences in our individually
preferred genre, and I encourage your most critical appraisal.

WHAT DEVELOPS IN ADULTHOOD?

In offering an answer, let me take a decidedly different and theoretically stronger position about development in general than Professor Atchley assumes. I take what he eschews as being an "expansionist" viewpoint. Namely, *development involves additions to reserve or adaptive capacity in mind and behavior across the lifespan* (Baltes, 1987; Featherman, 1987). When the child learns mathematics and begins to reason with symbolic logic rather than with concrete arithmetic operations, this is development. The reason is that the new procedural skills and knowledge provide a comparatively broader base for cognitive and behavioral adaptation to a wide, but not necessarily exhaustive, set of situations and real-world problematics that are present *or may be present* in the near future. Procedural skills and knowledge provide an expansion of the capacity to adapt to an additional range of complexity in the environment, giving the child with these capacities a "competitive edge," so to speak, compared to the child with merely concrete arithmetical approaches. Not all children expand their reserve capacities for performance of these tasks upon demand, and others who develop in this framework may not retain this expertise through lack of use (Denney, 1982).

Similarly, the gains of cognitive wisdom in later adulthood and old age by some individuals (Baltes, Dittmann-Kohli, & Dixon, 1984), and training gains in fluid intelligence that restore developmental losses (Willis, 1985), illustrate gains and restorations of adaptive capacity, that is, development. So, too, do the cardiovascular improvements that occur with jogging for those of us at middle age.

I do not pursue a controversial corollary, namely, that each specialization and each gain in reserve capacity may potentially entail a loss or erosion of former abilities and of adaptive capacity in situations in which these skills are highly useful. Development involves specialization and, hypothetically, both gains and losses. Whether losses occur depends, in part, on the degree and level of specialization and on the social ecology of the task—what the task demands are and what the supportiveness or competitiveness of the social setting is (see Hatano & Inagaki, in press; Featherman & Peterson, 1986, for a related view). I prefer to designate the losses of adaptive capacity, that is, the reductions of developmental reserve as *aging*. Because gains and losses are potentially possible across the entire life span, both development and aging are not age-graded processes. (See Featherman & Shavit, 1988, for an example of development and aging in intellectual functioning during adolescence in Israel, as related to differently structured educational experiences. For a more complete exegesis of the construct of development and its relationship to specialization, see Dixon & Baltes, 1986; Featherman & Peterson, 1986.)

With this working definition of development in hand, let me turn to adult development and the durable idea of "developmental tasks" (e.g., Havighurst, 1951). The important question to ask about development in any life period, be it childhood or adulthood (or whatever other abstractions from the flow of the life course we make and label as a life period) is: development of what for what? It is a neofunctionalist question, linking individuals' minds and behaviors to the flow of social situations through the life course. The idea of distinctive developmental tasks permits the analytical abstraction of life periods and the qualitative distinction of one period from another. If there is to be an assessment of the impact of demographic factors in adult development, it must deal with the historically specific developmental tasks of adulthood.

So, it is not sufficient to ask how migration affects the mind of an adult and to comment on some hypothesis about mass culture, pluralistic thinking, and identity diffusion, as Atchley's analysis suggests. This is a person-by-situation, ahistorical, adevelopmental perspective that is the genre of social psychology. Atchley's frame of reference about migration and "development" could just as easily apply to childhood. By contrast, one must ask: "What are the developmental tasks of adulthood, as differentiated from those of preceding and succeeding life periods, and how is migration intertwined as an influence on and/or reflection of this developmental agenda?" The latter is a historical and evolutionary question, for the idea of developmental tasks connotes an agenda for socialization that can and does change with the culture and times (see Atchley, 1983, for an illustration of this general point). If we focus on the unique developmental tasks of adulthood, our purview of what specific changes in mind and behavior (or in Atchley's universe of ideas and skills) to monitor for developmental, functional significance is delimited.

Thus, what are the developmental tasks of contemporary American adulthood (not necessarily adulthood in abstraction from time and place) for which demographic structures and processes are of high relevance? Following the suggestion of Freud, Erikson (1959, 1963), and Smelser and Erikson (1980), let me emphasize what I believe to be one of the most demanding—loving *and* working. Note I underscore the conjunction as a single developmental task or task complex. The task complex involves expressing a sustained emotional commitment to another or others that is not evoked out of self-interest, a characteristic of mind and behavior sometimes labeled "generativity." At the same time it involves a subjective sense, confirmed by the responses from key others, of personal effectiveness and agency at tasks regarded as important or significant in one's community. This is sometimes called *productive competence*; and very often in our cultural context, its most salient (but not only; see Kahn, 1984) instances involve tasks for which the value is great enough to warrant a monetary evaluation, such as paid work. Were the culturally defined and self-selected targets for loving the same as those for working, the tasks of adulthood—adult development—might be rather more simple than it seems to be for many American men and women (see Gilligan, 1982, for some speculations).

Indeed, at the conclusion of my remarks, I sugggest that a confluence of demographic factors and trends seems to be making it very difficult for many adults to be loving and working—to achieve both generativity and productive competence. Following a brief digression, I suggest what some difficulties are, where they come from, and how the developmental agenda of loving and working in contemporary adulthood feeds back to social and demographic structures.

WHAT CAN WE LEARN FROM A POPULATIONIST ANALYSIS OF ADULT DEVELOPMENT?

Before taking up my own brush and painting this picture with emboldened abandon, let me digress momentarily. I want to return to my second point of disagreement with Professor Atchley's emphasis of a demographic analysis (looking at fertility, migration, and mobility as influences on adult development) over a population analysis. By population analysis, perhaps better called population–person analysis (i.e., Featherman & Lerner, 1985), I refer to a behavioral model linking social structures to individual behavior in a reciprocally causal or influential relationship. My main differences with Atchley's contrasts are ones of emphasis.

There are three key ideas in the population–person model of development on which I want to draw later in my remarks. Briefly, the first is that individuals' behaviors not only affect their own development but those of others as well. One instance of this idea, in evolutionary form, is the contingent influence of one generation on another and of preceding cohorts on subsequent ones. There are many classical examples of this idea, including Karl Mannheim's (1952) on intellectual "generations" and the sociology of change in cultural knowledge systems; Norman Ryder's (1964, 1965) essays on the cohort as a linking construct between personal biography and history; Pitirim Sorokin's (1959) analysis of the persistence and change in the American class system via mechanisms of intergenerational transmission of values, human capital, and wealth; and Richard Easterlin's (1980) assessment of cohort destinies of fortune or misfortune as a function of their relative size in the age-stratification system (Riley, 1985). An interesting aspect of this general phenomenon, namely, that our individual behaviors leave a legacy of opportunities and constraints for others, is that cohorts of strangers rather than generations of relatives are often the more powerful influences on our lives and their courses. The opposite pattern prevailed in early industrial and preindustrial society (Featherman, in press).

A second idea in the population–person model is that individuals are not just passive recipients of the structural constraints and opportunities that they inherit from the cake of custom and the (unjust) desserts of their predecessors; they influence their own and other's destinies (e.g., Lerner & Busch-Rossnagel, 1981). Children, even infants, affect the development of their parents; wives, that of their husbands, and so on. This principle has led to a questioning of the concept of the normal "family life cycle," with its characterization of the domestic household in terms of a unitary, nearly universal developmental history of structure and composition that channels a typical course of children's and parents' developments across families (Vinovskis, 1988).

Third, sometimes the development that occurs in one life period can lead to loss of reserve capacity in another life period. This may occur because what has comparatively greater adaptive value earlier in life may not continue to add to developmental reserves that are required or maximally beneficial for adapting successfully in another (with different developmental tasks). This idea has many examples from evolutionary and comparative biology, for it simply restates the fact that adaptive success is always relative to prevailing ecological conditions. It is only in some hypothetically stable society that development in one life period might predict individual differences in adapting to the developmental tasks in another period (Featherman, in press).[1]

I believe these three ideas illustrate an essential difference between a population–person analysis and a demographic analysis. The former is explicitly ecological and evolutionary–historical; the other, descriptive and enumerative. Although both might be applied to describe person-by-situation interactions and be useful for a social psychology of adulthood, the population–person approach is more amenable to developmental analysis. This is the case because it incorporates specific ideas about the evolution of contextual systems (societal development), about individual ontogeny (individual development), and about how they are related in ecological, adaptional terms within specific historical circumstances.

---

[1]A biological example of this idea comes from pleiotropic gene action that may help explain the onset of senescent declines with advanced age. For example, the very gene action that deposits calcium to strengthen bones during the prereproductive years, enhancing the skeletal integrity of mother and infant and improving their survival probabilities, also may lead to hardening of the arteries and eventual death in the postreproductive years (Kirkwood, 1985). A behavioral example is the case of developing a "type-A" approach to achievement tasks, which at some suboptimal level may have quite beneficial career outcomes during adulthood but prove to be fatal if not redirected and modulated during retirement or late old age.

WHAT MAJOR CHANGES ARE UNDERWAY
IN ADULTHOOD AND IN ADULT DEVELOPMENT
IN THE AMERICAN POPULATION?

With my own model of development and of population analysis at hand, let me sketch with glossing brevity at least one change that also illustrates the applications of the foregoing guiding ideas about adult development and population process. In doing so, I am indebted to the more penetrating and exhaustive analyses of sociodemographic trends by several colleagues (see Bumpass, 1986; Bumpass & Sweet, in press; Cherlin, 1981; Davis, 1984; Garfinkel & McLanahan, 1987, for details).

The issue is the conjunction of loving and working in adulthood, its relationships to gender role expressions for American men and women, and the developmental linkages between the adaptive capacities of these adults in adulthood and the reserves for individual development later in the old age period. Let me focus more on women for whom the changes seem most profound and perhaps more problematic.

Several demographic trends are converging to transform the ways in which loving and working as life problems or tasks are handled by American women. The first is the rise of marital dissolution and the decline in prevalence of married households as developmental contexts. Although divorce rates have climbed steadily since the Civil War and recently plateaued, no demographer forecasts a long-term reversal of the rate. Relatedly, the rate of marrying continues to decline across successive cohorts, and the most recent estimate is that 30% of contemporary women may never marry. Among the native population of Americans (discounting immigrants), perhaps as many as 30% of women will remain childless by choice.

A second important trend for women reflects rising participation in the paid economy. Women are attending and completing higher education at a greater rate than men in their cohorts, a very new phenomenon. By the end of the decade, half or more of the paid labor force will be women, may of whom have young children in the household. Some significant fraction of these women — perhaps as many as a half — will head mother only families. What is striking in contemporary trends is the pace at which the sex ratio of workers is closing in both the early prime working ages and the pre- and postretirement years. This reflects the relatively greater difficulties not heretofore faced by young male workers and the rising tendency for men to exit the paid labor force prior to traditional retirement age at a greater rate than their wives or female family heads.

What is worth underscoring about the second trend is that it has occurred despite lingering and marked sex segregation of jobs and work and nearly unchanging sex differentials in the earnings of workers with similar experience and work effort (Fuchs, 1986).

Where do these trends come from? What do they signal about societal and individual development and perhaps their interrelationship? In suggesting answers to these questions, I want to emphasize two related sources of influence, as implied by the person–population model of adult development. First are sources arising from individual actions of self-efficacy (Bandura, 1980), that is, adults finding personal expressions of loving and working within a variety of niches within contemporary society. Second are more historical sources stemming from a century and a half of industrialization and modernization as cultural themes, expressing global qualities of macrosocietal and institutional change and therefore of changes in the context of adult socialization for the population as a whole.

Let me begin with the historical factors that we "inherit" from the behaviors and the demographic and life-course choices of previous generations and cohorts. First, the rise of factory employment for women in the 19th century and then the transformation of the industrial economy into a service one has spurred the rate of working for pay outside the home. This, in turn, seems to raise the incentives for contemporary women to remain in school to complete higher educational degrees, which serve as the entry credentials for better paying jobs in this expanding sector.

Second, jobs outside and away from the home for men (and only for unmarried women) in the 19th century eroded the more exclusive family-based economy that produces goods and services. This development helped to put in place the persisting sex-segregated market for types of work, including housewifery as an occupation and expression of productive competence (Tilly, 1985). But cyclical post–World War II economic pressures on the domestic household and rising opportunities for hard wages in the modern service economy for women have transformed further the relative attractiveness of housewifery and the realistic availability of alternative expressions of productive labor (Oppenheimer, 1982). For both men and women, these historical trends have also transformed the cultural meaning of productive competence in adulthood to encompass the idea of economic worth and degree of economic independence or individuality, based on one's "career" in the paid labor force.

Third and related, cultural values of individualism and independence, latent since the founding of American society, are given more open and full expression in the more affluent industrial and postindustrial society (Lesthaeghe, 1983). The foregoing transformations in the economy created opportunities for greater explorations of self-selected goals rather than of those either dictated by or heavily contingent upon family and kin (Elder, 1978; Hareven, 1977). Thus, life-course choices regarding loving and working are set within themes of self-actualization and self-interest for both men and women.

What is important about this thumbnail interpretive history for the social structural context of adult development is that the trends and their underpinnings signal long-term changes in the specifics of adult development. In reading Professor Atchley's exegesis of the baby-boom phenomenon and its impact on contemporary adult development, I am led to infer that perhaps the effects might be cyclical, as Easterlin has suggested (1980); or at least the aberrations that this phenomenon might have caused in the educational systems and labor market might be mitigated as cohort succession replaces larger with smaller cohorts. Although the demographic analysis of cohort fertility and succession might lead us to this expectation (and to his credit Professor Atchley does not forecast this outcome), the longer historical view suggests additional forces, more linear than cyclical, and implying qualitative shifts in the expression of loving and working.

This brings me to the second major set of factors behind the trends in loving and working, those that reflect individual action and self-efficacy rather than the broad sweep of societal transformation. Of course, the two sets are not independent. The trends in divorce, in married versus less traditional family forms, in childlessness, and in paid careers for women reflect a seemingly new self-oriented calculus about the life course. It seems to be one based more on economic rather than on religious, moral, or kinship considerations. It appears to be based heavily on self-interest and self-actualization (the "me generation"). It is an economic calculus putatively based on the rational choice among competing risks, namely opportunity costs and present value of future actions.[2]

In this self-oriented economic calculus, contemporary women in particular seem to be expressing cultural values for independence and seeking optimal contexts for its achievement. Loving and working are set within this action context, and the specifics of nuptuality, fertility, migration, and socioeconomic mobility—the demography—follow from this decisional process (and also from the global historical transformations discussed earlier). For example, long-term emotional commitments sealed and reinforced by legal marriages may not be a rational choice for growing fractions of women, even though the majority of a cohort still becomes married. The life-course costs of a highly likely divorce and headship of a mother only family can be devastating; their anticipation lowers the present value of married life and children, even though for some, espe-

---

[2]At least this is the model of decision making about the life cycle that social scientists from different disciplines are applying to understand the actions of contemporary individuals and couples (e.g., England & Farkas, 1986; Fuchs, 1983). Blumstein and Schwartz (1983) give more qualitative approaches.

cially for minority women, the fate of single parenthood may be the only available option for adult living (Garfinkel & McLanahan, 1987). If we add into the equation of costs and opportunity costs the options for greater economic independence that lie in the marketplace, the logistical and relational difficulties faced by dual career couples, and the unequal division of household-maintenance tasks and lesser leisure for women, we might conclude that the divorce rates, the rise in more temporary emotional commitments, the declining (economic) value of children, and the expansion of independent self-expression are synergistically related.

In short, the trends of change in adult development may be self-fueling. The aggregation of individuals' life-course decisions and the economic calculus of loving and working are no less important for the future of American demography than the life-course decisions of prior cohorts have been for contemporary adult development. Loving and working have always been the developmental tasks of adulthood. What has changed, and will continue to change, is the variety and means of their specific expression.

DOES DEVELOPMENT LAST FOREVER?

In closing my commentary, I return to my definition of development and to sketch some speculations about the future of adult life and its connection to life in old age. In doing so, I want to emphasize an earlier point, namely, that development in one life period does not necessarily imply successful adaptation with different developmental tasks in later life periods. This idea is consistent with the life cycle "spiral" of developmental challenges and the necessary, but not sufficient, resolutions that are precursors of later development (e.g., Erikson, 1963).

Let me assume, as I have, that contemporary trends in American demography—the rising divorce rate, the declines in the near universality of marriage and parenthood as the framework for loving and generativity—are expressions of new modes of working out the developmental task of loving and working. If so, then the trends actually may be consistent with developmental gains for many adults. For some women, the developmental gain could be greater independence and a somewhat closer equality with men, at least on dimensions of economic independence and perceived productive competence based on working in the paid economy. An additional gain in developmental reserve may be a more balanced commitment to self-oriented and other-oriented goals and to a corresponding moral orientation less restricted to either particularistic or universalistic principles (e.g., Gilligan, 1982).

By attaining developmental specialization in loving and working, contemporary adults both gain and lose. The losses, for both men and women, may include the lack of sustained and reciprocated commitments and attachments to spouses and children. Although such losses may not adversely affect the developmental reserves essential for the tasks of adulthood, the absence of lifelong close kin, especially children, may redound into a major developmental deficit in old age. This could be most severe for women, whose greater longevity and (at least in contemporary cohorts) frailty frequently forces their reliance on daughters and other kin for sustained care and other interpersonal reserves associated with the developmental tasks of "old" old age.

Let me illustrate the basis for this speculation. Antonucci and Jackson (1985) have argued, from limited empirical evidence, that older adults enter old age with a "bank account" of social support, that is, the balance of debits and credits of help received and given through life. If one has a positive balance, then in times of need the "norm of reciprocity" permits one to ask for help with relatively low risk of refusal or embarrassment. But in advanced age, the convoy of one's life partners is smaller or composed of shorter termed replacements, and the balance in the bank may not be favorable. By following this reasoning, we can understand why elders seem highly likely to expect not their peers but their children, in whom they have invested heavily through life, to assist them with chronic burdens.

Further, Rodin (1986) has reviewed a growing literature that attempts to link self-efficacy and control over one's life course to stress, disease, and death. She concluded that the linkages become stronger with advanced age. It may be that one's adult children are critically important to this resource of self-efficacy and control in certain critical aspects of old age. I have in mind the control over the course of one's dying, a major developmental task in the final life period.

Gerontologists like Victor Marshall (1980) remind us that episodes of institutionalized living, especially just prior to death, are typically part of the life world of old old age. Langer (1979), Langer and Rodin (1976), and Margret Baltes and her colleagues (Baltes & Reisenzein, 1985) document the extraordinary difficulties faced by institutionalized and especially frail elderly in maintaining control over the processes of their own dying (an active "mindfulness" in this socially routinized and austere ecology) and the motivation for independent self-care simultaneously. Although the costs and benefits of institutionalized living and staff-provided care vary according to the needs of different elderly, becoming institutionalized (avoiding it or maintaining a sense of control within it) present a major developmental task for many elderly.

I suggest that one's children become a highly valuable part of one's developmental reserve in these contexts. They provide a potentially alternative source of long-term care in some cases and, when institutionalization does occur, of sustained social contact and alliance in negotiating the conditions of death with medical professionals and administrators.[3] As contemporary adults reach old age, will the developmental behaviors that expanded their reserves for adaptation to adulthood equip them well for adaptation to the developmental challenges of the final life period? I have suggested that the answer may not be positive for all of us. A rational choice for adult living without sustained commitments to risky marriages, unreliable spouses, and child rearing may expand an individual's developmental reserves in one life period when the agenda is loving and working; such a rational calculus for modern adulthood may limit one's reserves subsequently.[4]

SUMMARY

Let me sum up and put away the broad brush. Understanding adult development and its embeddedness within society requires more than the principles of social psychology as incorporated by the social structure and personality genre within sociology. It requires a strong concept of what development is and an acknowledgment of bioculturally constituted developmental tasks that define and demarcate developmental periods. In portraying the setting of adult development within the life course and other developmental tasks, I have tried to illustrate a further aspect of human development; namely, that developmental gains and losses are mutually interrelated. Expansions of developmental reserves of adaptive

---

[3]More affluent modern adults seem to take a short-run rather than a life-span view of the value of children. When adults in developing and high fertility societies (Cain, 1985) and minority Americans with high and early fertility (Furstenberg, 1976; Hogan & Kitagawa, 1985) were compared, the more advantaged appear to disregard or to find substitutes for the developmental and economic benefits of children.

[4]To my mind, this hypothetical relationship illustrates a behavioral parallel with the biological phenomenon of the pleiotropic genetic effect, which may underlie biological aging and link it to the reproductive vigor of our species (see Kirkwood, 1985). In no way are my remarks about the possible developmental value of children intended as prescriptive; neither are my remarks about the developmental assets and liabilities for women, or men, of careers of loving and working. My purpose is entirely didactic in order to illustrate ways of looking at adult development from a life-span perspective and within a historical, evolutionary framework. This is the essence of the population–person model (Featherman & Lerner, 1985), in which the concept of development acknowledges gains and losses of adaptive reserves and resources.

capacity in mind and behavior need not necessarily lead inexorably to development in subsequent life periods.

In juxtaposing adult development and demographic structures, I have taken a somewhat different approach than offered by Professor Atchley, although the differences are more of emphasis than substance. In my population, rather than demographic, analysis of adult development I have emphasized the historical evolutionary roots of both contemporaneous aspects of adulthood and future prospects for change in adult development. The population–person model I have used to sketch the course of adult development, historically and ontogenically, acknowledges the causal links among individual action, historical legacy, and future of adulthood. Adult development is understood only partially by the social psychology of the here and now. Adult development is a historical and evolving phenomenon.

Apropos of this last idea, let me leave you with one impulsive swipe with the brush of speculation. Surely there are limits to the range of possible expressions of adult development both now and in the future. Demographic and other social structures in Professor Atchley's remarks illustrate this generalization. If my speculations about the functional value of children in old age are correct and if finding substitutions for these functions are difficult to arrange (either by personal action or by public policy), then there may be feedback from the developmental problems of old age to the developmental adaptations of adults.

That is, analysts of marital and childbearing patterns in the 21st century may discover some reversals in trends of the last decades that heretofore have been viewed as the nearly linear extensions of modernization and individuation (e.g., Bumpass & Sweet, in press). These hypothetical reversals, or stabilizations in steady-state variation, would not reflect the same rational calculus of more immediate economic decision making that, at least, we analysts tend to apply to understand the demographic behavior of contemporary adults. Rather, if my speculative scenario holds, the limits to contemporary trends in adult development may arise from life-span anticipations of lengthy old age in a society unable or unwilling to provide formal, institutionalized solutions for the problematics, the developmental tasks of an extended life span for the many who live them. Ironically, it may be the evolutionary development of very old age as a life period that precipitates a rediscovery of the developmental values of children, of the abiding emotional commitments to life partners, and of the bank of social support therefrom. Lengthy old age could transform (not restore to a former state) the nature of loving *and* working in adulthood in ways that projections only from the historical record could not forecast.

REFERENCES

Atchley, R. C. (1983). *Aging: Continuity and change.* Belmont, CA: Wadsworth.

Antonucci, T. C., & Jackson, J. S. (1987). Social support, interpersonal efficacy, and health: A life course perspective. In L. Carstensen & B. Edelstein (Eds.), *Handbook of clinical gerontology* (pp. 291–311). New York: Pergamon.

Baltes, M. M., & Reisenzein, R. (1985). The social world in long-term care institutions: Psychological control toward dependency? In M. M. Baltes & P. B. Baltes (Eds.), *The psychology of control and aging* (pp. 315–344). Hillsdale, NJ: Lawrence Erlbaum Associates.

Baltes, P. B. (1987). Theoretical propositions of life span developmental psychology: On the dynamics between growth and decline. *Developmental Psychology, 23,* 611–626.

Baltes, P. B., Dittman-Kohli, F., & Dixon, R. A. (1984). New perspectives on the development of intelligence in adulthood: Toward a dual-process conception and a model of selective optimization with compensation. In P. B. Baltes & O. G. Brim, Jr. (Eds.), *Life-span development and behavior* (Vol. 6, pp. 33–76). New York: Academic Press.

Bandura, A. (1980). Self-referent thought: A developmental analysis of self-efficacy. In J. H. Flavell & L. D. Ross (Eds.), *Cognitive social development: Frontiers and possible futures* (pp. 200–239). New York: Cambridge University Press.

Blumstein, P., & Schwartz, P. (1983). *American couples: Money, work, sex.* New York: Morrow.

Bumpass, L. L. (1986, June). *Marriage and childbearing in the demographic transition.* Lecture presented at the 25th Anniversary Symposium, Population Studies Center, University of Michigan, Ann Arbor.

Bumpass, L. L., & Sweet, J. A. (in press). *American families and households.* New York: Russell Sage Foundation.

Cain, M. (1985). Fertility as an adjustment to risk. In A. Rossi (Ed.), *Gender and the life course* (pp. 145–160). New York: Aldine.

Cherlin, A. J. (1981). *Marriage, divorce, remarriage: Social trends in the United States.* Cambridge, MA: Harvard University Press.

Dannefer, D. (1984). Adult development and social theory: A paradigmatic reappraisal. *American Sociological Review, 49,* 100–116.

Davis, K. (1984). Wives and work: The sex role revolution and its consequences. *Population and Development Review, 10,* 397–417.

Denney, N. W. (1982). Aging and cognitive changes. In B. B. Wolman (Ed.)., *Handbook of developmental psychology* (pp. 807–827). Englewood Cliffs, NJ: Prentice-Hall.

Dixon, R. A., & Baltes, P. B. (1986). Toward life-span research on the functions and pragmatics of intelligence. In R. J. Sternberg & R. K. Wagner (Eds.), *Practical intelligence: Nature and origins of competence in the everyday world* (pp. 203–235). New York: Cambridge University Press.

Easterlin, R. (1980). *Birth and fortune.* New York: Basic Books.

Elder, G. Jr. (1978). Family history and the life course. In T. Hareven (Ed.), *Transitions: The life course in historical perspective* (pp. 17–64). New York: Academic Press.

England, P., & Farkas, G. (1986). *Households, employment, and gender.* New York: Aldine.

Erikson, E. H. (1959). Identity and the life cycle. *Psychological Issues, 1,* 50–100.

Erikson, E. H. (1963). *Childhood and society* (2nd ed.). New York: Norton.

Featherman, D. L. (1986). Biography, society and history: Individual development as a population process. In A. B. Sørensen, F. Weinert, & L. Sherrod (Eds.), *Human development and the life course.* Hillsdale, NJ: Lawrence Erlbaum Associates.

Featherman, D. L. (1987). *Work, adaptive competence, and successful aging: A theory of adult cognitive development.* Lecture presented at the Ninth World Congress to the International Society for the Study of Behavioral Development, Tokyo, Japan.

Featherman, D. L. (in press). Societal change, the life course, and social mobility. In A. Weymann (Ed.), *Handlungspielräume reihe: Der mensch als soziales und personales wesen*. Stuttgart: Ferdinand Enke Verlag.

Featherman, D. L., & Lerner, R. M. (1985). Ontogenesis and sociogenesis: Problematics for theory and research about development and socialization across the lifespan. *American Sociological Review, 50,* 659–676.

Featherman, D. L., & Peterson, J. G. (1986, November). *Adaptive competence in work careers: Socialization for successful aging*. Paper presented at the annual meeting of the Gerontological Society of America, Chicago.

Fuchs, V. R. (1983). *How we live: An economic perspective on Americans from birth to death*. Cambridge, MA: Harvard University Press.

Fuchs, V. R. (1986). Sex differences in economic well-being. *Science, 232,* 459–464.

Furstenberg, F. F., Jr. (1976). *Unplanned parenthood: The social consequences of teenage childbearing*. New York: Free Press.

Garfinkel, I., & McLanahan, S. S. (1987). *Single mothers and their children: A new American dilemma*. Washington, DC: Urban Institute.

Gilligan, C. (1982). Adult development and women's development: Arrangements for a marriage. In J. Giele (Ed.), *Women in the middle years* (pp. 89–114). New York: Wiley.

Hareven, T. K. (1977). Family time and historical time. *Daedalus, 106,* 57–70.

Hatano, G., & Inagaki, K. (in press). Two courses of expertise. In S. Stevenson, H. Azuma, & S. Halenta (Eds.), *Child development and education in Japan*. San Francisco: Freeman.

Hauser, P. M., & Duncan, O. D. (1959). *The study of population*. Glencoe, IL: Free Press.

Havighurst, R. J. (1951). *Developmental tasks and education*. New York: Longmans.

Hogan, D. P., & Kitâgawa, E. (1985). The impact of social status, family structure and neighborhood, or the fertility of black adolescents. *American Journal of Sociology, 90,* 825–855.

House, J. (1977). The three faces of social psychology. *Sociometry, 40,* 161–177.

Kahn, R. L. (1984). Productive behavior through the life course: An essay on the quality of life. *Human Resource Management, 23,* 5–22.

Kirkwood, T. B. L. (1985). Comparative and evolutionary aspects of longevity. In C. E. Finch & E. L. Schneider (Eds.), *Handbook of the biology of aging* (pp. 27–44). New York: Van Nostrand Reinhold.

Langer, E. J. (1979). The illusion of incompetence. In L. C. Perlmuter & R. A. Monty (Eds.), *Choice and perceived control* (pp. 301–313). Hillsdale, NJ: Lawrence Erlbaum Associates.

Langer, E. J., & Rodin, J. (1976). The effect of choice and enhanced personal responsibility for the aged. *Journal of Personality and Social Psychology, 34,* 191–198.

Lerner, R. M., & Busch-Rossnagel, N. A. (1981). Individuals as producers of their development: Conceptual and empirical bases. In R. M. Lerner & N. A. Busch-Rossnagel (Eds.), *Individuals as producers of their development: A life-span perspective* (pp. 1–36). New York: Academic Press.

Lesthaeghe, R. (1983). A century of demographic and cultural change in Western Europe. *Population and Development Review, 9,* 411–435.

Mannheim, K. (1952). The problem of generations. In P. Kecskemeti (Ed.), *Essays on the sociology of knowledge* (pp. 276–322). London: Routledge & Kegan Paul.

Marshall, V. W. (1980). *Last chapters: A sociology of aging and dying*. Monterey, CA: Brooks-Cole.

Oppenheimer, V. K. (1982). *Work and the family: A study in social demography*. New York: Academic Press.

Riley, M. W. (1985). Age strata in social systems. In R. H. Binstock & E. Shanas (Eds.), *Handbook of aging and the social science* (2nd ed., pp. 369–414). New York: Van Nostrand Reinhold.

Rodin, J. (1986). Aging and health: Effects of the sense of control. *Science, 232,* 1271–1276.

Ryder, N. B. (1964). Notes on the concept of a population. *American Journal of Sociology, 49,* 447–463.

Ryder, N. B. (1965). The cohort as a concept in the study of social change. *American Sociological Review, 30*, 843–861.

Shavit, Y., & Featherman, D. L. (1988). Schooling, tracking, and teenage intelligence. *Sociology of Education, 61*(1), 42–50.

Smelser, N., & Erikson, E. H. (1980). *Themes of love and work in adulthood.* Cambridge, MA: Harvard University Press.

Sorokin, R. P. (1959). *Social and cultural mobility.* London: Free Press.

Tilly, L. A. (1985). Family, gender, and occupation in industrial France: Past and present. In A. S. Ross (Ed.), *Gender and the life course* (pp. 193–212). New York: Academic Press.

Vinovskis, M. A. (1988). The historian and the life course: Reflections on recent approaches to the study of American family life in the past. In P. B. Baltes, D. L. Featherman, & R. M. Lerner (Eds.), *Life-span development and behavior* (Vol. 8, pp. 33–59). Hillsdale, NJ: Lawrence Erlbaum Associates.

Wells, L. E., & Stryker, S. (1988). Stability and change in self over the life course. In P. B. Baltes, D. L. Featherman, & R. M. Lerner (Eds.), *Life span development and behavior* (Vol. 8, pp. 191–229). Hillsdale, NJ: Lawrence Erlbaum Associates.

Willis, S. L. (1985). Towards an educational psychology of the adult learner. In J. E. Birren & K. W. Schaie (Eds.), *Handbook of the psychology of aging* (pp. 818–847). New York: Van Nostrand Reinhold.

2

Behavior-Relevant Ecological Factors

M. Powell Lawton
Philadelphia Geriatric Center

The overall topic of this book lends itself comfortably to a consideration of the transactions between the older person and the environment. In order to address this topic, I repeat a considerable number of previously discussed ideas before going on to an extension of these ideas as stimulated by the task of preparing this chapter. In the most general terms possible, I discuss how the older person's functioning is maintained at optimal levels by particular uses of the environmental context. This discussion involves consideration of a number of dualities such as person and environment, competence and incompetence, docility and proactivity, challenge and security, openness and closedness, and affective self-regulation and permeability.

Although I turn next to an extended consideration of what I mean by "environment," it is necessary to indicate at the outset that the social structure in my terms represents only one aspect of the larger construct, the environment. I also acknowledge that I find it impossible to discuss constructs of the types mentioned in a way that portrays adequately their dynamic, changing and interrelated nature. The language of process, temporal state, and development must be supplied by those more gifted in this way than I. Perhaps static end states are a necessary beginning in my attempt to differentiate poorly understood dynamic processes. In any case, any dualities to which I've referred must be implicitly viewed as continua—"things" in process—and inherently related to one another.

PERSON AND ENVIRONMENT

One of the oldest problems in psychology is how to deal with the logical contradiction involved in viewing person as an entity distinct from environment. At the most basic level, environment exists only through the mind. Thus, can environment be said to be describable exclusive of the sensory and cognitive processes? Ittelson (1973), for example, said: "Environment is an artifact created in man's own image" (p. 18). From an entirely different perspective, Gibson (1979) has affirmed the unity of person and environment though the physical energy of physical structures common to both and through the construct of "affordance," that is, behavior-relevant stimulus information inherent in the object and simultaneously specifying the person's potential for using that information.

The environmental psychologists in their empirical research endeavors have often affirmed the unitary nature of person and environment but have resorted to *linking* person and environment constructs rather than to dealing with them as a single system. Those who study the topic "environmental cognition," for example, have pursued such tasks as determining how connotative meanings are assigned to environmental objects (Kasmar, 1970), how large-scale environments become cognitively apprehended (Lynch, 1960), how older people schematize "home" (Rubinstein, 1987), or how people find their way in traversing a new environment (Weisman, 1981).

The major stream of research that deals with "perceived quality of life" in fact represents the study of people's subjective evaluative representations of the external world in such limited sectors as job, home, family, uses of leisure time, and so on (Campbell, Converse, & Rodgers, 1976).

For each of these approaches, the researchers assume that there is a person attempting to feel, comprehend, or manipulate an environment and that there is some transactional process whereby "the environment is brought into the person" or "the person enters into the environment." When environmental psychology has proceeded toward application and intervention, the heuristic necessity of talking about person *and* environment is clear: Ways of characterizing the central tendencies and individual differences in persons and environment are necessary if we are to design housing, affect the growth of cities and neighborhoods, or fashion usable objects for people. Thus, the raw materials for environmental design become such nontransactional attributes as personal values, personal preferences, or personal competences on the person side; and such attributes as social-area census characteristics, social networks, neighborhood amenities, or housing quality on the environment side. In fact, some progress has been made in "removing the person" from some environmental measures. For example, one can count the number of people living alone in a census tract, measure the amount of fallen plaster in a dwelling unit, or even gain a fair amount of consensus in rating the affective quality of environments (Russell & Lanius, 1984).

The Person

With the previous explanation having been offered for the utility of talking separately about person and environment, let me proceed to define these two central features of my discussion. The aspects of the person that are most central to this discussion are what I refer to as "personal competences" and "personal resources."

Competence and Incompetence. White (1959) defined competence as the process by which the person learns to interact effectively with his or her environment. The process includes "visual exploration, grasping, crawling and walking, attention and perception, language and thinking, exploring novel objects and places, manipulating the surroundings and producing effective changes in the E" (p. 329). The *motivation* is "effectance," and the experience is "a feeling of efficacy." White thus seemed to view competence as a dynamic process subsuming both givens residing in the person and "becomings." My own definition of competence includes primarily intrapersonal givens: Competence is the ability to respond adaptively, as judged by social norms, in the domains of physical health, activities of daily living (ADL), sensorimotor and perceptual functions, and cognition. Figure 2.1 depicts a schema in which I try to view personal competences defined behaviorally in hierarchical fashion. The left-most domains — biological health, functional health (ADL), and to some extent cognitive ability — are more "basic" in that they have a clear link to biology, are vulnerable to changes in health, but resistant to major change with experience. I also call them basic because I see them as having a strong connection to the soma of the individual, independent of the context.

Those domains of behavioral competence on the right — time use and social behavior — are related to biology and health and may have some considerable stability over a lifetime; but they are above all determined by personal preference, social norms, and environmental opportunity. Yet competence in most examples indicated in Fig. 2.1 is measurable in terms of some specified norms, whether that be, for example, for blood pressure in millimeters of mercury or for a social consensus that it is better to have more friends than few.

As I've written in greater detail elsewhere (Lawton, 1982), time use and social behavior are not seen as characteristics residing within the person in the same way that basic biological, sensory, motor, and cognitive competence are. For our present purpose, the important factor is that in the aging process most people retain their competences in most areas, but chronic disease, sensory impairments, social ageism, or personal losses also become statistically more prevalent. My goal in this discussion is to further our understanding of how people optimize behavioral and psy-

COMPLEX

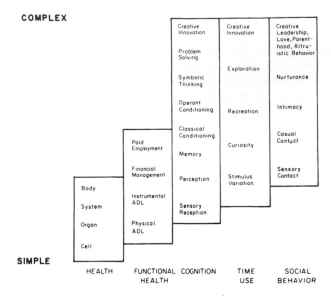

SIMPLE

| | HEALTH | FUNCTIONAL
HEALTH | COGNITION | TIME
USE | SOCIAL
BEHAVIOR |

FIG. 2.1 Hierarchy of behavioral competence

chological outcomes even in the face of negative change or diminished personal opportunity structure.

Personal Resources.   The other person attribute is harder to specify. Personal resources include *efficacy* and *affective self-regulation.* Within these categories, the object of one's action may be either the environment or the self. Efficacy is the normatively judged quality of the behaviors developed to deal with the environment. Thus each example of competence mentioned in White's (1959) definition may be evalutated in terms of how well they succeed in managing the relationship between the person and the environment. In keeping with Bandura's (1977) use of the term, efficacy is exhibited behaviorally in specific situations and is thus a more variable and much more environmentally linked characteristic than is competence. Competence is necessary for efficacy, and it is competence expressed through efficacy that leads to one's more general ability to respond to environmental press (Murray, 1938). Efficacy by one route begins with a personal need, desire, or preference followed by an environmental search for a means to satisfy the need; a choice of the appropriate environmental resource or an active effort to create such an environmental resource; and a behavior designed to use the resource. Alternatively, an environmental press may demand a response from the person; the evaluated quality of that response constitutes the efficacy of that occasion. Thus efficacy may be exhibited in either proactive or reactive form.

Efficacy has a subjective as well as an objective (behavioral) aspect: The expectation that one will deal with the environment and emerge with a favorable outcome is subjective efficacy.

The object of one's transactions with the environment may be one's affective life as well as one's behavior. People seek positive affective experiences and minimize negative affective experiences. Affective self-regulation represents one's success in keeping the type, amount, quality, and conditions of affective stimulation, and one's responsiveness to such stimulation, within the bounds of one's personal needs, preferences, and ability to manage.

This concept is based on the idea that people not only respond affectively to environmental situations that instigate such responses, they also actively search for situations with a probability of providing particular kinds of affective experience. People may also search their internal needs, motivations, and memories for affective experience. Efficacy thus represents successfully directed behavior; affective self-regulation is successfully directed emotion. They are linked by cognitive processes discussed next.

Of course, a person is much more than the aggregate of competence and resources. These two aspects are emphasized, however, because they lend themselves particularly well to the prediction of outcomes resulting from people's transactions with the environment.

Environment

At this point, it is necessary to offer a more extended look at what is meant by environment. *Objective environment* may be defined as all that originates outside the skin of the person. Despite the theoretical difficulties of making such a distinction, our concepts must be translated into attributes capable of being measured. One way of doing so is to make the inside–outside distinction, the inside or transactional variety having been alluded to previously. I find it convenient to think of five gross categories, all of which can be identified, counted, or measured in c.g.s. independently of the target person (Lawton, 1970).

The *personal environment* consists of other individuals who interact with the person. For example, a spouse, relatives, members of the household, therapists, co-workers, and so on can, if necessary, be identified archivally. Friends can be identified behaviorally in most cases. The qualitative aspects of the personal environment, for example, whether a person is considered a confidant, is a transactional environmental attribute.

The *small group environment* consists of groups in which the person is a member. This level is a salient and differentiable domain of environment to the extent that group-determined forces that are neither purely personal nor simply social institutional forces impinge on the person. For example, pressure to conform behaviorally or ideationally, reinforcement of behavior, or affirmation of the person's competence may emerge because of unique properties of small groups, such as a group goal, a group expectation, or a group selection of the person to fill a specific role within.

The *suprapersonal environment* is the modal characteristics of the aggregate of people physically proximate to the person, who may or may not have some personal relationship to that individual. The age characteristics of other tenants in an apartment building, the dominant ethnic character of one's neighborhood, and the educational background of one's co-workers are examples of suprapersonal environmental characteristics. The degree of congruence between a personal characteristic and a corresponding suprapersonal characteristic constitutes a transactional aspect of the suprapersonal environment.

The *social environment* consists of all characteristics of the social structure at a level of aggregation beyond any personal characteristic. For example, culture, values, social norms, laws, organizations, and other social institutions fall into this environmental category. Again, the way in which these forces are recognized, interpreted, and acted on is an aspect of the transactional environment.

The *physical environment* is all that is inanimate. As was true when I wrote in 1970, there is still no convincing taxonomy of the physical environment. One way to impose such order is to use a geographic perspective, where one begins with the microenvironment of personal space then proceeds to the dwelling unit, the neighborhood, and the community, and so on. But then there is the natural versus the person-made, the simple versus the complex, and countless other ways of classification. How and whether such multiple dimensions can be used to organize the physical environment hierarchically is not known.

The terms *situation, milieu,* and *context* have often been used to represent aspects of the environment (Frederiksen, 1972; Sells, 1963). Some examples might be a social intervention, the workplace, or any "behavior setting" specified by Barker (1968). These situations are too complex to be treated as entities. Instead, they require characterization in multivariate terms; we use units that fall into the five environmental categories previously mentioned to do this.

To repeat, it may sometimes be necessary for researchers to confine their attention to some aspect of the external environment in order to use or plan for its use. A population count is a case in point as a planning-relevant aspect of the suprapersonal environment. Population count (or population density) has been shown to be relevant to the behavior of many individuals. Whether a given population count is perceived as "small" or "large" depends on the processed meaning of the population fact to a particular individual. For example, Wohlwill and Kohn (1973) determined that Harrisburg was "quiet" and "small" to transplanted New Yorkers but "noisy and large" to rural migrants from the South. A final comment: Each of the five classes of objective environment has a transactional aspect, the particular environmental attribute as perceived by the person.

I repeat these definitions at some length in order to anchor my discussion. Unquestionably, my statements on "the social environment" do no justice to the rich construct "the social structure." However, it is important, first, to specify the social environment independently of the target person (usually by consensus or by aggregating the opinions or observations of large numbers of people). Second, like any other aspect of the environment, the social environment can arouse or activate the individual. Third, the social environment may be perceived, apprehended, and interpreted by the person, and thus is transactional. Finally, it is people who create social structure; therefore the volitional, proactive contribution of the person to the social structure needs to be acknowledged. This chapter deals with environment as a general class, and much of the discussion of environment is relevant to social structure as an aspect of environment.

In parallel with the choice to view the person in terms of competences, Nahemow and I (Lawton & Nahemow, 1973) similarly found it convenient to characterize environment in terms of Murray's (1938) concept of "press," the extent to which an environment demands a response from the person. We schematized this relationship between personal competence and environmental press, shown in Fig. 2.2, in which the evaluated quality of outcome of the behavior or internal state occasioned by a person of competence level A faced with environmental press level X is represented by a point on the surface of the figure (point P in this case).

Figure 2.2 illustrates that favorable behavioral and affective outcomes are likely to result from a match between personal competence and environmental demand. An excess of press over competence at a particular time occasions maladaptive behavior and negative affect, as does a deficiency of press with respect to competence. We compared overdemand to stress, underdemand to deprivation. Among the principles illustrated here, there is no level of competence so high as to be invulnerable to extraordinary press levels and no level of competence so low as to have no range of positive outcome. Another principle appears to be that a given amount of objective change in press level would affect the outcome disproportionately more for low-competence people than for high-competence people. We called this "the environmental docility hypothesis." We were led to this generalization by research showing physically healthier tenants in planned housing to be geographically unconstrained in choosing new friends and therefore better able to attain the favorable outcome of selective friendship choice. Those in poorer health were more

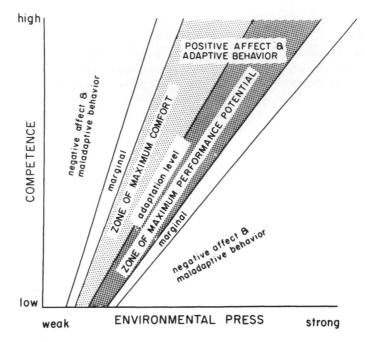

FIG. 2.2 Diagrammatic representation of the behavioral and affective outcomes of person–environment transactions

vulnerable to the press of physical distance and thus were limited to only the most proximate neighbors as friends (Lawton & Simon, 1968).

DOCILITY AND PROACTIVITY

The environmental docility hypothesis has been used widely as the theoretical rationale underlying the attempt to encourage favorable outcomes by special environmental design targeted at people with lowered competence. Ideally an incremental improvement in the environment should disproportionately enhance outcome for the more disabled as compared to the effect of the same improvement for the most competent. Such an assertion has guided the activity of planners, architects, and other designers in search of competence-maintaining design features.

It should be clear to everyone that such a strategy puts the professional in the active role and the older person in the passive role; that is, the older person is a recipient and user of a built environment designed by others. This one-way effect of environment on the person is, of course, only part of the story (Lawton, 1980). A research finding not supportive of the docility hypothesis was reported by Lieberman and Tobin (1983), who studied the effect of postrelocation environmental quality on the well-being of older hospitalized mental patients. Rather than finding the most impaired to be most responsive to improved environments, they found that the best postrelocation environments had their strongest effects on the least impaired.

This study led me back to some of Frances Carp's recent writings (1984) in which she discussed the limitations of our press-competence model, pointing out that we had not dealt with people's needs and preferences. She noted that the environment was characterized not only by demands but by resources and opportunities. It seems clear that this thinking represents a good focus for improving the model.

If we examine Fig. 2.2 again, it is possible to substitute personal resources for competence and environmental resources (its continuum ranging from few to many) for press, as has been done in Fig. 2.3. At low levels of personal resources, there is a relatively narrow range of environmental resources available to the person within the favorable outcome zones. Environmental opportunities beyond that range are presumed to be unusable by the low-competent person, either because they are too

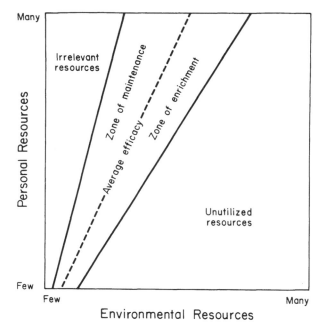

FIG. 2.3 Environmental docility and proactivity are both affected by personal resources and, in turn, affect perceived resources. Only proactivity leads to environment change

demanding, not personally salient, or simply out of reach and therefore irrelevant. For the person of higher competence, the environment is richer because the greater proportion of all that is "out there" in the objective environment is presumably within range of use should the person's needs and preferences point in that direction.

The critical distinctions between the original model and the revised one are that (a) the environment is differentiated into resources and demands and (b) the stance of the person may be either passive or active. As a companion to the environmental docility hypothesis, the environmental proactivity hypothesis states that the greater the competence of the person, the greater the number of environment resources that may be used in the pursuit of personal needs and wishes. Thus, a response may be prevented or shaped by environment demand, and conversely the person may shape his or her own environment in such a way as to afford a desired response.

Environmental docility and environmental proactivity are classes that represent neither a person attribute nor an environmental attribute, but they signify person–environment transactions. Personal efficacy and affective self-regulation may occur equally within the context of either a docile or a proactive stance. A schematic attempt to depict the constructs discussed thus far is shown in Fig. 2.4. As an open system, it can be seen

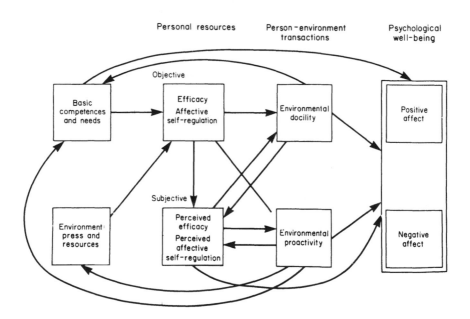

FIG. 2.4 Environmental proactivity model

that in addition to the causal sequences implied by the foregoing discussion, the effective use of both docile and proactive processes feeds back toward subjectively perceived resources and toward competence. Environmental proactivity also can affect environment, and the feedback from proactivity to both competence and environment then proceeds in the forward causal flow. Figure 2.4 attempts to clarify that the environment as well as the person is a dynamic, changing process not a fixed given. Therefore it must be understood that any measure of the five classes of objective or transactional environments must be defined in time as narrowly as the person's "status" must be measured.

A gap that remains is when docility will occur and when proactivity will occur. It is necessary once more to disclaim the categorical nature of these properties of the behavioral system and to acknowledge that few responses are activated in purely proactive or docile fashion. Nonetheless, it is clearly worthwhile to search for predictors of one behavior or the other, such as the degree of proactivity or docility that afford greater precision than would predictions based solely on the gross level of general competence.

Another aspect of Figs. 2.2 and 2.3 may give some assistance in this task. Our model originally posited a theoretical line along which all exact correspondences between competence and press level were arrayed. "Adaptation level," after Helson (1964), is the point for any given level of competence at which the level of environmental press is neither "high" nor "low" but exactly balanced. Such a quality may conceivably be objectively determined. For example, the following level may be determined by the industrial psychologist: the point of adequate performance quality attainable by an employee of known skill working under a quota requirement set to the average of that skill level.

The subjective or hedonic aspect of adaptation level is more familiar and is the basis of my discussion. Nahemow and I (Lawton & Nahemow, 1973) suggested that the point at which press and competence are in balance is also a point of affective neutrality. At this point, adaptation to press level has occurred, awareness of incoming stimulation is minimal, and concurrent behavior is relatively effortless and adequate in quality. Taking off from Wohlwill's (1966) elaboration of the Yerkes–Dodson law for sensory stimulation, we applied the curve shown in Fig. 2.5 to our model. Wohwill described any departure in stimulus strength from adaptation level as being hedonically positive. He used as an example the person sitting motionless in a tub. The person totally adapted to tepid water would react with mild pleasure to either a slight rise or a slight fall in temperature as more water is added. As stimulus stength increases (i.e., water becomes very hot or very cold—high node to right of AL), a point comes when pleasure diminishes and eventually displeasure (pain, strain)

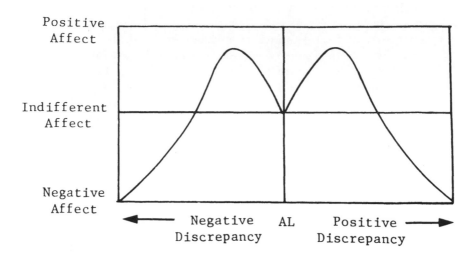

FIG. 2.5 Discrepancy from adaptation level

begins. A similar turnaround ensues as stimulation decreases (boredom, sensory deprivation — in this example excessive lack of variation in temperature, movement, or cutaneous stimulation).

Wohlwill's curve should be viewed as being imposed perpendicular to the plane of our competence-press model. Nahemow and I accept this hedonic hypothesis and add to it a motivational hypothesis, again an adaptation of the Yerkes–Dodson law. That is, we suggest that a mild increase in press strength is motivating and will elevate the person's quality or quantity of behavioral response. We called this slight mismatch between competence and press the "zone of maximum performance potential," suggesting that meeting the challenge of demand in increments above AL is the route toward elevating competence. Pleasure also results from mild decreases in press level. This opposite incongruity between competence and press is accompanied by a reduction in effort. This mild excess of competence over press was called "the zone of maximum comfort" in which security characterizes the context.

Up to this point, the description of the Wohlwill (1966) model has referred to the docile stance; that is, a change in environmental press level is an antecedent that produces the affective and behavioral changes noted. Once more, this direction of causality represents most of our interventions, whatever the type of environment we are describing. We may prescribe a challenging intervention for one person–environment combination and a supportive intervention for another.

Equal time for the proactive side demands that we investigate mechanisms leading people to initiate change in their environments. This question is of critical importance in the study of older people. It is probably fair to say that the great majority of the gerontological literature has been devoted to pathology, impairment, decrement, deprivation, and isolation, all of these negatives viewed as unwanted invasions from the outside, whether biological, psychological, or social. Without recounting the supporting data, it is clear that although these conditions become statistically more frequent as age increases, the majority of older people cannot be characterized in these ways. As many have said, it is likely that such undervaluing of the ages as a class, both by the population in general and by older people themselves, actually detracts from their behavioral competence.

The argument is not intended only to affirm the existence of high levels of competence in many older people. Much more important is to understand that challenge and proactivity can be part of every person's existence. Our task is to specify the conditions under which proactivity occurs and under which its exercise has favorable outcomes. As we suggested in relation to competence and press, there is no person with so few resources as to be unable to increase the supply of environmental resources by choosing wisely or actively altering the environment in his or her favor.

How people accomplish this task must be understood in terms of a system of competences, motivations, affective responses, and controls whose goal is growth and breadth/depth of experience to the maximum degree possible, given the maintenance of a required level of security. Six reasonable hypotheses follow from this basic premise:

1. Environmental proactivity is stronger or more frequent as competence increases.

2. Environmental affordances, specifically, are more likely to be discerned by those with greater cognitive ability.

3. Objective efficacy and affective self-regulation, together with their subjective cognates, are intervening variables between competence and the person–environment transactions labeled docility and proactivity.

4. The motivational energy of environmental proactivity has neural origins in the processes of affective arousal and cognitive and motor activation.

5. Both affective arousal and the maintenance of focused attention on behavioral goals are self-regulated; success in such self-regulation leads both directly to environmental proactivity and indirectly to proactivity by enhancing perceived efficacy.

6. Proactivity is seen as leading to increased psychological well-being; it also acts reciprocally to increase perceived efficacy, increased environmental resources, and increased competence. The successful use of docile behavior may have similar outcome, with one important exception: Docility accepts environment as given, or changes only its perceived aspect, whereas proactivity may succeed in altering the environment in such a way as to amplify its effects on efficacy and well-being.

The Neural Origins of Proactivity and Docility

The concept of self-regulation requires further elaboration. The theoretical bases for self-regulation may be found in both neurophysiology and perceptual and cognitive psychology. The opposing neural control processes identified by Pribram and McGuinness (1975), arousal and activation, provide a basis for inferring a self-motivated system for person–environment relations.

Arousal is mediated by noradrenergic transmitters and is a neural activity that adapts and decrements quickly to constant stimuli but is alert to novel stimuli. This system tends to be holistic in its organizing of stimulus information and is primarily a right-hemispheric operation. By contrast, the dopaminergic system is attuned to focused attention, perceptual monitoring, and maintenance of a state of readiness for motor behavior. Activation is primarily a left-hemispheric, sequential cognitive-processing system. All these summary statements oversimplify very complex functions, however, particularly the fact that a complicated array of cross-system checks and balances maintains synchrony between the two systems (thought of as another system called "effort" by Pribram & McGuinness, 1975). For example, affective control appears to be achieved not only by the habituation capacity of the arousal system but also by the cognitive and inhibitory mechanisms of activation system.

These systems — cognitive analysis and vigilance, on the one hand, and global affective orienting response, on the other — may be viewed as self-initiated propensities that one is capable of modifying by learning and continued action. Throughout the life span, these two systems are the motivating factors that we can associate with environmental proactivity and ultimately with psychological well-being.

The sequential processing capacity of the activation system lends itself well to the development and elaboration of cognitive schemata that transform the external environment into knowable terms. Neisser's (1976) definition of a schema as "a structure that directs perceptual activity and is modified as it occurs" (p. 14) points to both a docile and proactive function. As the repository of past cognitive activity, a schema brings some familiarity to one's environment. The template for comprehension is already there. The schema also leads the person to new learning. Again from Neisser (1976): "Anticipatory schemata prepare the perceiver to accept certain kinds of information rather than others and thus control the activity of looking. Because we can see only what we know to look for, it is those schemata (together with the information already available) that determine what will be perceived" (p. 20).

The neurological aspect of such self-directed exploration is expressed by Pribram and McGuinness (1975).

> The interaction between behaving organisms and their environment is not one-sided. The organism is not just a switchboard for income stimulation. Rather, the essence of behaving organisms is that they are spontaneously active, generating changes in the environment often by way of highly programmed, that is, serially ordered, responses. (p. 124)

Elsewhere they say: "The attention involved is voluntary, in the sense that it is initiated by some input event" (p. 133), and increasing competence results from "increasing the complexity of the neuronal model [the neural cognitive schema], an ecoding process described as 'chunking' the information" (p. 134).

The purposeful distinction of the environment into what is familiar and secure, on the one hand, and what must be assimilated and is therefore challenging, on the other, constitutes one self-regulatory task. Referring once more to the press-competence model, the focal task is for the person to comprehend a large array of environmental possibilities and to choose for his or her own behavioral arena those that are within the realm of his or her comptences to respond to. Growth in competence comes from successful problem solving and continued elaboration of one's cognitive schemata of environment and self. Self-maintenance occurs when the choice is for the familiar and may involve an affirmation of perceived efficacy in the absence of challenge.

This hypothesis may thus be stated: Efficacy and subjective efficacy may be maintained by docile behavior, but enhancement of efficacy occurs only through proactive behavior. In Fig. 2.4, it can be seen that docile behavior reinforces efficacy through feedback to competence. Proactive behavior reinforces efficacy through both competence and environmental enhancement. The revised proactivity model depicts the self-directed growth aspect of cognitive challenge, including the search for new learning and environmental contexts.

In parallel fashion, the environmental stimuli leading to arousal have been called "collative" (Berlyne & Madsen, 1973). These include novelty, complexity, unusual stimulus amplitude or pattern, or change in familiar or habituated stimuli. The evolutionary survival value of the orienting response is expressed in the global affective response pattern to novel

stimuli that may range from positive to negative. The amount of deviation of environmental demands from adaptation level in the press-
competence model has been suggested as the primary determinant of subjective well-being, excessive deviations being associated with negative
states. The revision also suggests that the proactive stance enables the person to search for and arrange environments with features that maximize
the person's attainment of his or her desired degree of arousal. That is,
affective self-regulation includes the efforts of people to enhance their
types, intensities, and qualities of emotional experience as well as their
efforts to moderate or diminish their range of affective experience. Thus
for some, maximizing positive affect will be the major preference; in ar-
ranging novel and potentially pleasurable situations for themselves, they
may take the risk of promoting novel situations that also evoke negative
affect. For others, a relatively neutral state, near adaptation level, will be
preferred. These people would presumably be adept in avoiding situations likely to evoke either negative or positive feelings. But this latter
group, in achieving a moderate-press lifestyle, nonetheless proactively designs its own context of stimulation. The revised proactivity model thus
describes the affective realm as well as the cognitive realm.

Viewing cortical activation as the medium for cognitive proactivity and
arousal as the medium for affective proactivity would be a gross oversim-
plification. Just as the nervous system is known to have an intricate system of interdependencies among units, the same is true at the level of
functioning individuals. We know that the motivation to create an intellectual challenge may have an affective outcome, or that obtaining a pleasure-
engendering environment requires careful planning. Thus we must continue to explore how people use cognitive, affective, and behavioral modes
to work in the service of an efficacious *self* and a state of favorable psychological well-being. It may be well to restate the basic dialectic: a ten-
sion between proactivity in the service of challenge, growth, and breadth
of experience and docility in the service of security, maintenance of function, and narrowed experience.

Docility and Proactivity in Personality Research

Aging in our society has been pictured as a transaction characterized by
docility. The withdrawal of middle-adulthood social rewards such as a place
in the labor force, a power that accompnies financial solvency, a responsibility for personal and familial decision making, for example, have been
cited as status reductions associated with an inner state of powerlessness.
The original statement of disengagement theory (Cumming & Henry, 1961)
explicitly posited a corresponding psychological process of relinquishment

of the reward structure associated with activity, striving, and engagement. Neugarten and her colleagues (1964, 1968) found evidence for the age-related replacement of a personality stance labeled "active mastery" with "passive mastery" or "magical mastery," a shift also reported in cultures very different from our own (Gutmann, 1969, 1971). The "rocking-chair syndrome" was one of several personality styles associated with favorable psychological adjustment in Reichard, Livson, and Peterson's (1962) study of normal aged. The weight of this and other later research at least supports the idea that passivity and reactivity are not necessarily psychologically debilitating.

Positive and Negative Affect. Figure 2.4 shows positive affect and negative affect as indicators of the most general outcome class, psychological well-being. In fact, evidence is mounting that not only do people distinguish subjectively between negative affect and positive affect (Diener, 1984; Russell, 1980; Warr, Barter, & Brownbridge, 1983) but also that the two aspects of psychological well-being have notably different antecedents (Bradburn, 1969; Costa & McCrae, 1980; Lawton, 1983). This topic is too complex to treat at length in this chapter. However, a hypothesis worthy of further exploration is that efficacy and self-regulation as they result in the transactional process of proactivity are differentially more likely to elevate positive affect than are the same degree of efficacy and self-regulation exercised in the service of docility. Conversely, competent docility is differentially associated with the reduction of negative affect. Thus, separate avenues to the maintenance of an overall state of psychological well-being arise through different mixes of proactivity and docility because, as Bradburn (1969) suggested long ago, happiness consists of the balance between negative and positive feelings.

Although the evidence is far from clear, there does seem to be an indication that both positive and negative affect are lower among older people. One problem with this finding is that most such evidence is cross-sectional, yet there is every reason to wonder whether cohort and period may not also confound such apparent age relationships in the affective as well as the cognitive area (Felton & Shaver, 1984). Should such age differences be confirmed as true age-related change, such a situation would at least be consistent with the idea that affect self-regulation represents one way of maintaining a favorable state of psychological well-being in the face of biological and social factors that tend to decrease one's personal competence and one's ability to manipulate one's environment proactively. That is, if one reduces the range of stimulus input, his or her choice of secure rather than challenging situations is likely to reduce novelty, emotional richness, and new learning; but at the same time, one also reduces the risks of taking on more affective involvement than he or she can tolerate. Thus, affective narrowing may be an age-related aspect of docility, one that helps maintain basic competence.

Carried too far, of course, this assertion can lead to the idea that passivity is the essence of old age and that programming for the elderly should reinforce such passivity. This conclusion was exactly what was deduced from the original statements of the disengagement theorists that disengagement was normative and that *only* the joint movement of both society and the individual to weaken the person's ties to society could eventuate in psychological well-being (Cumming & Henry, 1961).

It is clear that society does program too few opportunities for positive affect and cognitive challenge to be elicited in older people. The press-competence model does, in fact, suggest that there is no level of competence so low that an increment of demand cannot elicit behavior an increment more complex than that exercised at adaptation level (see Fig. 2.2). Figure 2.3 similarly suggests that there is no level of personal resource so low as to prevent *some* increment in the environmental resources that can be effectively used (i.e., positive affect as the result of novel stimulation). Our programs for older people, whether activity programs conducted in senior centers, "treatment" in nursing homes, or generalized incentives toward dependency built into our national policy regarding aging, have ignored the whole half of the motivational system that deals with proactivity, challenge, and positive affect. We must acknowledge the possiblity that passive mastery as an age-related phenomenon may result at least as much from a lack of accessible environmental resources as from an endogenous process of biological aging.

Enhancing Proactivity.   Most evidence regarding the effects of proactivity is indirect. It is possible, for example, to view self-initiated environmental change as an example of proactivity and to point to substantial positive results that have followed relocation to "retirement areas" of the country (Bultena & Wood, 1969; Longino, McClellan, & Peterson, 1980) or to planned age-segregated housing (Carp, 1966; Lawton & Cohen, 1974). Conversely, research such as that of M. M. Baltes (Baltes, Honn, Barton, Orzech, & Lago, 1983; Baltes, Kindermann, Reisenzein, & Schmidt, in press) has demonstrated very convincingly that passive behavior is the only type regularly rewarded in institutions for the aged. Nonetheless, naturalistic research has thus far been unable to disentangle the complex causal processes implied by such models as that shown in Fig. 2.4. Thus it may well be up to experimental researchers to provide new convincing information regarding the responsiveness of older people to deliberate attempts that enhance their opportunities for proactivity.

The research performed by Langer, Rodin, Schulz, and their associates (Langer & Rodin, 1976; Langer, Rodin, Beck, Weinman, & Spitzer, 1979;

Rodin & Langer, 1977; Schulz, 1976; Schulz & Hanusa, 1979) used the setting of the nursing home to devise interventions into the presumed dependency-inducing milieu such that predictability and perceived control would be enhanced (reviewed at considerable length in Rodin, Temko, & Harris, 1985). In these studies, interventions such as orientation of residents to the desirability of personal control; ways of maximizing the predictability of the environment; and concrete opportunities to exert control (e.g., caring for a plant) proved to have consequences such as increased psychological health, physical health, and even lower mortality. Rodin et al. (1985) reviewed this research as well as some other studies that did not confirm the control-enhancement hypothesis. In the process, they raised other questions that are central to the press-competence model, such as whether there are occasions when greater opportunity for control may constitute a threat and whether there are individual personality differences in the desire for control, which enter into a person–environment transactional element (docility or proactivity in the press-competence conception).

There are clearly many unanswered questions left at this stage of research. The control-enhancement hypothesis is in need of replicated testing by other investigators, with people of differing levels of competence, in different environmental context, and with more of the model elements shown in Fig. 2.4. However, the basic plan of experimentally varying the level of actual or perceived control afforded needs to be maintained in continuing this stream of research.

CONCLUSION

The press-competence view of well-being in later life has been extended by further consideration of personal efficacy and self-regulation, together with the way these intrapersonal factors relate to the environment. This transactional process may be considered in terms that have been called environmental docility and environmental proactivity. Both docility and proactivity may lead to psychological well-being and in turn enhance personal competence. Only proactivity shapes the environment, however; thus proactivity, when exercised in a range that maintains at least a minimal level of congruence between person and environment, represents a unique pathway toward growth and the experience of positive affect. There are conditions under which docility and reduction in affective range represent self-chosen and adaptive response to a reduction of competence due to biological aging or constriction of environmental opportunity. Conversely, there are special pathways to increased psychological well-being that come through proactivity. Such pathways are available to every person regardless of basic competence, the difference being in level of attainable increase in competence and level of control over environment, not in level of attainable psychological well-being.

REFERENCES

Baltes, M. M., Honn, S., Barton, E. M., Orzech, M., & Lago, D. (1983). On the social ecology of dependence and independence in elderly nursing home residents: A replication and extension. *Journal of Gerontology, 38*, 556–564.

Baltes, M. M., Kindermann, T., Reisenzein, R., & Schmid, U. (in press). Further observational data on the behavioral and social world of institutions for the aged. *Psychology and Aging.*

Bandura, A. (1977). Self-efficacy: Toward a unifying theory of behavioral change. *Psychological Review, 84*, 190–215.

Barker, R. G. (1968). *Ecological psychology.* Stanford, CA: Stanford University Press.

Berlyne, D. E., & Madsen, K. B. (Eds.). (1973). *Pleasure, reward, preference.* New York: Academic Press.

Bradburn, N. (1969). *The structure of psychological well-being.* Chicago: Aldine.

Bultena, G., & Wood, V. (1969). America's retirement community: Bane or blessing? *Journal of Gerontology, 24*, 209–218.

Campbell, A., Converse, P. G., & Rodgers. W. (1976). *The quality of American life.* New York: Russell Sage Foundation.

Carp, F., & Carp, A. (1984). A complementary/congruence model of well-being or mental health for the community elderly. In I. Altman, M. P. Lawton, & J. Wohlwill (Eds.), *Human behavior and the environment: The elderly and the physical environment.* (pp. 279–336). New York: Plenum.

Carp, F. M. (1966). *A future for the aged.* Austin: University of Texas Press.

Costa, P. T., & McCrae, R. R. (1980). Influence of extraversion and neuroticism on subjective well-being: Happy and unhappy people. *Journal of Personality and Social Psychology, 38*, 668–678.

Cumming, E., & Henry, W. E. (1961). *Growing old: The process of disengagement.* New York: Basic Books.

Diener, E. (1984). Subjective well-being. *Psychological Bulletin, 95*, 542–575.

Felton, B. J., & Shaver, P. (1984). Cohort variation in adults' reported feelings. In C. Z. Malatesta & C. E. Izard (Eds.), *Emotion in adult development* (pp. 103–123). Beverley Hills, CA: Sage.

Fredericksen, N. (1972). Toward a taxonomy of situations. *American Psychologist, 27*, 114–123.

Gibson, J. J. (1979). *The ecological approach to visual perception.* Boston: Houghton Mifflin.

Gutmann, D. (1969). *The country of old men: Cross-cultural studies in the psychology of later life.* Ann Arbor: Institute of Gerontology, University of Michigan.

Gutmann, D. (1971). Changes in mastery style with age: A study of Navajo dreams. *Psychiatry, 34*, 289–300.

Helson, H. (1964). *Adaptation level theory.* New York: Harper & Row.

Ittelson, W. H. (1973). Environment perception and contemporary perception theory. In W. H. Ittelson (Ed.), *Environment and cognition* (pp. 1–19). New York: Seminar Press.

Kasmar, J. V. (1970). The development of a usable lexicon of environmental descriptors. *Environment and Behavior, 2*, 153–169.

Langer, E., & Rodin, J. (1976). The effects of choice and enhanced personal responsibility for the aged. *Journal of Personality and Social Psychology, 34*, 191–198.

Langer, E. J., Rodin, J., Beck, P., Weinman, C., & Spitzer, L. (1979). Environmental deter-minants of memory improvement in late adulthood. *Journal of Personality and Social Psychology, 27*, 2000–2013.

Lawton, M. P. (1970). Ecology and aging. In L. A. Pastalan & D. H. Carson (Eds.), *Spatial behavior of older people* (pp. 40–67). Ann Arbor: Institute of Gerontology, University of Michigan.

Lawton, M. P. (1980). Environmental change: The older person as initiator and responder. In N. Datan & N. Lohmann (Eds.), *Transitions of aging* (pp. 171–1973). New York: Academic Press.

Lawton, M. P. (1982). Competence, environmental press, and the adaptation of older people. In M. P. Lawton, P. G. Windley, & T. O. Byerts (Eds.), *Aging and the environment: Theoretical approaches* (pp. 33–59). New York: Springer.

Lawton, M. P. (1983). The dimensions of well-being. *Experimental Aging Research, 9*, 65–72.

Lawton, M. P., & Cohen, J. (1974). The generality of housing impact on the well-being of older people. *Journal of Gerontology, 29*, 194–204.

Lawton, M. P., & Nahemow, L. (1973). Ecology and the aging process. In E. Eisdorfer & M. P. Lawton (Eds.), *Psychology of adult development and aging* (pp. 619–674). Washington, DC: American Psychological Association.

Lawton, M. P., & Simon, B. (1968). The ecology of social relationships in housing for the elderly. *Gerontologist, 8*, 108–115.

Lieberman, M. A., & Tobin, S. S. (1983). *The experience of old age.* New York: Basic Books.

Longino, C. F., McClelland, K. A., & Peterson, W. A. (1980). The aged subculture hypothesis. *Journal of Gerontology, 35*, 758–767.

Lynch, K. (1960). *The image of the city.* Cambridge, MA: MIT Press.

Murray, H. (1938). *Explorations in personality.* New York: Oxford University Press.

Neisser, U. (1976). *Cognition and reality.* San Francisco: W. H. Freeman.

Neugarten, B. L. (1964). *Personality in middle and late life.* Chicago: University of Chicago Press.

Neugarten, B. L. (1968). Adult personality: Toward a psychology of the life cycle. In B. L. Neugarten (Ed.), *Middle age and aging.* Chicago: University of Chicago Press.

Pribram, K. H., & McGuinness, D. (1975). Arousal, activation, and effort in the control of attention. *Psychological Review, 82*, 116–149.

Reichard, S., Livson, F., & Petersen, P. G. (1962). *Aging and personality.* New York: Wiley.

Rodin, J., & Langer, E. J. (1977). Long-term effects of a control-relevant intervention with the institutionalized aged. *Journal of Personality and Social Psychology, 35*, 897–902.

Rodin, J., Timko, C., & Harris, S. (1985). The construct of control: Biological and psychological correlates. In M. P. Lawton & G. L. Maddox (Eds.), *Annual Review of Gerontology and Geriatrics* (Vol. 5 pp. 3–55). New York: Springer.

Rubinstein, R. (1987). *The home environments of older people: Psychosocial processes relating person to place.* Unpublished manuscript, Philadelphia Geriatric Center, Philadelphia.

Russell, J. A. (1980). A circumplex model of affect. *Journal of Personality and Social Psychology, 39*, 1161–1178.

Russell, J. A., & Lanius, U. F. (1984). Adaptation level and the affective appraisal of environments. *Journal of Environmental Psychology, 4*, 119–135.

Schulz, R. (1976). Effects of control and predictability on the physical and psychological well-being of the institutionalized aged. *Journal of Personality and Social Psychology, 1976, 33*, 563–573.

Schulz, R., & Hanusa, R. H. (1979). Environmental influences on the effectiveness of control and competence-enhancing interventions. In R. A. Monty & L. C. Perlmutter (Eds.), *Choice and perceived control.* (pp. 315–337). Hillsdale, NJ: Lawrence Erlbaum Associates.

Sells, S. B. (Eds.). (1963). *Stimulus determinants of behavior.* New York: Ronald Press.

Warr, P., Barter, J., & Brownbridge, G. (1983). On the independence of positive and negative affect. *Journal of Personality and Social Psychology, 44*, 644–651.

Weisman, J. (1981). Evaluating architectural legibility: Way-finding in the built environment. *Environment and Behavior, 13,* 189–204.

White, R. W. (1959). Motivation reconsidered: The concept of competence. *Psychological Review, 66,* 297–333.

Wohlwill, J. F. (1966). The physical environment: A problem for a psychology of stimulation. *Journal of Social Issues, 22,* 29–38.

Wohlwill, J. F., & Kohn, I. (1973). The environment as experienced by the migrant: An adaptation-level view. *Representative Research in Social Psychology, 4,* 135–164.

Adaptation and the Aging Human

Kenneth M. Weiss
Pennsylvania State University

TWO FATHERS

The topic of this book has led me to think of my own family experience. My father spent his working life in a huge bureaucratic organization. Somewhat of a free spirit, he became dissatisfied with the organization after many years there. Because of their excellent retirement plan, he was able to retire in 1970 at age 55.

Since his retirement, he has become successful in two entirely separate areas of creative art and a functionary in various organizations; he swims or plays tennis on a daily basis and has traveled the country and the world. He has been hospitalized for a few ailments, none of them serious, and remains as sprightly today as he has ever been.

My father's father also retired at about the same age. He, too, lived for more than two more decades following his retirement. However, they were years of depressing, decreasing economic and physical well-being. Although initially as lively and active as his son, my father's father lost his teeth, his sight, his hearing, his continence, and, toward the end, his competence.

Both my father and his father were of sound economic means when they retired, and both of sound mind and body. Both had healthful lifestyles and inquiring minds. They were as genetically close as any two individuals other than identical twins. But the ends of their lives were at the antipodes of the aging experience.

What am *I* to look forward to? How should I plan for it? Do fathers' experiences presage that of their sons'? Successful adaptation requires information, which an adapting organism uses in knowing how to react, how to plan. What is my information?

This story has no moral, but it does have a point. It is the difficulty we may have in attempting to specify, or even to evaluate, the nature of the interaction between the aging person and his/her environment, and perhaps that we be wary of our natural tendency to attribute to the individual a greater capacity to control events than he or she may in fact have.

Dr. Lawton has written extensively about different ways in which organisms may adapt to the environment, and how different patterns of activity may be harbingers of different aging experiences. To discuss the details of those points is not my area, but I would like to discuss adaptation in humans in relation to aging. The meaning of the term *adaptation* as used here is close to Dr. Lawton's concept of transactions between individual and environment aimed at optimizing functioning.

ARE HUMAN BEINGS ADAPTIVE

It is difficult to make systematic sense of the idea that human beings use their personal and environmental resources in a way that is adaptive. Dr. Lawton has provided a schematic figure with these two attributes as the axes. Using this, we can think of adaptiveness in the following way. A level of adaptiveness (say, A) can be assigned to each point in the plane spanned in one dimension by personal resources (p) and in the other by environmental resources (e), thus constructing an adaptive surface: $A = f(p, e)$. This can be thought of as a Z axis on a three-dimensional graph. At any time, t, an individual will be at some coordinate and have an adaptive level specified by the adaptive surface, that is, $A(t) = f[p(t), e(t)]$. Over his or her lifetime, the individual experiences total adaptation equal to the sum of the values $A(t)$.

Human beings do not all aim for the same region in the p-e space, at least so far as we can currently measure it; so there may be substantial interindividual differences in the adaptive surface. It is not obvious how we can objectively determine the relative level of adaptiveness corresponding to each point (p, e). More precisely, what kind of function defines this surface of adaptation? What does the plot actually look like?

It is not clear even that the general shape of the adaptive surface is similar for different individuals; that is, that the same "zones" would be judged by outside observers to be the most adaptive, or the most sought, by different individuals. Chance events may lead to discontinuities in this surface as individuals move along it over time in an effort to optimize their lives in some sense. Individual genetic differences; idiosyncracies of personal, social, and life-history circumstances; "self-defeating" behavior; and individually variable perceptions of p and e may also play havoc with anyone's attempt to be specific or quantitative about this aspect of adaptation.

Perhaps in the end, we do not typically behave in a rigorously adaptive way.

What Would the Adaptive Goals of the Aging Individual Be?

Most of us may think that we know roughly what we aim for in life and how we would like to spend our older years. There may be many satisfactory goals, that is, a multiple-peak adaptive surface. I imagine that the elderly themselves would feel, to the extent of their ability, that they are trying to bring about a certain kind of life for themselves. But is this true in fact?

At the very least, we can think of many examples of behavior that are not calculated to maximize the worldly well-being of the individual in the usual sense. Let us consider cigarette smoking. Other than dramatic self-inflicted trauma, there is little in today's society more likely to be destructive to one's life and health than the use of tobacco, and this danger is generally understood. Smoking is a part of the environment and also relates to the personality of the smoker; we ought to be able to assign it to a region in the p-e space. But what value of A would pertain to this region? Are smokers maladapted? By diminishing the personal resources of the individual, does smoking in fact move him or her in a maladaptive direction over time? Is the individual's total lifetime adaptiveness less than it would have been without smoking?

These may seem like trivial questions. But given that we are mortal, is it maladaptive to trade pleasure for time? Can we say that the level of adaptiveness experienced by the smoker is lower than if he or she abstained from the habit? Do the lowered adaptive levels that occur with progressive emphysema, or the discontinuity caused by death from smoking-related lung cancer, lead to a net lower lifetime adaptiveness? Health consequences can be accounted from the public policy point of view, but how can the same be done from the point of view of individual perceptions?

Some who are middle aged or older will read this discussion, and I would venture that some readers are hypertensive, substantially overweight, or have had a heart attack. Do they follow their doctor's advice? Do they take their medicines regularly? Do they follow dietary and exercise regimens? Get enough sleep? If not, they are in the majority—but are they adaptive? Should we judge adaptiveness as we would be judged? As the ideal, or the actual mean or mode?

The other side of the coin may be as instructive. Are those who faithfully follow healthful diets on an adaptive path? If we suppose that a healthy lifestyle really does increase longevity, is that behavior adaptive in regard to a satisfactory old age? A glance at the nursing home population would suggest that this is not necessarily so. Nothing about low-fat diets is supposed by anyone, so far as I know, to be proof against Alzheimer's disease, arthritis, cataracts, or sensorineural hearing loss. Yet "wellness" behavior is practiced most by those with the most personal and environmental resources, those whom we would expect to have high A values.

Because psychological factors are central to the topic of this book, we might seriously consider those with a true belief in an afterlife. For such persons, the state of the body or the length of earthly life may be less relevant. Where does the internally depicted world, which extends to all areas of life as well as to an afterlife, fit on the adaptive surface? In other ways, societal values may conflict directly with health-related ones, so that seeking prestige or approval may entail risks and stresses detrimental to longevity or health.

Even persons who single-mindedly pursue specific goals are in fact traversing discontinuous geography, filled with gaps and chasms that can neither be known nor foreseen. Thus may the smoker, whose pleasure in life is maintained by his or her habit, be moving steadily toward a fatal discontinuity—feeling well adapted all the way to the edge.

What Are the Adaptive Goals of the Population?

Human beings are biological creatures, molded by many millennia of evolution. During these millennia, and even in the biological legacy handed to the earliest humans by their mammalian forebears, adaptation has involved reacting to the immediate needs of survival, food seeking, mate choice, and child rearing. Issues of survival and well-being beyond the years of economic productivity were unimportant and generally beyond the reach of biological evolution. Human populations have little experience with postreproductive survival as the norm.

It is highly likely that the amount of genetic variability in relation to aging processes is considerable. This is the expected result of the accumulation of mutations whose effects are expressed only later in life, beyond the ability of natural selection to affect them. This theoretically expectable variability in senescence is borne out clearly in the variability in health experiences of the elderly. This variation extends from the purely biological to the cognitive.

From the population point of view, that is, from the perspective of research on public policy, public health, and the like, it might be possible to specify criteria for judging the success of societal actions in terms of mean levels of adaptiveness. For example, actions that increase longevity, reduce the postretirement total of inpatient hospital days, or even reduce the variability in age of death might be objective measures of a successful program. Such programs would have to accomplish this in some way by taking account of the variability in the subject individuals, and this may mean to overcome that variability. Such goals could come directly into conflict with the individual, because biomedical measures calculated to increase collective longevity might do so at the expense of increased morbidity, for example, in general or at least in some individuals; or as is currently taking place, reduced hospital days saving public funds at the expense of individual well-being.

This raises the question of innovativeness and proactivity. It is not at all clear that evolution favors — in humans or any other species — innovativeness. What most characterizes mammalian social behavior is stereotyped activity, that is, expertise at maintaining the status quo. Mammals are driven to maintain homeostasis. More often that not, from a biological point of view, change is threatening. This can affect public policy in at least two ways. First, many elderly may be best served if we consider how to help them maintain their status quo rather than provide resources for innovativeness (i.e., perhaps we need to be very careful about assigning higher adaptive value to proactivity as opposed to docility, at least as a general rule). Secondly, environments favoring flexibility may nonetheless fail to provide real options for many people. They may be wasted resources for those for whom physical, mental, or even socioeconomic history may prevent successful use of the resources even if present.

Should attitudes toward innovativeness change in old age? Perhaps; the elderly are freed from many of the competitive constraints placed on the young. Still, though there are many exceptions, the stereotype of the elderly as conservative in personal habits and traditional in attitude is probably not an empty one. To what extent might the exceptions, the innovators, be concentrated in the academic segment of society — do our views mirror those of the clientele whose needs our research is designed to serve? Some caution should be exercised in order that the conventional persons not be penalized if they cannot or choose not to innovate. In many traditional and more complex human societies, to be an inactive elder is to have a place of honor.

CONCLUSION

These are thoughts of an outsider to psychosocial research, one whose interests are in the quantitative aspects of human genetic variation, in the genetic determinants of biological aging, and in the evolution of these characteristics. One who knows little about the determinants of normal affective behavior cannot presume to contribute much of substance to the general nature of Dr. Lawton's views.

However, it is wise to be cautious in making assumptions about adaptiveness in people, especially in regard to judging or evaluating it. The closer we may look at the problem, the more elusive it may become. Hence, evaluating, predicting, or engineering proactivity (or any other personal approach to the world) may be a tenuous endeavor on any other than an individual basis. This complexity in human beings makes the problem of public policy toward the aging more difficult, but is itself one spice of life of which we should take advantage.

Youthful Designs for Research on Aging: A Response to Lawton's Theoretical Challenge

Urie Bronfenbrenner

In his thought-provoking chapter for this volume, M. Powell Lawton argues the necessity for, and then goes on to propose, a conceptual framework for conducting research on aging that is more complex than the models currently in use. Specifically, he calls for more differentiated constructs in three domains:

1. A conceptualization of the aging *person* in terms of the individual's psychological orientations toward the environment (e.g., openness vs. closedness, competence vs. incompetence)
2. A more differentiated analysis of the *environment* in terms of proximal versus distal domains, ranging from face-to-face interactions to broader institutional and cultural contexts.
3. An examination of developmental outcomes as a function of the *match* between the *personal* and *environmental resources* located in each of the first two domains.

Within this broad conceptual framework, Professor Lawton further delineates particular characteristics of the person and the environment that interact to produce differing developmental outcomes. Three features of this formulation are especially noteworthy. First, he views resources as having two aspects: objective and subjective. For example, in adopting Bandura's concept of *efficacy*, he distinguishes between efficacy as manifested in performance, on the one hand, and, on the other, the person's belief in his or her own capacity to be effective. Second, Lawton proposes a major dichotomy between *environmental docility* as opposed to *proactivity*, with the latter being regarded as essential for effecting environmental change. Third, with respect to developmental outcomes, he differentiates between positive and negative psychological well-being in order to test the hypothesis that these two types of end states "have noticeably different antecedents."

All three distinctions are important because they provide paired conceptual contrasts for correcting an oft noted, but still prevalent one-sided emphasis in research on aging, aptly summarized by Professor Lawton in the following passage:

> It is probably fair to say that the great majority of the gerontological research literature has been devoted to pathology, impairment, decrement, deprivation, and isolation, all of these negatives viewed as unwanted invasions from the outside, whether biological, psychological, or social. Without recounting the supporting data, it is clear that, although these conditions become statistically more frequent as age increases, the majority of older people cannot be characterized in these ways.

For me, Professor Lawton's proposals for a more differentiated paradigm for studying person–environment interaction in development are especially gratifying, given my own efforts along similar lines. This is not the place to describe the results of that endeavor, which are readily available elsewhere (for the most recent reports, see Bronfenbrenner, 1986a, 1986b, in press). What I would like to do, however, is to call attention to some theoretical and methodological contributions in other domains of developmental research outside the field of aging that, in my view, support, complement, and further the scientific implementation of the conceptual system Professor Lawton has presented in Chapter 2.

In particular, these contributions address a dilemma that Lawton highlights in the concluding section of his chapter. He notes that although there are a few studies dealing with proactive orientations on the part of the individual, on the one hand, or proactive potentials of the environment, on the other, the designs are comparatively simplistic. In his words, "Naturalistic research has thus far been unable to disentangle complex processes implied by such models as that shown in Fig. 2.4. Thus, it may well be up to experimental researchers to provide new convincing information regarding the responsiveness of older people to deliberate attempts that enhance opportunities for proactivity."

There can be no doubt that, ceteris paribus, the planned experiment remains the strategy of choice for investigating causal processes of whatever kind, including, by the way, even the most simple ones. But "other things" are rarely "equal." In particular, planned experiments tend to be extremely expensive and often difficult, if not impossible, to carry out because of social, political, ethical, and ideological considerations. Fortunately, however, in recent years developmental scientists, typically working at earlier stages of the life course than old age, have been employing complex naturalistic designs that, although admittedly not fully meeting the requirements of Professor Lawton's ideal paradigm, do shed light on at least some of the critical issues he has raised. Putting the issue more precisely, there is no single study that one can cite as a "best example," but if one looks at a range of different, well-designed investigations, each including a combination of elements that makes a significant contribution in its own right, one can begin to see possibilities for cumulative convergence and integration.

The basic prototype for this emergent design is what I have called a *process–person–context model* (Bronfenbrenner & Crouter, 1983). As the name implies, such a model provides for analyzing variation in developmental processes as a function of the interplay between the characteristics of the developing person and the environmental systems in which that person participates. One of the earliest but, in my judgment, still one of the best examples is found in a series of studies by Tulkin (1970), all growing out of his doctoral dissertation. The research is especially noteworthy because it illustrates the phenomenon of model convergence and integration, in this instance within the work of a single investigator. Moreover, in contrast to more recent studies that take advantage of newly developed and highly sophisticated statistical techniques, Tulkin provides pursuasive evidence for fairly complex causal linkages with nothing more than mean differences and correlations at his disposal. Finally, reference to Tulkin's research seems especially appropriate in this discussion of Professor Lawton's chapter because of the anticipatory reinforcement it provides, at an operational level, for a number of Lawton's key theoretical distinctions.

Tulkin's aim was to study the influence of socioeconomic status on socialization processes in a sample of 10-month-old female infants and their mothers. In his first published study, authored jointly with his mentor Jerome Kagan (Tulkin & Kagan, 1972), he showed that middle-class mothers engaged in more reciprocal interactions with their infants, especially in the sphere of vocalization. He also noted that middle-class homes contained more toys and manipulatable objects and fewer barriers to the infant's locomotion.

Nicely in accord with Professor Lawton's first major dichotomy, Tulkin's next publication (Tulkin & Cohler, 1973) shifted from the objective to the subjective realm by focusing on the mother's belief systems about herself and her baby. To begin with, the authors posited and found that middle-class mothers were more likely to subscribe to statements stressing the importance of perceiving and meeting the infant's needs, the value of mother–child interaction, and the moderate control of aggressive impulses. The documentation of such differences in belief, however, was not the investigators' primary interest. They then went on, as Professor Law-

ton would have them do (see his Fig. 2.4), to examine the interrelationship between the subjective and objective spheres; that is, between the
mothers' beliefs and their behaviors. Once again, the nature of the findings confirms the importance of Lawton's theoretical distinctions. In the
Tulkin and Cohler's (1973) words:

> The unique contribution of the present study is the significant relationship
> between maternal attitudes and childrearing behavior. Specifically, middle-
> class mothers whose attitudes reflected the encouragement of reciprocity
> (i.e., that infants can communicate, and that mothers can understand and
> respond) more often held their infants in a face-to-face position, respond-
> ed to infant's vocalizations, imitated infants' vocalizations, gave the infants
> objects to play with, and responded more frequently to the infants' frets.
> (p. 102)

Even though Tulkin's research provides both confirmation and com-
plementarity for Lawton's theoretical ideas, there is one noteworthy difference between the implicit assumptions of the former and the explicit
formulations of the latter with respect to directionality of causal processes. Thus, Tulkin and Cohler appear to assume that it is the mother's belief in her own effectiveness that then leads her to act more effectively.
By contrast in Lawton's Fig. 2.4, the causal arrow points in the opposite
direction; it is the person's objective performance that is seen as producing a self-image of an efficacious person. In the absence of stated grounds
favoring one alternative over the other, this seems to be an instance in
which each model maker could profitably consider the other's formulation for possible adoption.

But it is the overlap between the two independently derived conceptualizations—one latent, the other manifest—that is so gratifying. Indeed,
when one consider the next analysis by Tulkin and Cohler (1973), the fan-
ciful image comes to mind of these two investigators, a quarter of a century ago, looking at a TV monitor that magically enabled them to peer
into the future and see Lawton's Fig. 2.4 filling the screen. Having duly
examined its second column, our prescient researchers shift the focus to
column 3, with its critical distinction between docile and proactive environments. For what Tulkin and Cohler's (1973) next analysis did was
to compare the magnitude of the behavior-belief correlations for middle-
class and working-class families. The result: "The association . . . was much
less pronounced for this group [working-class] than for the middle-class
sample" (p. 102). In considering possible explanations for this contrast,
the authors noted that several working-class mothers had remarked during the interview that although they believed mothers in general could
influence an infant's development, they themselves felt powerless to do
so given the circumstances of their lives.

Both the finding and its interpretation lend themselves readily to a reformulation in terms of Lawton's dichotomy between environmental "docility" versus "proactivity." The first is an attribute more characteristic of working-class life, the second of middle-class life. I advisedly use the term "life" rather than "environment" because, as Lawton emphasizes: "Environmental docility and environmental proactivity are classes that represent neither a person attribute nor an environmental attribute, but they signify person–environment transactions." To apply the dichotomy to the present case, in the middle class world both objective opportunities and proactive personal beliefs are widely prevalent and reciprocally enhance each other. By contrast, in working class environments a corresponding prevalence and dynamic operate to reinforce both objective limitations and subjective docility toward one's surroundings. As a result, personal efficacy, although present among individuals in both contexts, finds much readier response in the first setting than in the second.

In accord with Lawton's formulation, the two kinds of worlds result in rather different developmental trajectories, not only for adults but for children as well. It is exactly this phenomenon that is documented in three additional studies by Tulkin. Thus, in two laboratory experiments, Tulkin hypothesized and found that middle-class infants cry more when separated from their mothers (1973a), but are better able to discriminate the mother's voice from that of an unfamiliar female of the same social class (1973b). Finally, several years later, Tulkin and Covitz (1975) reassessed the same youngsters after they had entered school. The children's performance on tests of mental ability and language skill showed significant relationships to the prior measures of reciprocal mother–infant interaction, strength of maternal attachment, and voice recognition when the children had been 10 months old. And once again, the observed correlations were higher for middle-class families. Even more important from a developmental perspective, the relationships of maternal behavior at 10 months to the child's behavior at age 6 were considerably greater than the contemporaneous relationships between both types of variables in the first year of life. The investigators, however, were quick to reject the hypothesis of a delayed "sleeper effect." Rather, they argued that mothers who believe and engage in adaptive reciprocal activity with their infants at early ages are likely to continue to provide age-appropriate environments as the child gets older, thus producing a cumulative trend. Or, to employ a more sophisticated formulation suggested by Lawton's conceptual model, such mothers are likely to continue to be both a product and a producer of environmental proactivity.

Taken together, the series of studies included in and growing out of Tulkin's doctoral dissertation exhibit and implement several critical features of Lawton's formulation. In particular, Tulkin's research does shed

light on how characteristics of the person, on the one hand, and both proximal and more distal environmental contexts, on the other, can influence
developmental processes and outcomes.

But Tulkin's cumulative design still does not meet all of Lawton's conceptual requirements. As I mentioned earlier, there is as yet no single line
of investigation that fully exploits the existing design potentials for analyzing, within a naturalistic study, the kinds of complex alternative and bi-
directional causal pathways specified in Lawton's conceptual framework.
For example, with all its merits, Tulkin's model is essentially unidirectional;
thus it fails to consider the extent to which the mother's behavior and
belief systems might be influenced by the characteristics of her baby.

Tulkin's design lacks yet another critical element not explicitly mentioned in Lawton's conceptual framework, but clearly is consistent with
it. I refer to the fact that Tulkin's design is purely dyadic; in particular,
no consideration is given to the possibility that the behavior of both
mother and infant might be influenced by the father. This omission is
hardly surprising for, as I have pointed out elsewhere (Bronfenbrenner
& Crouter, 1983), it was not until the late 1970s that studies of parent–child
interaction expanded beyond a two-person to a *three-person model*. By the
1980s, the results of such investigations had demonstrated the construc-
tive impact of the presence of such "third parties," not only within the
family but outside as well (Bronfenbrenner, 1986a). In so far as I have
been able to determine, a comparable design development has still to take
place in studies of aging. For example, as yet there appears to be no substantial body of evidence on the influence of adult children (including
children-in-law) on the well-being and development of their elderly
parents.

The foregoing comment relates to yet another element missing in
Tulkin's 1970 design but since incorporated in many studies of children,
adolescents, and young adults. Although Tulkin employs measures of performance and behavior in school as developmental outcomes, his analyses
of process and context are confined to a single setting: the family. More
recently, a growing number of studies have systematically examined the
developmental impact of processes taking place both within and between
two or more settings, such as family and school, school and peer group,
family and workplace, and so on (for a summary of this research, see Bronfenbrenner, 1986a). I have referred to such designs as *mesosystem models*.
Models of this kind are particularly appropriate for analyzing the simultaneous effects of the different levels of the environment distinguished
in Professor Lawton's conceptual schema, but the scientific potential of
these designs is yet to be fully exploited in studies of aging. For example,
mesosystem models would be particularly appropriate for investigating
the well-being and development of elderly persons living apart from their
families. In such studies, a critical element would be the extent, nature,

content, and reciprocity of *linkages* between settings in the form of visits, phone calls, letters, gifts, and so on.

The necessary limitations of a discussant's remarks preclude a comprehensive treatment of recent design innovations that could be applied for analyzing some more complex features of Lawton's proposed conceptual framework for research on aging; but at least one additional element of the *process–person–context* paradigm needs to be mentioned in this regard. It pertains to a feature in Lawton's framework that is particularly important in research on human development; namely, his schema goes beyond a single-step cause-effect model to posit a set of sequential, sometimes alternative causal pathways. Especially in studies of development, such a sequential causal chain takes on yet another dimension: It extends over time along what Elder (1974, 1985) has referred to as the life course.

The term *life course* is to be distinguished from the more familiar concept of *life span*, primarily because it has quite different implications for research design. To be sure, the strategy of choice for both domains is a longitudinal study, but the former requires an element not usually present in a conventional follow-up investigation. Thus most longitudinal studies document and analyze changes over time in characteristics of the individual. A study of the life course requires, in addition, the analysis of changes over time occurring in the environment as well. I have referred to this type of design as a *chronosystem model* (Bronfenbrenner, 1986a, in press). An example is found in the work of the Finnish psychologist Lea Pulkkinen (1982, 1983). Using a longitudinal design, she examined the influence of environmental stability and change on children's development from 8 to 20 years of age. The "steadiness" versus "unsteadiness" of family living conditions was measured by the occurrence of such events as the number of family moves, changes in day care and school arrangements, parental absences, and altered conditions of parental employment. Greater instability in the family environment was associated with greater submissiveness, aggressiveness, and anxiety among children in later childhood and adolescence, and higher rates of criminality in early adulthood. The influence of environmental stability turned out to be more powerful than that of socioeconomic status.

Although Pulkkinen's use of a chronosystem model has yielded important scientific findings, her design omits an essential element of a process–person–context model, an element also emphasized in Lawton's conceptual framework. Thus, Pulkkinen made no attempt to investigate whether environmental stability had any differential effects depending on characteristics of the person, even with respect to so simple a feature as the sex of the child. In other words, her analyses did not allow for possible person–context interactions. And even within the framework of her chronosystem model, she did not examine possible alternative environmental pathways through the life course.

A fuller implementation of a process–person–context model invites both types of analyses. This opportunity is currently being exploited in the continuing follow-up of Glen Elder's (1974) classic studies of *Children of the Great Depression*. In their recent work, Elder and his colleagues (for references, see Bronfenbrenner, 1986a) make ingenious use of structural equations to demonstrate the critical role of the personality characteristics of both parents and children in determining alternative courses of subsequent development in response to the impact of economic hardship. For example, the presence in the family of an irritable father or an irritating child significantly increased the likelihood that unemployment would have long-range negative consequences for the subsequent development of the younger generation. The fact that neither Elder, nor anyone else to my knowledge, has examined the possible buffering or facilitating developmental impact of *positive* personal characteristics of parents and children highlights the importance of Professor Lawton's conceptual distinctions in this regard.

The principal aim of these remarks, however, is not solely to underscore the theoretical merits of Lawton's complex conceptual schema for advancing scientific studies of aging but also to demonstrate that some of the more sophisticated research designs currently being used in studies of development at earlier ages are beginning to approach, at an operational level, the demanding conceptual requirements of Lawton's theoretical framework. In short, the time has come when it is not only desirable but possible to translate theory into practice. Indeed, that is exactly what Elder has done in the latest study (Caspi & Elder, 1986) of his "Children of the Great Depression", who now average 70 years of age and thereby "represent one of the oldest panel studies in operation" (p. 20). It is significant, especially given the title of these remarks, that the first author of the research report is not Glen Elder himself but Avshalom Caspi, a representative of the new generation of developmental researchers of the 1980s, equally at home in theory and method. Using longitudinal data on 79 women from the 1900 generation of the Berkeley Guidance Study, the authors show "how social and psychological factors interact over time in the course of successful aging" (p. 18). Given the scope and rigor of the research model employed and the theoretical significance of the findings, it is difficult to imagine a more fitting and timely response to Professor Lawton's probing intellectual challenge or a more gratifying note on which to conclude these comments.

REFERENCES

Bronfenbrenner, U. (1986a). Ecology of the family as a context for human development. *Developmental Psychology, 22*, 723–742.

Bronfenbrenner U. (1986b). Recent advances in research on human development. In R. K. Silbereisen, K. Eyferth, & G. Rudinger (Eds.), *Development as action in context: Problem behavior and normal youth development* (pp. 287–309). Heidelberg & New York: Springer-Verlag.

Bronfenbrenner, U. (in press). Interacting systems in human development: Research paradigms, present and future. In N. Bolger, A. Caspi, G. Downey, & M. Moorehouse (Eds.), *Persons in context: Developmental processes*. New York: Cambridge University Press.

Bronfenbrenner, U., & Crouter, A. (1983). The evolution of environmental models in developmental research. In P. H. Mussen (Ed.) *Handbook of child psychology: Vol. I, history, theory, and methods* (pp. 357–414). New York: Wiley.

Caspi, A., & Elder, G. H., Jr. (1986). Life satisfaction in old age: Linking social psychology and history. *Journal of Psychology and Aging, 1*, 18–26.

Elder, G. H., Jr. (1974). *Children of the Great Depression*. Chicago: University of Chicago Press.

Elder, G. H., Jr. (1985). *Life course dynamics: Trajectories and transitions*. Ithaca, NY: Cornell University Press.

Pulkkinen, L. (1982). Self-control and continuity in childhood to late adolescence. In P. Baltes & O. Brim (Eds.), *Life span development and behavior* (Vol. 4, pp. 64–102). New York: Academic Press.

Pulkkinen, L. (1983). Youthful smoking and drinking in a longitudinal perspective. *Journal of Youth and Adolescence, 12*, 253–283.

Tulkin, S. R. (1970). *Mother–infant interaction in the first year of life: An inquiry into the influences of social class*. Unpublished doctoral dissertation, Harvard University, Cambridge, MA.

Tulkin, S. R. (1973a). Social class differences in attachment behaviors of ten-month-old infants. *Child Development, 44*, 171–174.

Tulkin, S. R. (1973b). Social class differences in infant's reactions to mother's and stranger's voices. *Developmental Psychology, 8*(1), 137.

Tulkin, S. R., & Cohler, B. J. (1973). Child-rearing attitudes and mother-child interaction in the first year of life. *Merrill-Palmer Quarterly, 19*, 95–106.

Tulkin, S. R., & Covitz, F. E. (1975). *Mother-infant interaction and intellectual functioning at age six*. Paper presented at the meeting of the Society for Research in Child Development, Denver, CO.

Tulkin, S. R., & Kagan, J. (1972). Mother-child interaction in the first year of life. *Child Development, 43*, 31–41.

Cohort Differences in Cognitive Aging: A Sample Case

Sherry L. Willis
The Pennsylvania State University

INTRODUCTION

For over two decades, the importance of studying adult intelligence within the context of sociocultural change has been recognized (Baltes, 1968; Riegel, 1976; Schaie, 1965). Empirical studies have focused primarily on the effect of cohort membership upon cognitive performance (Schaie, 1983). When individuals of different birth cohorts have been assessed at the same chronological age, the level of performance on a variety of psychometric ability measures has been shown to vary by birth cohort.

From the early studies on cohort differences in adult intellectual performance, empirical research and theoretical discussion have taken three directions. First, there is continuing empirical research on defining cohort differences in the *direction* and *rate* of cognitive development and decline (Schaie & Hertzog, 1983, 1986). Second, there has been discussion of the specific social structures and mechanisms that may be associated with cohort differences in cognitive performance. Of particular interest has been the relationship between change in certain structural indices (e.g., educational level, occupational status) and cohort differences in the level of intellectual performance (Abeles & Riley, 1987; Baltes, Cornelius, & Nesselroade, 1979; Kohn & Schooler, 1983). Third, new conceptualizations of the constructs of cohort and period have been recently proposed that extend definitions of cohort beyond that of birth cohort and define period in ways other than in linear time dimensions (Featherman & Peterson, 1986; Schaie, 1986a).

In this chapter, we consider issues related to the first two questions by using a sample case. We examine in detail the relationship between changes in educational level, as a social indicator, and cohort differences in inductive reasoning ability. In this sample case, a positive cohort trend is manifested for both the social indicator and the cognitive ability. Let me begin, however, with the big picture and briefly summarize some recent findings regarding cohort differences in the direction and rate of change in cognitive performance for a variety of abilities.

EXAMINATION OF COHORT PROGRESSIONS
FOR THREE ABILITIES

There has been the tendency to summarize cohort effects in cognitive functioning as representing a uniformly positive cohort trend in which an increase in level of performance occurred from cohort to cohort, when these cohorts were compared at the same chronological age. However, as increasing numbers of birth cohorts have been examined for a variety of mental abilities, the early summaries describing a positive trend have been found to be much too simplistic (Schaie & Hertzog, 1983).

Cohort trends in intellectual performance are multidirectional, and the rate of change between successive cohorts varies widely (Schaie, 1986b). This can be illustrated by examination of the differences between successive cohorts for three of the Thurstone (1938) primary abilities: *inductive reasoning, spatial orientation, and number.*

Brief Description of the Data Base

The data to be discussed come from the Seattle Longitudinal Study (SLS; Schaie, 1983), a multiwave panel study that used as its population frame the membership of a metropolitan health maintenance organization. Participants were community-dwelling adults randomly selected from seven-year age intervals included in each panel (ages 25, 32, 39, 46, 53, 60, 67, 74, 81). Data were collected at 7-year intervals from 1956 to 1984.

Throughout the study, subjects have been assessed on five of Thurstone's primary mental abilities, and demographic information has been obtained at each data collection point. The data presented are based on an independent random sampling model in which each cohort at each age was assessed by means of a separate sample, thus controlling for possible effects of testing, reactivity, and experimental mortality. These analyses involved a sample of 768 subjects.

Inductive Reasoning

Cohort differences on inductive reasoning come closest to showing a positive, linear cohort progression. The top section of Fig. 3.1 presents cumulative mean differences in inductive reasoning performance for 10 birth cohorts (1889, 1896, 1903, 1910, 1917, 1924, 1931, 1938, 1945, 1952), when compared at the same chronological ages.[1] Although there is a clear linear trend, there are, however, significant differences in the *rate* of progression between successive cohorts. Relatively steep increments up to the 1931 birth cohort are shown, with slower decelerating increment thereafter. Cohort progressions vary by gender. On inductive reasoning,

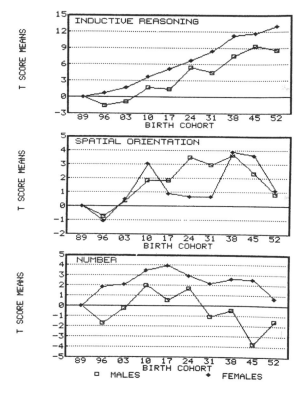

FIG. 3.1. Cumulative cohort differences for three of Thurstone's primary mental abilities: inductive reasoning, spatial orientation, number.

[1]We obtained cohort differences by taking the differences between means for each pair of cohorts at all common age levels. We then obtained cohort difference estimates by averaging across all estimates to avoid undue weighting in terms of differential sample sizes. We constructed cohort gradients by cumulating cohort difference estimates across cohorts.

women exhibited a quite regular, positive linear trend. The cohort pattern for men is positive but less regular.

Spatial Ability

The cohort progession for spatial orientation is much more irregular, with distinct gender differences in the overall pattern (middle section of Fig. 3.1). There was a generally positive trend for early cohorts of men, reaching an asymptote for the 1924 to 1938 birth cohorts. Women reached an initial peak for the 1910 cohort followed by a drop for the 1917 to 1931 cohorts. Both males and females exhibited a sharp drop for the 1945 and 1952 cohorts.

Number Ability

A very different pattern is shown for number ability, involving simple addition and subtraction computations (bottom section of Fig. 3.1). A peak was reached by the 1910 cohort and was maintained through the 1924 cohort, followed by a negative trend. Men reached an earlier asymptote by the 1910 cohort, and there followed a "stair-step" decrement until 1945 with some recovery for the 1952 cohort. Women exhibited a greater increment from base, reaching a peak with the 1917 cohort followed by a plateau then a decline for the 1952 cohort.

This brief overview of cohort progressions for three primary abilities illustrates that the direction of cohort effects varies across abilities, with some abilities showing positive, linear trends across the cohorts studied and other abilities exhibiting curvilinear or even negative cohort progressions. The rate of change between the successive cohorts studied varies widely also.

COHORT DIFFERENCES IN INDUCTIVE REASONING: A MORE DETAILED LOOK

We now begin a more intensive examination of cohort differences for one important primary ability—inductive reasoning—and consider possible social indicators associated with cohort effects for this ability.

Inductive reasoning has been defined as the ability to identify one or more logical rules or principles critical to the solution of a particular problem type, coupled with the ability to utilize these rules in future problem solutions (Thurstone, 1938). This ability is frequently assessed by Letter or Number Series tests in which the subject is shown a series of letters or numbers and asked to identify the next letter/number in the series.

This primary ability is represented in a number of psychometric models of intelligence (Cattell, 1971; Guilford, 1967; Thurstone, 1938) and more recently has been studied in computer simulations of problem solving (Simon & Kotovsky, 1963). Inductive reasoning has been of interest to gerontologists because it is one of the abilities exhibiting relatively early age-related decline. Previous analyses from the SLS on inductive reasoning ability indicated that significant age-related decline occurred in people in their mid-60s. However, analyses of the 1977 data suggest that for more recent cohorts, age-related decline may occur as early as the mid-50s (Schaie & Hertzog, 1983).

As you may recall from Fig. 3.1, there has been a positive, linear cohort progression for inductive reasoning, but the rate of increment has slowed down for recent successive cohorts. This linear cohort progression is evident in Fig. 3.2, which shows selected cohort comparisons at five ages (46, 53, 60, 67, 74 years). That is, Fig. 3.2 presents a time-lag comparison of five sets of two cohorts: birth cohorts (1924, 1917, 1910, 1903, 1896) assessed in 1970 at the ages of 46, 53, 60, 67, and 74 years compared with the birth cohorts (1938, 1931, 1924, 1917, 1910) assessed in 1984 at the same ages.

Note in Fig. 3.2 that at all five ages the cohorts assessed in 1984 performed at a higher mean level than the same-age cohorts assessed in 1970, indicating a positive cohort trend. Age differences are also apparent in that earlier cohorts at both times of measurement performed at a lower mean level than more recent cohorts. Of particular interest to us in this chapter is the greater magnitude of differences shown for the cohorts com-

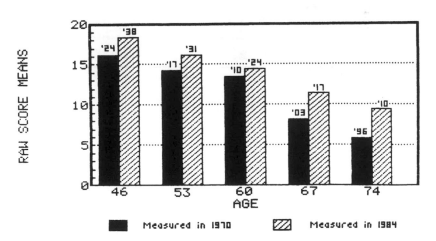

FIG. 3.2. Cohorts measured on inductive reasoning ability in 1970 compared with cohorts at the same age measured in 1984. Cohort comparisons are shown at five ages (46, 53, 60, 67, 74). Birth years are indicated for each cohort comparison.

pared at older ages (i.e., at ages 67 and 74; cohorts 1903 vs. 1917, 1896 vs. 1910). Differences for cohorts compared in middle age are much smaller (i.e., at ages 46, 53, and 60; cohorts 1924 vs. 1938, 1917 vs. 1931, 1910 vs. 1924). These reductions in the magnitude of cohort effects across age groups suggest a slowing down in the rate of the positive cohort progression observed for inductive reasoning.

Gender Differences

Figure 3.3 presents these cohort comparisons separately for males and females. Significant cohort differences were found for males only at age 74, with a trend toward a significant difference ($p < .09$) at age 67. There are no significant differences between male cohorts compared in middle age. In contrast, significant cohort effects were found for females within all age comparisons. Although the magnitude of cohort differences for women were somewhat greater for the comparisons made at the older ages, the differences were significant at all ages.

In summary, the data suggest a slowing down of the positive cohort progression for inductive reasoning, with smaller differences between cohorts compared in middle age than between cohorts compared in old age. This slowing of a positive cohort trend is most evident for males, with nonsignificant differences between cohorts compared in middle age. For women, there is evidence of a continued positive cohort progression, with significant cohort comparisons at all ages examined. At all ages, females assessed in 1984 performed at a higher level than cohorts of the same age assessed in 1970.

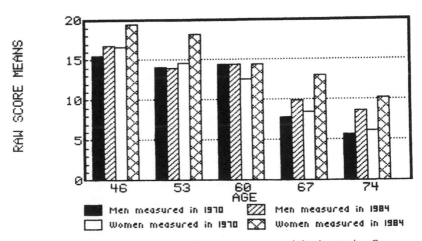

FIG. 3.3. Cohort comparisons of inductive reasoning ability by gender. Cohorts measured in 1970 compared with cohorts at the same age measured in 1984.

Social Indicators and Cohort Effects
for Inductive Reasoning

We next ask whether contextual variables related to inductive reasoning performance can be identified, and do they exhibit the same pattern of cohort progression as that decribed for inductive reasoning? Educational level is a likely candidate given that it has been shown in numerous studies to be significantly related to a variety of cognitive abilities. Indeed, in the gerontological literature, educational level has been reported in several studies to account for a greater proportion of variance in cognitive performance than chronological age. Our regression analyses indicate that 20% of the variance in inductive reasoning scores for the cohorts studied can be accounted for by educational level alone.

Cohort Differences in Educational Level.   The top section in Fig. 3.4 presents mean cohort differences in educational level at the five ages at which cohort comparisons were made (ages 46, 53, 60, 67, 74). Significant cohort differences were found at each of the five ages. In every case, the birth cohort assessed in 1984 exhibited a significantly higher mean educational level than the cohort assessed at the same age in 1970.

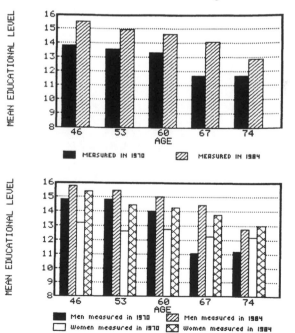

FIG. 3.4. Cohort comparisons of mean educational level for cohorts assessed in 1970 and for cohorts at the same age, assessed in 1984. Top section represents total group; bottom section, gender.

The bottom section in Fig. 3.4 shows cohort differences in educational level separately for males and females. There were significant cohort differences for women for all comparisons, except at the oldest age (74 years). In contrast, cohort differences are shown for males only at the two oldest ages (67, 74); the male birth cohorts compared at ages 46, 53, and 60 did not differ significantly in mean educational level, suggesting a slowing of a positive cohort progression for males similar to that shown for inductive reasoning.

Cohort Differences in Inductive Reasoning Residualized for Educational Level. Given the similarity in the cohort progressions for inductive reasoning ability and educational level for the cohorts studied, we examined changes in the magnitude of cohort differences in inductive reasoning when the effects of educational level were partialled out. Figure 3.5 (top section) presents the cohort comparisons in inductive reasoning performance with the effects of educational level partialled out. There were significant cohort differences only between the cohorts compared at the oldest age level (74). No other cohort comparison is statistically significant. The data in Fig. 3.2 (top section) indicates significant cohort effects at all ages; whereas, in Fig. 3.5, cohort differences are significant only for cohorts compared at age 74.

The bottom section of Fig. 3.5 presents the same data separately for

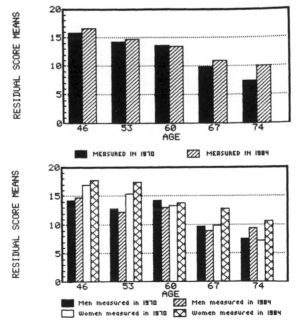

FIG. 3.5. Cohort comparisons of inductive reasoning ability with effects of educational level partialled out. Top section represents total group; bottom section, gender.

males and females. Whereas cohort comparisons for women had been significant at all ages (Fig. 3.2, lower section), significant effects remained only for cohorts compared at the two oldest ages when education was controlled (Fig. 3.5). Recall that differences for males were shown only for the cohorts compared at age 74, and these effects were also eliminated when variability associated with educational level was partialled out.

THE NATURE OF COHORT DIFFERENCES IN INDUCTIVE REASONING

As I have examined the graphs showing cohort differences in intellectual functioning, I have often wondered as to the nature of the specific behavioral differences between cohorts reflected in these cohort progressions. Performance on psychometric measures of intelligence, such as the Thurstone Inductive Reasoning test, has traditionally been measured by the number of correct responses given by the subject. The question arises of whether the positive cohort progression for inductive reasoning reflects an increase in accuracy, an increase in speed of problem solving, or some combination. For example, recent cohorts may have attempted more test items, thereby increasing the number of items answered correctly (i.e., increasing their test score), although the level of accuracy may not have differed for the two cohorts. Accuracy, in this context, is defined as the proportion of items answered correctly out of the items attempted. Alternatively, the number of items attempted may not have increased across cohorts when compared at the same age; but more recent cohorts may have become more accurate, answering a greater proportion of attempted items correctly. Some combination of increased accuracy and problem-solving speed may also be reflected in these cohort effects.

These types of questions have been prompted by paradigmatic shifts in the study of cognition with greater emphasis given to information processing and componential analyses of cognitive behavior (Rybash, Hoyer, & Roodin, 1986; Salthouse, 1986; Sternberg & Berg, 1987). However, many long-term studies of adult cognition have been based on a psychometric approach to intelligence (Owens, 1953; Palmore, 1970; Schaie, 1983), yielding data in a form not readily amenable to address many issues of concern within an information-processing approach.

To examine alternative hypotheses regarding the nature of cohort effects, we compared cohort differences in accuracy (proportion of attempted items answered correctly), versus cohort differences in speed of problem solving.[2] Figure 3.6 (upper section) presents cohort differences

---

[2]The total cohort difference score can be partitioned into that part associated with differences in accuracy and the remaining part resulting from a difference in the number of items attempted (i.e., speed of problem solving). An accuracy difference score was computed to examine cohort differences in accuracy when adjusted for cohort differences in the number of items attempted. We derived the accuracy difference score by computing the expect-

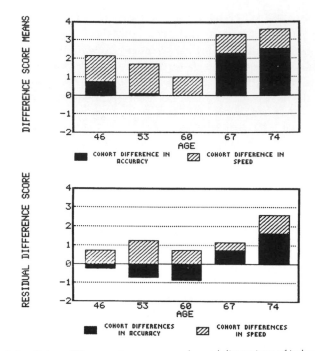

FIG. 3.6. Cohort differences in accuracy and speed dimensions of inductive reasoning performance. Upper section shows raw differences; lower section shows differences residualized for effects of educational level.

in accuracy and speed of problem solving at each of the five ages at which cohort comparisons were made. In agreement with Fig. 3.2, the magnitude of cohort differences was greater for cohorts compared at older ages. Of particular interest, however, are the qualitative differences in the nature of the effects for cohorts compared at different ages. For cohorts compared at ages 67 and 74, the cohort effects were due primarily to differences in level of accuracy; the more recent cohort at each age was more accurate than the earlier cohort at the same age. In contrast, for cohorts compared at ages 46, 53, and 60 years, cohort effects were due primarily to differences in speed of problem solving; the more recent cohort at each age attempted more test items than did the earlier cohort at the same age. For cohorts compared at age 46, we see some difference associated with increased accuracy, but it is small when contrasted with

---

ed score for the more recent cohort (assessed in 1984) in each comparison, if accuracy was the same for the two cohorts when compared at the same age. We computed the expected score by multiplying the number of items attempted by the more recent cohort times the accuracy rate for the earlier cohort (assessed in 1970). The cohort difference in accuracy equals the observed score for the more recent cohort minus the expected score for that cohort. We computed the cohort difference in problem-solving speed by subtracting the accuracy difference score from the total cohort difference score.

the cohort differences associated with increased accuracy for cohorts compared at ages 67 and 74.

Finally, we examine the nature of cohort differences when the effects
of educational level are partialled out. The lower section of Fig. 3.6
presents cohort differences in accuracy and problem-solving speed under these conditions. As would be expected given the proportion of variance accounted for by educational level, the magnitude of the cohort
differences was much reduced and, in most cases, was no longer statistically significant. With regard to the nature of cohort differences, we see
that effects for cohorts compared at ages 67 and 74 were still primarily
associated with positive cohort increments in level of accuracy. However,
for cohorts compared at ages 46, 53, and 60, the positive cohort trends
were totally associated with increases in speed of problem solving, and
there was a slight negative trend in accuracy level for cohorts compared
at those ages.

DIFFERENTIAL COHORT PROGRESSIONS:
SOME IMPLICATIONS

The research on cohort effects on cognitive functioning indicate that cohort progressions differ across mental abilities in direction and rate. Cohort progressions are multidirectional. For some abilities, such as inductive
reasoning, a positive linear cohort trend has been manifested in the past,
whereas curvilinear or negative trends have been shown for other abilities. Furthermore, there is considerable variability in the rate of change
across cohorts. For example, there appears to be a slowing of the positive
cohort trend for inductive reasoning ability.

To the extent that abilities, such as inductive reasoning, are important
in the daily functioning of individuals, this slowing of positive cohort
progressions has important societal implications. Current cohorts entering old age are significantly advantaged cognitively compared with previous cohorts at the same age. This advantage in cognitive competence
should facilitate their dealing with many complexities and demands of
later adulthood. The relative advantagement of those currently entering
old age bodes well for society, given the rapid increase in the number
of elderly living into old, old age.

If we consider also the slowing of the positive cohort progression for
inductive reasoning, there is the implication that current older adults will
be at less disadvantage when compared with middle-aged adults than were
prior cohorts in old age. Indeed, with the slowing of the positive cohort
progression, the magnitude of cohort differences are of the size that may
be reduced or eliminated via cognitive training and educational interven-

tions (Willis, 1985; Willis & Schaie, 1986). The potential of educational interventions for diminishing cohort differences is further supported by our analyses indicating that cohort effects could be significantly reduced by partialling out cohort differences in educational level.

This discussion needs to be tempered by the recognition that the study of cohort effects in old age reflects not only cohort differences in the *level* of ability performance achieved but also possibly cohort differences in the *rate* of age-related change. That is, the cohorts assessed at ages 67 and 74 in 1970 may have experienced somewhat greater age-related change by those ages than did the cohorts assessed at the same ages in 1984, given demographic trends in average life expectancy, medical treatment of chronic diseases, and so on.

The implications of the slowing of positive cohort progressions are somewhat less rosy when we consider future generations of older adults. As the magnitude of cohort differences decreases, there is the implication that future generations of older adults will enter old age with little cognitive advantage over their predecessors. Yet, there is little doubt that the complexities and demands of daily living will continue to increase in the next few years. There is the implication, then, that the cohorts of adults entering old age in the next two decades may be in comparatively greater need of societal supports or educational interventions to assist them in dealing with the increasing complexities of daily demands.

The data examined in this chapter indicate further that the rate of change in cohort progressions may vary by gender. The slowing of the positive cohort progression for inductive reasoning ability was more pronounced for men than for women. The importance of examining cohort progressions separately by gender and by other individual difference variables suggests other societal implications. The data indicate that the relative cohort advantagement of current and future generations entering old age may vary by gender. Given the data suggesting that the positive cohort trend for inductive reasoning ability appears to have slowed more for males than for females, it follows that current middle-age females will be relatively more advantaged entering old age, compared to previous cohorts, than will males of the same age/cohort. This bodes particularly well for these individuals as well as for society, given that women are more likely than men to experience old age widowed, alone, and with fewer financial resources.

We have also attempted to examine in more detail the specific behaviors related to cohort differences in cognitive performance. Our analyses suggest that cohort progressions may reflect qualitative as well as quantitative shifts. Cohorts may differ not only in their level of cognitive performance but also qualitatively in the nature of their behaviors underlying these cohort differences. These qualitative shifts from accuracy to speed in the nature of cohort differences in reasoning ability may be related to slowing cohort progressions in social indicators, such as educational level; this trend is most notable for the cohort comparisons made at the ages of 46, 53, and 60. Note that when the effects of education are partialled out of the reasoning ability scores, the remaining positive cohort effects solely reflect increases in the speed of problem solving rather than increases in accuracy. The implication is that secular trends in social indicators may be related not only to quantitative cohort differences in cognitive functioning but also to qualitative shifts in the nature of the cohort differences.

THE ROLE OF SOCIAL INDICATORS
IN THE ACQUISITION AND MAINTENANCE
OF COGNITIVE ABILITY

Our colleagues in sociology have differentiated between macro- and microlevels of social structure as they impact psychological functioning. Macrolevel structure involves large social units and includes society as a whole, whereas microlevel structure involves the immediate social environment of the individual. We suggest that within a life-span perspective, we need to differentiate between macro- and microlevel social structures that impact the *acquisition* of intellectual skills and abilities in young adulthood, as against social structures that influence the *maintenance* of intellectual functioning in middle and later adulthood. A major developmental task of childhood and young adulthood is the acquisition of a certain level of proficiency in basic cognitive skills, such as written and oral language, computation, and abstract reasoning. However, in adulthood and old age, the primary intellectual demands focus on the application, maintenance/restoration, and compensation of these cognitive skills and abilities (Baltes & Kliegl, 1986; Schaie, 1977–1978). In work and family life, the adult is called on to apply the cognitive knowledge base and skills acquired in early schooling. In middle age, the individual must expend increasing effort in maintaining and restoring cognitive skills. Although the average middle-aged individual has not experienced significant age-related decline in cognitive ability, rapid technological and societal change may render previously acquired skills and knowledge base obsolete or in need of updating and restoration. Finally, in old age, the individual is faced with the increasing possibility of physical and contextual losses and, thus, must selectively determine in what cognitive domains to compensate for these losses.

Middle age is characterized by considerable stability in basic mental abilities (e.g., inductive reasoning) and increased expertise in specific knowledge bases relevant to the individual's career or life tasks. The research of Glaser (see his discussion following this chapter) and others has indicated that individual differences in basic mental processes may not be particularly relevant once an expert knowledge system is in place. However, given rapid technological change and the current knowledge explosion, the middle-aged adult is increasingly faced with the threat of technical obsolescence in those areas of expertise acquired in young adulthood. We believe that the basic mental abilities, such as inductive reasoning, may again become important in middle age when the individual is faced with the radical reorganization of previous knowledge bases or with the acquisition of new knowledge structures. For example, Garfein (1986) has recently trained middle-aged adults with little or no prior computer literacy to use spread sheet software. He found fluid abilities to be significant predictors of the middle-age adult's ability to master this technology.

The mechanisms by which social structures impact acquisition of intellectual functioning may be quite distinct from the way in which social structures impact maintenance and compensation of cognitive ability. In the acquisition of cognitive abilities, social structures may be influential in determining the *level* of intellectual performance achieved by a particular cohort. By contrast, in middle and later adulthood, social structures may influence primarily the *rate of change* in intellectual performance as the individual copes first with technological and societal challenges then with age-related change in old age.

Level of performance on many ability tests has been shown to be highly related to level of educational attainment. Featherman (Featherman & Peterson, 1986) has noted the cohort trends toward increasing age-gradedness in the transitions into adulthood. As age-gradedness increases, the timing and duration of transition events into adulthood become more uniform across cohorts. For example, laws governing compulsory schooling have contributed to the age-gradedness in education of the young. The timing and duration of basic schooling is, consequently, being experienced more uniformly by successive cohorts. Likewise, increase in the number of years of compulsory schooling has contributed to a decrease in cohort differences in median educational attainment.

The continuing positive cohort trend in female's postsecondary educational attainment is important, also, given gender differences in the relationship between educational attainment and career development in midlife. Educational attainment is important for both men and women in acquiring their first jobs in young adulthood. For men, later job experience and training become increasingly important in determining the career moves and advancements achieved in midlife. However, for women, occupational achievements in midlife are more consistently related to their first jobs and, thus, to educational attainment.

Of particular interest to those of us studying adult development are the macro- and microsocial structures that impact the *maintenance* of cognitive functioning in middle and old age. Three lines of recent research suggest that certain dimensions of the workplace environment are associated with intellectual viability in middle and later adulthood. First, there is the salient work of Kohn and Schooler (1983) examining reciprocal relationships between work complexity and intellectual flexibility. Second, Featherman (this volume) has proposed some provocative ideas that suggest how an individual's knowledge and skills acquired in the workplace may impact his or her adaptation to old age. Third, our own work (Willis & Tosti-Vasey, 1986) describes the personal characteristics and work environment dimensions that foster professional updating and productivity in midcareer faculty. These three lines of research suggest that there may be "spillover" or transfer from skills and abilities acquired in the workplace to more general dimensions of cognitive functioning, and that these effects are likely to persist on a long-term basis.

Specific dimensions of the work environment have been identified as being related to maintenance and enhancement of intellectual functioning. Kohn and Schooler (1983) have reported that more complex work environments, entailing a variety of challenging job demands in which people and ideas are involved and the worker has considerable autonomy in determining work priorities, are related to enhanced intellectual flexibility. In our own research with midcareer faculty, we have found that continued scientific productivity is related to having breadth and diversity in job demands. Work that either underutilizes the professional's skills or, conversely, results in overspecialization is particularly disadvantageous. Enhancement of a college faculty's intellectual skills, for example, is hampered by repetitive teaching of a limited number of courses. Overspecialization is dangerous in midcareer, because it not only limits diversity in job assignments but also renders professionals in some technical fields more vulnerable to obsolescence from sudden shifts in the direction of their professional discipline.

In the Kohn and Schooler research (1983), work with people was found to be more complex than work with things. We have found that the role of colleagues is particularly important in professional productivity and competence in midlife. Peers are the most widely used source of technical information. Our choice of information channels is influenced by ease of accessibility, and our colleagues are often the most accessible resource. In addition, peers influence one's perception of the work environment, including norms or standards of work effort and achievement.

SUMMARY

In this chapter, we have discussed issues related to the direction and rate of cohort progressions for cognitive abilities using inductive reasoning ability as a sample case. Cohort progressions for mental abilities are multidirectional and dynamic. We have observed that the positive, linear progression for induction appears to be slowing for cohorts currently in middle age. The direction and rate of cohort progressions vary by gender. For inductive reasoning, cohorts of males compared in middle age exhibited less of a cohort effect than did females from the same cohorts.

Our analyses have suggested that cohort effects in cognitive performance reflect qualitative as well as quantitative differences. There is suggestive evidence that the slowing in some positive cohort trends may also involve qualitative shifts in the nature of cohort effects. Comparisons of cohorts at middle age indicated that these effects were primarily associated with differences in speed of problem solving rather than with differences in level of accuracy.

We have demonstrated that social indicators, such as educational level, can account for considerable variability associated with cohort effects. After residualizing for educational effects, we found no significant differences in ability level for cohorts compared in middle age. However, significant cohort effects remained for cohorts compared at older ages.

We have suggested that in further explorations of the relationship between social indices and cognitive functioning across the life span, it will become increasingly important to differentiate between social indicators that primarily impact acquisition of cognitive ability as oppose to indicators that impact maintenance of cognitive competence in middle and old age. Indicators related to acquisition are more likely to influence peak level of ability performance, whereas indices associated with maintenance of cognitive competence impact cohort differences in the rate of cognitive change in later life.

Although the classroom is the environment most commonly associated with acquisition of cognitive skills, several lines of research indicate that the workplace is an important environment for the maintenance and enhancement of cognitive competence in midlife. Diverse, challenging work assignments, autonomy in decision making, and stimulation and information provided by colleagues have been implicated as important dimensions of the work environment that foster enhancement and maintenance of intellectual competence in midlife. It has been suggested that abilities and skills honed in the workplace are important in coping with challenges of later life. Executive planning and problem-solving skills developed on the job may be particularly useful in decision making in old age. However, the contextual variables and cognitive processes that facilitate the transfer of previously acquired knowledge and skills to dealing successfully with the problems of old age remain to be identified and examined. Adult development and social change represent a dialectical process. The impact of social indicators and psychological development upon each other will, therefore, continue to change and must be studied as a dynamic system.

ACKNOWLEDGMENT

The research reported in this chapter was supported by a grant (AGO3544) from the National Institute of Aging. We gratefully acknowledge the enthusiastic cooperation of members and staff of the Group Health Cooperative of Puget Sound.

REFERENCES

Abeles, R. P., & Riley, M. W. (1987). Longevity, social structure and cognitive aging. In C. Schooler & K. W. Schaie (Eds.), *Cognitive functioning and social structure over the life course* (pp. 161–175). Norwood, NJ: Ablex.

Baltes, P. B. (1968). Longitudinal and cross-sectional sequences in the study of age and generation effects. *Human Development, 11*, 145–171.

Baltes, P. B., Cornelius, S. W., & Nesselroade, J. R. (1979). Cohort effects in developmental psychology. In J. R. Nesselroade & P. B. Baltes (Eds.), *Longitudinal research in the study of behavior and development* (pp. 61–87). New York: Academic Press.

Baltes, P. B., & Kliegl, R. (1986). On the dynamics between growth and decline in the aging of intelligence and memory. In K. Poeck, H. J. Freund, & H. Ganshirt (Eds.), *Neurology* (pp. 1–17). Heidelberg: Springer.

Cattell, R. B. (1971). *Abilities: Their structure, growth, and action.* Boston: Houghton-Mifflin.

Featherman, D. L., & Peterson, T. (1986). Markers of aging: Modeling the clocks that time us. *Rsearch on Aging, 8,* 339–365.

Garfein, A. (1986, November). *Microcomputer proficiency in later middle-aged adults: Teaching old dogs new tricks.* Paper presented at the meeting of the Gerontological Society of America, Chicago.

Guilford, J. P. (1967). *The nature of human intelligence.* New York: McGraw-Hill.

Kohn, M. L., & Schooler, C. (1983). *Work and personality: An inquiry into the impact of social stratification.* Norwood, NJ: Ablex.

Owens, W. A., Jr. (1953). Age and mental abilities: A longitudinal study. *Genetic Psychology Monograph, 48,* 3–54.

Palmore, E. (Ed.). (1970). *Normal aging: Reports from the Duke Longitudinal Study, 1955–1969.* Durham, NC: Duke University Press.

Riegel, K. F. (1976). *Psychology of development and history.* New York: Plenum.

Rybash, J. M., Hoyer, W. J., & Roodin, P. A. (1986). *Adult cognition and aging.* New York: Pergamon.

Salthouse, T. A. (1986) *A theory of cognitive aging.* Amsterdam: North Holland.

Schaie, K. W. (1965). A general model for the study of developmental problems. *Psychological Bulletin, 64,* 91–107.

Schaie, K. W. (1977–78). Toward a stage theory of adult cognitive development. *Aging and Human Development, 8,* 129–138.

Schaie, K. W. (1983). The Seattle Longitudinal Study: A twenty-one year exploration of psychometric intelligence in adulthood. In K. W. Schaie (Ed.), *Longitudinal studies of adult psychological development* (pp. 64–135). New York: Guilford.

Schaie, K. W. (1986a). Beyond calendar definitions of age, time and cohort: The general developmental model revisited. *Developmental Review, 6,* 252–277.

Schaie, K. W. (1986b, September). *Social context and cognitive performance in old age.* Paper presented at the meeting of the American Sociological Association, New York.

Schaie, K. W., & Hertzog, C. K. (1983). Fourteen-year cohort-sequential studies of adult intelligence. *Developmental Psychology, 19,* 531–543.

Schaie, K. W., & Hertzog, C. (1986). Toward a comprehensive model of adult intellectual development: Contributions of the Seattle Longitudinal Study. In R. J. Sternberg (Ed.), *Advances in human intelligence* (Vol. 3, pp. 79–118). New York: Academic Press.

Simon, H., & Kotovsky, K. (1963). Human acquisition of concepts for sequential patterns. *Psychological Review, 70,* 534–546.

Sternberg, R., & Berg, C. (1987). What are theories of adult intellectual development theories of? In K. W. Schaie & C. Schooler (Eds.), *Cognitive functioning and social structure over the life course.* Norwood, NJ: Ablex.

Thurstone, L. L. (1938). *Primary mental abilities.* Chicago: University of Chicago Press.

Willis, S. L. (1985). Towards an educational psychology of the adult learner: Cognitive and intellectual bases. In J. E. Birren & K. W. Schaie (Eds.), *Handbook of the psychology of aging.* (2nd ed., pp. 818–847). New York: Van Nostrand Reinhold.

Willis, S. L., & Schaie, K. W. (1986). Training the elderly on the ability factors of spatial orientation and inductive reasoning. *Psychology and Aging, 1,* 239–247.

Willis, S. L., & Tosti-Vasey, J. (1986). *Professional obsolescence and updating in midcareer faculty.* Unpublished manuscript, Pennsylvania State University, University Park.

Knowledge-Derived Competence

Robert Glaser
Learning Research and Development Center
University of Pittsburgh

As an outsider to the aging business, at least to its study, I am impressed with what has been and can be learned substantively and methodologically from the Seattle Longitudinal Study data base. The objective of Professor Willis' work — to describe the direction and rate of cognitive change for age differences in various birth cohorts — is significant for increasing our knowledge of the aging process. The various abilities she describes show interesting progressions, asymtotes, and peaks that seek explanation. Gender differences and comparisons at older ages are shown to be related to what has occurred in our society over the past 20 years. Particularly incisive are the findings on inductive reasoning, which we know correlates with school success in younger ages and, as Willis points out, with performance on "right or wrong" answer tests of daily activities in older adults. For this psychometrically defined ability of reasoning, the good news is that the scores of older people of today are up relative to those of older people of years ago; the bad news is that, although the scores of middle-aged people are slightly better than those of the past, they are relatively less so when compared with older people.

Even more interesting to me is Willis' attempt to undertake a deeper analysis of the meaning of global test scores, although I would quibble with her calling the analysis *componential* (the term's now generally accepted meaning is found in articles by Sternberg, 1977, and Pellegrino & Glaser, 1979). Nevertheless, in the attempt to understand the progressions and retrogressions of cognitive aging, such detailed analysis of test scores is an important endeavor. The data obtained on changes in accuracy and response speed (or number of items attempted) indicate that older people show an increase in accuracy; middle-agers show increases in speed,

113

with middle-aged women showing that the birth cohort increase is still partially related to accuracy. I wish that I could explain this. I can speculate: Perhaps older groups have learned that they need to be more careful on tests, and middle-agers are still opting for the test-taking strategy of hitting as many items as they can.

Certainly, the deeper analysis of the test score changes that Willis studied are important in the effort to work toward the cognitive constructs and social-environmental explanations underlying them. In keeping with this goal, I would like to offer some thoughts for the future—a future, as I see it, in which we have designed assessment instruments that are built on a more modern theory of cognition than were traditional psychometric measures. (Perhaps as a bridge, these newer measures can be correlated both with the older measures and with criteria of performance in old age so that a richer picture of the constructs necessary to understand cognitive aging can be obtained.) In these remarks, I offer only observations on one facet, the contribution of an emerging cognitive theory of knowledge acquisition.

THE ROLE OF KNOWLEDGE STRUCTURES
IN THE DEVELOPMENT OF COMPETENCE

In a discussion of the psychological aging process and changes in cognitive competence, I believe that we need to consider the structures and schemas of knowledge that become better articulated over the individual's course of living and accumulating experience in the world. It is increasingly apparent from data and theory in various domains of study—developmental psychology, memory development, expert and novice problem solving, and artificial intelligence—that organized, specific knowledge is a significant factor in the quality and power of a person's thinking and problem-solving in concert with the power of more general intellectual or cognitive processes. This is the theme that I pursue in my remarks. It follows from this that emphasizing primarily the assessment of general intellectual processes tells only part of the story.

Recent advances in cognitive science now make it clear that processes of competent performance are derived to a significant extent from the availability of organized knowledge as well as from global qualities or aptitudelike processes of thinking. In various situations and in the course of aging, psychologists must accord equal importance to knowledge as a generating source of cognitive process as they had previously accorded to the "pure processes" of memory, induction, spatial visualization, and so forth.

We can elaborate on this general proposition by recounting investigations in several domains of human competence—namely, in studies of the development of cognitive capabilities in children: the development of expertise in adult performance (involving the representation, automatization, and proceduralization of performance); the relationship between general and specific cognitive skills used in learning and problem solving; and the growth of executive, self-regulatory, monitoring, and elaboration skills that develop with cognitive competence in performance and learning. Consider the following findings and speculations.

1. *Studies of children's memory and classification tasks show a superiority of performance that is attributed to the influence of knowledge organization in a content domain in addition to the exercise of memory strategies as such.* The reorganization of knowledge in children's conception of biological phenomena as a result of school instruction and world experience, for example, shows that learning and problem solving are greatly influenced by new information and its restructuring. Whereas children 4 to 7 years old conceive of all living things in terms of human characteristics, older children organize their knowledge of these characteristics in terms of biological functions (Carey, 1985). These changes in the knowledge base produce sophisticated cognitive performance that might be interpreted as an abstract change in their abilities. However, such changes appear to come about when the child acquires new knowledge structures that make available mental representations that enable new kinds of thinking and inferencing. As developmental psychologists have devoted increasing attention to changes in children's specific content knowledge, knowledge of specific domains has emerged as a crucial dimension of development. Increases in domain knowledge are now seen to underlie changes previously attributed solely to the global growth of capabilities and strategies.

2. *In adults, the salience of structured knowledge is apparent in studies of expertise and expert/novice contrasts.* These investigations show that the intuitions of competent individuals are facilitated by their recognition of structured patterns and the quality of their problem perceptions. This ability to recognize patterns in events that are experienced determines how a problem or situation is represented and interpreted and how the situation is solved and acted upon. In general, the knowledgeable individual sees the deep structure rather than the surface structure of a problem, sees the principles inferred from the given features, and the knowledge in terms of procedures for its applicability in a given situation (Chi, Glaser, & Rees, 1982). Familiar situations often entail rapid intuitive action that reveals how expert perceptions are enabled by specific knowledge. Unfamiliar situations require more general cognitive activities, and rapid

representation may be precluded. Unfamiliar situations may need to be rerepresented a number of times through inferences and analogical procedures before an actionable representation is arrived at; or general heuristics and general memory search processes may be necessary to define these unfamiliar situations. Interpreting problem-solving competence in both familiar and unfamiliar domains as a factor in the course of psychological aging, therefore, becomes a key issue.

3. *To illuminate the differences betwen specific and general competencies, Newell (1980) introduced an apt metaphor—a cone of problem-solving methods.* At the base of the cone, the broad end, there exists a large set of specific powerful routines applicable to performance in specific knowledge domains. They are powerful in that once they are accessed, problem solution should follow, assuming they are executed properly. At the apex or tip of the cone, there are a few, relatively speaking, highly general but "weak" routines. They are general in that they are applicable to almost any problem-solving situation, but they are weak in that they alone will not lead to specific problem solution. Such general routines include, for example, means-end analysis, subgoal decomposition, exhortations to stay on task and monitor progress, and so on. Thus, as we move up or down the cone, there are trade-offs between generality and power, between so-called strong methods and weak methods. The strong methods are learned in the context of specific domains, the general methods are acquired as more generalized habits of thinking (perhaps as a part of general intelligence or as abstracted competencies induced from a variety of specific experiences). The interesting question is how this dimension of performance—the interaction between specific and general cognitive skills—relates to changes in intellectual competence with age.

4. *Another increasing dimension of cognitive skill from childhood onward is the growth of metacognition, executive control processes, self-regulation, and other such mechanisms.* Essentially, these are mechanisms that evaluate and monitor performance. Information-processing models of cognition generally attribute powerful operations to an executive system capable of evaluating its processing activities. Such executive systems are aware of their capacity limitations; they are aware not only of their capabilities but also of their appropriate use; they plan and schedule activities; they monitor and evaluate outcomes; and they terminate performance at appropriate times. Such control processes are apparent in work on the development of children's knowledge of their own capabilities (Brown, Bransford, Ferrara, & Campione, 1983; Flavell, Friedrichs, & Hoyt, 1970); in studies of comprehension monitoring (Markman, 1985) and of effort and attention allocation (Schneider & Shiffrin, 1977); and in general analyses of self-regulation and forms of editing and error correction in problem solving. The development of these executive performances appears to be another dimension that can be investigated in studies of psychological aging.

5. *Related to the mechanisms just mentioned is the distinction between automatic and controlled processing.* William James lucidly described this processing in 1896:

> The great thing . . . in all education is to . . . fund and capitalize our acquisitions, and live at ease upon the interest of the fund. *For this we must make automatic and habitual, as early as possible, as many useful actions as we can,* and guard against the growing into ways that are likely to be disadvantageous to us. . . . The more of the details of our daily life we can hand over to the effortless custody of automatism, the more our higher powers of mind will be set free for their own proper work. There is no more miserable human being than one in whom nothing is habitual but indecision. . . . Full half the time of such a man goes to the deciding, or regretting, of matters which ought to be so ingrained in him as practically not to exist for his consciousness at all. (p. 122)

In recent years, automatic and controlled processing have become the subject of quite advanced research and theorizing. "Automatic processing is a fast, parallel process that is not limited by short-term memory, that requires little subject effort, and that demands little direct subject control. Controlled processing is a comparatively slow, serial process that is limited by short-term memory constraints, that requires subject effort, and that provides a large degree of subject control" (Schneider, 1985, pp. 296–297; Schneider & Shiffrin, 1977). This distinction raises many interesting questions relevant to the growth of competence with increasing age and expertise. On the one hand, the development of automatic processes permits much more memory space to be applied to conscious action. On the other hand, the automatization of acivities may preclude amenability to further development because they are so ingrained—another aspect of psychological aging (Brown et al., 1983).

HOW FINDINGS ON KNOWLEDGE STRUCTURES
APPLY TO THE MEASUREMENT OF COGNITIVE AGING

The measurement of cognitive aging should be driven more than it is by the emerging cognitive theory of knowledge acquisition. We now realize that people who have learned concepts and skills over a long period of time have acquired a large collection of schematic knowledge structures. These structures enable understanding of the relationships inherent in their knowledge. We also know that someone who has learned to solve problems and make inferences has acquired a set of cognitive procedures attached to knowledge structures that enable actions that influence learning, goal setting, and planning. At various stages of proficiency and in the course of aging, there exist different integrations of knowledge, different degrees of procedural skill, and differences in rapid access to memory and in representations of tasks to be performed. An important characteristic of the measurement of ability in cognitive aging, then, should be assessment of knowledge structures and their related cognitive processes.

Measurement of this kind, as I envision it, is at an early stage. Many ideas needed are yet to be worked out, but I can speculate on a tentative set of dimensions comprising components of cognitive proficiency that might underlie assessment. Consider the following factors.

1. *Knowledge Organization and Structure.* As cognitive proficiency is attained in a domain, elements of knowledge and components become increasingly interconnected so that proficient individuals access coherent chunks of information rather than disconnected fragments. The knowledge of less proficient individuals is fragmentary, consisting of isolated definitions and superficial understandings. The degree of fragmentation and structuredness and the degree of accessibility to interrelated chunks of knowledge become dimensions of assessment.

2. *Depth of Problem Representation.* It is now well known that novices recognize the surface features of a problem or task situation, and more proficient individuals go beyond surface features and identify inferences or principles that subsume the surface structure. This ability for rapid recognition of underlying principles could be assessed by appropriate pattern recognition tasks in verbal and graphic situations. Certain forms of representation may be highly correlated with details of an individual's ability to carry out a task or solve a problem.

3. *Quality of Mental Models.* People develop mental models of phenomena and situations with which they work. The nature of these representations is determined by what is useful for the tasks that need to be performed and the level of effort required. The nature of these models indicates not only the levels of task complexity that a person is capable of handling but also the level at which life demands force people to think.

4. *Goal Orientation of Procedures.* Carrying out procedures is an important aspect of many skills. However, they cannot be measured in rote fashion; they must be assessed in terms of the effective goals guiding them. The relationship between task understanding and efficient conduct of procedures is an important aspect of cognitive proficiency, and effective measurement should de-emphasize rote and piecemeal assessment of procedural skills that does not focus on adaptability to performance goals.

5. *Automaticity and Task Integration.* When subtasks of a complex activity require simultaneous demands for attention, the efficiency of the overall task is affected. This fact has particular implications in the assessment

of the interaction between basic skills and advanced components of cognitive performance. Although component processes may work well when tested separately, they may not be efficient enough to work together. A slow, or inefficient, component process in interaction with other processes can lead to breakdowns in overall proficiency. If a task consists of an orchestration of basic skills and higher level strategic processes, then an assessment procedure should be able to diagnose the inefficiencies in this complex performance.

6. *Proceduralized Knowledge.* Modern learning theory has suggested that the course through which we acquire components of knowledge proceeds from an initial declarative form to a more useful procedural form. In the early stage we can, for example, know an item of specialized vocabulary without knowing the conditions under which that item of knowledge is applicable and is to be used most effectively. Studies of the differences between experts and novices indicate that beginners may have requisite knowledge, but this knowledge is not bound to the conditions of its applicability. When knowledge is accessed by experts, it is always associated with indications of how and when it is to be used appropriately. This progression can be considered a factor in assessing cognitive proficiency.

7. *Metacognitive and Self-Regulatory Skills.* These skills develop with maturity, and they may be less developed in people with performance difficulties. It is likely that these skills appear in various forms and levels of competence over a wide range of individuals. An especially interesting characteristic of these skills is that they may be the particular aspect of performance that facilitates transfer to new situations. Individuals can know a rule or procedure that improves their performance on certain tasks, but it is also important that they know how to adapt the rule to other situations and how to monitor its use. Self-regulatory activities of this kind are important skills to be assessed in studies of cognitive aging.

CONCLUSION

Overall, the research reported by Willis astutely describes age patterns and progressions in the general cognitive processes identified by psychometric analyses, as well as general methods and heuristic processes uncovered in early information-processing studies of human problem solving on knowledge-lean tasks. However, I suggest that these broadly applicable processes are only part of individual variation in cognitive proficiency and that much else resides in domain-specific processes nurtured over the course of life-span development. Complimentary to the work reported by Willis and her colleagues, I would like to see attention paid also to the processes of knowledge-derived competence.

REFERENCES

Brown, A. L., Bransford, J. D., Ferrara, R. A., & Campione, J. C. (1983). Learning, remembering, and understanding. In J. H. Flavell & E. M. Markman (Eds.), *Handbook of child psychology* (pp. 77–166). New York: Wiley.

Carey, S. (1985). *Conceptual change in childhood.* Cambridge, MA: MIT Press.

Chi, M., Glaser, R., & Rees, E. (1982). Expertise in problem solving. In R. Sternberg (Ed.), *Advances in the psychology of human intelligence.* Hillsdale, NJ: Lawrence Erlbaum Associates.

Flavell, J. H., Friedrichs, A. G., & Hoyt, J. D. (1970). Developmental changes in memorization processes. *Cognitive Psychology, 1,* 324–340.

James, W. (1896). *The principles of psychology.* New York: Henry Holt.

Markman, E. M. (1985). Comprehension monitoring: Developmental and educational issues. In S. Chipman, J. Segal, & R. Glaser (Eds.), *Thinking and learning skills (Vol. 2): Research and open questions* (pp. 275–292). Hillsdale, NJ: Lawrence Erlbaum Associates.

Newell, A. (1980). One final word. In D. T. Tuma & F. Reif (Eds.), *Problem solving and education: Issues in teaching and research* (pp. 175–189). Hillsdale, NJ: Lawrence Erlbaum Associates.

Pellegrino, J. W., & Glaser, R. (1979). Cognitive correlates and components in the analysis of individual differences. In R. J. Sternberg & D. K. Detterman (Eds.), *Human intelligence* (pp. 61–88). Norwood, NJ: Ablex.

Schneider, W. (1985). Training high performance skills: Fallacies and guidelines. *Human Factors, 27*(3), 285–300.

Schneider, W., & Shiffrin, R. M. (1977). Controlled and automatic human information processing: I. Direction, search, and attention. *Psychological Review, 84*(1), 1–66.

Sternberg, R. J. (1977). *Intelligence, information processing, and analogical reasoning: The componential analysis of human abilities.* Hillsdale, NJ: Lawrence Erlbaum Associates.

Training-Controlled Social Structure?

Timothy A. Salthouse
Georgia Institute of Technology

Not too long ago I attended a conference in which a participant provided a set of guidelines for what one should say when serving as a discussant. To the best of my memory, his prescription included four major components. The first was *praise*, in which the discussant extols the many virtues of the work being presented, if for no other reason than to justify the time he or she spent reading the speaker's text and deciding what he or she was going to say about it. The second component was *qualification*, in which the discussant brings the author of the target material back to reality by mentioning limitations of the work that could be overcome by extensions of the research, which may or may not be practical or even possible. The third suggested aspect of the discussant's role was *gentle criticism* because the author failed to place greater emphasis on issue X, and X happens to be whatever topic the discussant is currently interested in. Finally, the prescription stated that the discussant's comments should finish with an *optimistic conclusion* by stating that although the major issues in this area have not yet been resolved, the research under discussion represents a very promising direction toward the achievement of that goal.

I more or less follow this outline in my discussion of Sherry Willis' chapter, but I want to point out that my laudatory comments about her work are not simply perfunctory because I truly believe that she is doing exceptionally fine work in a very important area. Moreover, it seems appropriate that Sherry Willis should speak about social structure and psychological processes because for many years she has investigated what is probably the most likely means by which social factors influence the behavior of a particular individual. That is, social structure seems to have its primary impact upon psychological processes by influencing either the quantity or the quality of experience received by an individual, and much of Willis' past research has focused on the effects of explicit manipulation of experience on cognitive functioning. In this respect, training research (and other attempts to experimentally manipulate experience) might be considered a sociocultural microcosm in that the effects of experiential variations on cognitive functioning are subjected to direct investigation. Of course, the degree of experiental variation possible in short-term studies is clearly limited relative to what probably occurs in the natural environment, but the ability to control this experience allows stronger inferences about the causal role of experience on cognitive functioning than would otherwise be possible.

There is now a sizable literature of training studies in which portions of an individual's experience have been systematically controlled, but Willis' are the best in several respects. For example, she invariably includes a no-training control group to determine whether the observed effects are actually attributable to the training and not to some other unspecified processes, she examines the stability or persistence of the training effects rather than simply assessing performance immediately after training, and she attempts to determine whether the effects are ability specific both by administering transfer tests and by making comparisons at the level of latent constructs.

This careful and programmatic research effort has yielded fairly definitive answers to most, but in my opinion not yet all, of the important questions that might be addressed in training studies. What I consider to be the four most important of these questions are listed in Table 1. The first question has been answered positively by nearly all researchers who have published training studies, even if only by virtue of the fact that a researcher is unlikely to report a study if the training was not found to be beneficial in at least some respects.

However, this initial question is not particularly interesting unless the training effects can be demonstrated to be reasonably stable and generalizable to other situations. In other words, for most purposes question 2 is more important than question 1 in that the practical and theoretical significance is considerably greater if experience is found to affect ability and not just performance. Many studies reported by Willis and her col-

TABLE 1
Four Questions Relevant to Training Studies

1. Does experience enhance cognitive performance?
2. Does experience enhance cognitive ability?
3. Are the effects of experience specific to certain groups of individuals? (e.g., Can only young dogs learn new tricks?)
4. (a) Is differential experience a determinant of age-related differences in cognition?
   (b) Can age-related decline in cognitive functioning be reversed with experience?

leagues have exhibited evidence for training effects at the ability level, thus the answer to the second question also seems to be yes. This is an important finding in the context of this book because it indicates that there are likely to be substantial effects of social structure on cognitive functioning to the extent that social structure influences the quality or quantity of an individual's experience.

The answer to the third question seems to be no because the currently available evidence appears to indicate that the benefits of experience are roughly equivalent for most groupings of reasonably healthy individuals. These findings clearly serve to refute the cliche that "old Dogs can't learn new tricks," and they imply that training-like interventions could be of immense practical importance. This is particularly true in the later years when, because of declining levels of performance, some older adults may need experiential interventions to function at a competent level.

Question 4 is by far the most controversial. Although I suspect that the answer to at least question 4a may eventually be found to be yes, I don't think the evidence is yet available to reach a firm conclusion. I would like to explain my position on this issue by considering the most recent of the Willis and Schaie training studies in greater detail. I illustrate the results of their training manipulations (Willis & Schaie, 1986) in Fig. 1, with the training results (vertical arrows) superimposed on a graph of the cross-sectional age trends (solid functions) for space and reasoning abilities (derived from Table 1, in Schaie, 1985). Although Willis and Schaie have generally contrasted the training effects with results from longitudinal studies, cross-sectional data may provide the more appropriate comparison. That is, because it is often assumed that experiential variation is minimized when a single generational cohort is used in a longitudinal study, the best estimate of the potential contribution of training-mediated experience effects might be obtained if these effects are compared with age-related trends from cross-sectional studies in which it is suspected that at least some of the observed performance differences are attributable to differences in experience. This is particularly true if one subscribes to the argument that cross-sectional studies confound age changes with cohort differences, and the latter are attributable to variations in the quantity or quality of experience of the type manipulated in training studies.

Both graphs in Fig. 1 indicate that the training effects can be quite substantial, with a benefit across several weeks of training averaging between ⅓ and ½ the magnitude of the cross-sectional decline evident across a range of 50 years. However, it is only speculative, although tempting, to suggest that because the depressed levels of performance can be enhanced with experiential interventions, it is experiential deprivation or disuse that is responsible for performance declining rather than remaining stable across adulthood. There appear to be at least two problems that must be resolved before this disuse interpretation can be supported on the ba-

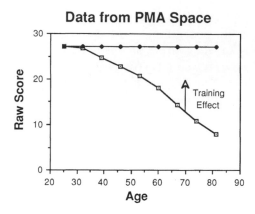

FIG. 1. Training effects (arrows in the context of observed cross-sectional trends (open symbols) and conceivable interpretations (solid symbols).

sis of results such as those illustrated in Fig. 1. Willis and Schaie (1986) have addressed these issues in their recent work, but the results currently available are not supportive of the disuse or differential experience interpretation and consequently fail to provide a secure basis on which we can reach a conclusion about the role of experience in producing, or reversing, age-rela d declines in cognitive functioning.

One problem with interpeting the finding that poor-performing individuals improve their performance with training as indicating that the cause of their disadvantage was lack of recent experience, is that there could have been equivalent improvement by the individuals who initially performed better. In this latter case, the function relating age to training-enhanced performance would not be the horizontal line representing age-invariant performance; instead the function would consist of a line parallel to the original but at uniformly higher levels. If the benefits of added experience are actually equivalent across the entire age range and not selectively beneficial only to those for whom prior experience was presumably deficient, then it seems unreasonable to suggest that a factor of differential experience was responsible for the initial performance differences.

Distinguishing between the possibilities of selective versus general training benefits clearly requires the examination of training effects in more than one group. Even with multiple groups the interpretations are not simple, however, as is revealed if we consider how different training outcomes might be interpreted from alternative theoretical perspectives. Table 2 summarizes some of these interpretations (under the assumption that the functions relating performance to experience are monotonic and similar across groups).

Notice that the only case in which the results are diagnostic in distinguishing between the differential-experience interpretation and an alternative biological-deterioration interpretation is when the training effects are greater for the initially disadvantaged group. At the present time, the biological-deterioration perspective does not seem able to account for a finding that older adults improve more than young adults with a short-term intervention (assuming there are no artifacts, such as a measurement ceiling, in either group). A selective benefit favoring the initially most disadvantaged would consequently weaken the plausibility of an irreversible, biologically based interpretation of the age-related cognitive differences and, at least indirectly, strengthen the plausibility of the alternative disuse interpretation.

Willis and Schaie (1986; Schaie & Willis, 1986) recently reported data relevant to this comparison, although instead of comparing adults of different ages they contrasted older adults identified as having declined in a

TABLE 2
Interpretability of Training Outcomes

Hypothesized Source of Cross-Sectional Trends	Training Outcome		
	$Y = 0$	$Y > 0$	$Y < 0$
Differential experience	Possible (e.g., Training affects different mechanism)	Possible (e.g., Learning rates differ)	Possible (e.g., Young near saturation on experience)
Biological deterioration	Possible (e.g., Training affects different mechanism)	Possible (e.g., Learning rates differ)	Impossible?

given ability over a 14-year period with those identified as not having declined. The reasoning behind this comparison is similar to that described previously, but the availability of longitudinal data allowed investigation of the additional question of whether the declines in cognitive functioning could actually be reversed.

Based on the distribution of scores in 1970, individuals were classified in 1984 as having remained stable or as having declined depending upon whether or not their 1984 score was lower, by a criterion amount, than their 1970 score. All individuals were then administered training geared toward either the spatial ability or the reasoning ability. The major results of the study showed that the training effects at the ability level were not selective because individuals identified as remaining stable or as declining over the past 14 years exhibited nearly equivalent improvement. Because the disadvantaged (declining) group benefited no more than the nondisadvantaged (stable) group, these findings cannot be unambiguously interpreted. (One of four interactions testing whether training effects were selectively greater for declining individuals than for stable individuals was reported to be significant at $p < .05$; but because this was discovered in the context of over 60 statistical comparisons, it may well have a chance occurrence.)

One possible reason for the equivocal results of the Willis and Schaie training studies may be that the classification of individuals as remaining stable or as declining could have been imprecise. Their classification system was based on whether individuals deviated from their earlier score by an amount greater than the standard error of between-individual scores. A possibly more desirable procedure for assessing the reliability of within-individual change might have been to obtain multiple observations from each individual at each measurement occasion, and then to use a statistical test to compare the two distributions of observations for each individual (cf. Salthouse, Kausler, & Saults, 1986). In this manner, the variability used to assess the reliability of the across-time differences is directly relevant because it is derived from the same individual rather than estimated from the across-individual variability, as was the case in the Willis and Schaie studies. This would obviously require considerably more testing time per individual at each measurement occasion, but some procedure such as this may be necesssary if one wants to obtain accurate assessments of across-time changes occurring within a given individual.

Another problem with using results from training studies as support for a differential experience interpretation of cognitive age differences is that the mechanisms of training-related improvement may not have been the same as those responsible for age-related decline. That is, even if training selectively benefits the disadvantaged (declining) group more than the advantaged (stable) group, the plausibility of a "deficit-reversal" interpetation of the training results would be low if different processes mediate age-related performance decline and training-related performance improvement.

Willis and Schaie (1986) have recently taken steps to address this concern by investigating the specific mechanisms responsible for the training and age-related decline effects. This is an important direction for future research, not only because of the previously mentioned theoretical reasons but also because identification of the mechanisms responsible for modifying performance should greatly improve the effectiveness of future training interventions and further increase our understanding of the fundamental nature of behavior-change effects.

However, I do have some reservations about Willis and Schaie's "componential" analyses based on correct and incorrect answers in highly speeded tasks. My concern has to do with the fact that incorrect answers can apparently originate for at least two quite different reasons: (a) erroneous processing due to low ability level and (b) incomplete processing due to greater emphasis on speed than on accuracy. These two factors do not seem distinguishable without further information, such as examination of speed-accuacy operating characteristics (e.g., Salthouse, 1979). Thus it is not clear what is reflected in separate analyses of number of items correct and number of items attempted (i.e., sum of number correct and number incorrect). I suspect it is not simply the case that the latter represents only speed and the former only accuracy, but it doesn't yet seem possible to determine exactly what they do reflect.

Because of this interpretation problem and because the initial results seem to indicate that the age and training effects exhibit somewhat different patterns of change on the component measures of correct and incorrect responses, it is still not known whether training improves performance by altering the same mechanisms responsible for the age-related declines. For this and the other reasons I have discussed, I do not think we have sufficient data currently to reach a conclusion on the issue of whether age-related differences in cognitive functioning are at least partially caused by differences in experience or whether provision of experience can truly reverse earlier declines.

CONCLUSIONS

In summary, the cognitive training research conducted by Willis and her colleagues over the last several years clearly establishes that social structure, if it is interpeted as influencing the quantity and quality of experience received by an individual, almost certainly influences cognitive functioning. Even though the available research seems to suggest that the training-related benefits are not selective (i.e., it has thus far been impossible to overcome relative deficits by manipulation of experience), the absolute magnitude of the improvements are substantial and indicate that the effects of social structure could be extremely large.

REFERENCES

Salthouse, T. A. (1979). Adult age and the speed-accuracy tradeoff. *Ergonomics, 22,* 811–821.

Salthouse, T. A., Kausler, D. H., & Saults, J. S. (1986). Groups versus individuals as the comparison unit in cognitive aging research. *Developmental Neuropsychology, 2,* 363–372.

Schaie, K. W. (1985). *Schaie-Thurstone adult mental abilities test manual.* Palo Alto, CA: Consulting Psychologists Press.

Schaie, K. W., & Willis, S. L. (1986). Can decline in adult intellectual functioning be reversed? *Developmental Psychology, 22,* 223–232.

Willis, S. L., & Schaie, K. W. (1986). Training the elderly on the ability factors of spatial orientation and inductive reasoning. *Psychology and Aging, 1,* 239–247.

Social Structure Effects and Experimental Situations: Mutual Lessons of Cognitive and Social Science

Carmi Schooler
National Institute of Mental Health

The central focus of this chapter is on how two important approaches to understanding the psychological aging process—the study of social structural effects on individual psychological functioning and the experimental investigation of the nature of cognitive functioning—can inform each other. Because my vantage point tends to be that of the social scientist, I can, of course, fairly easily discern the difficulties that social science findings pose for cognitive science. On the other hand, I am aware that, no matter how great these difficulties are, if social scientists are interested in how social structure affects what people think, they must come to grips with the central topic of cognitive research—how people think.

In particular, if, following Marx (1964), Mannheim (1954), and Merton (1968), social scientists are concerned with how individuals' vantage points in the social system affect their belief systems, then they must understand the psychological laws through which people generalize what they have learned in one context to another. On the other hand, as we see in this chapter, the findings of both social and cognitive research indicate that the very ways in which people think and quite possibly generalize are affected by their social structurally and culturally determined experiences. Such findings cast strong doubt on the view, apparently held by many cognitive researchers, that cognitive processes are essentially the same among all normal individuals. Because we cannot take such similarity for granted, it would seem wrong for us to generalize about cognitive functioning from the performance of whatever subjects come most readily to hand.

My personal conviction that much of what cognitive and social scientists can learn from each other concerns one or another form of generalization comes from my attempt to explicate the psychological significance of the central findings of an extensive series of studies that Melvin Kohn, I, and our colleagues (1983) conducted on the psychological effects of occupational conditions. One of our central findings is that doing self-directed, substantively complex work leads to increased intellectual flexibility. Although we have demonstrated this causal relationship in countries of widely diverse cultures (United States, Japan, Poland), under a variety of different conditions (paid employment, school work, women's housework), and at different stages in the life span (students, younger workers, older workers), we have isolated neither the specific characteristics of the environment nor the exact cognitive mechanisms through which this process takes place.

As a first step toward doing so, I attempted to integrate our findings with those of other studies in the psychological and sociological literature. The resultant literature review (Schooler, 1984a) revealed a substantial amount of evidence for the rough-hewn, but more general hypothesis that environmental complexity from any source leads to effective cognitive functioning across all stages of the life span. This effect was shown to occur both as the result of experimental manipulation of matched subject groups and through statistical examination of social structural conditions linked to environmental complexity (Schooler, 1972a). However, although a reasonable case could be made for this general hypothesis, the surveyed literature provided few clues about the nature of the mechanisms through which environmental complexity has such effects. Almost without exception, the studies that dealt with the effects of environmental complexity seemed to regard the individual's cognitive functioning as a black box — whose input and output might be measured — but whose internal processes remain a mystery.

It therefore seemed reasonable to turn to the work of cognitive scientists in order to form more explicit hypotheses about what takes place within individuals when their cognitive processes are affected by the complexity of their environments. In doing so, I quickly realized that my problems dovetailed with some of those faced by cognitive scientists in at least one crucial aspect — the interrelated problems we both faced over issues of generalization. On the one hand, I was concerned with how people generalize what they learn in dealing with complexity in one environment (e.g., work) to dealing with complexity in another (e.g., cognitive tests in an interview; Kohn & Schooler, 1969, 1983 or leisure time activities, Miller & Kohn, 1983). What cognitive studies might reveal about such generalization seems vital for gaining an understanding of the mechanisms through which environmental complexity and environmental conditions determined by social structure have their psychological effects. On the other hand, the discoveries of cognitive psychology about the various effects of experience on cognitive processes show us that experimental cognitive scientists must learn from social structural ones — the necessity of insuring the generality of cognitive findings by studying wide and, if at all possible, representative samples of individuals.

In the remainder of the chapter, I will first show how, given the non-representative nature of their subjects, the very findings of cognitive science experiments about how what is learned in one situation is carried over to another cast doubt on the generalizability of their conclusions. Next, I look at what the facts and theories of learning generalization can tell us about mechanisms through which social-structurally determined environmental conditions have their cognitive effects. Then, I examine some convergences between the findings of cognitive and social science research on the characteristics of the immediate environment that affect cognitive functioning. I conclude by discussing the convergence between some social and cognitive scientists in an increasing awareness of problems caused by not taking the larger social context into account when attempting to explain cognitive functioning.

COGNITIVE FINDINGS
AND EXPERIMENTAL SUBJECTS

An examination of the major journals in which cognitive psychological experiments are published reveals that the overwhelming majority of such experiments are conducted with college students as subjects. Only occasional studies are conducted with experts, pathological subjects (usually amnesiacs), or those at one or the other end of the life course. Not only are representative population samples never used, but a range of individuals with different social-structurally or culturally determined experiences are rarely included in the same study. Such an omission might not be that important if there were good reasons to believe that experience does not affect the nature of thinking. However, although it may be appropriate for neuroscientists to assume that a neuron of a particular type in one individual, or species, functions pretty much like any other neuron of the same type, many findings and theories of cognitive researchers strongly suggest that individuals' thinking processes are strongly affected by their experience.

It should, however, not be too surprising that cognitive psychologists have paid scant attention to the possibility of social structural effects on psychological functioning. Experimental social psychologists, whom one might expect to be more aware of the possibility of such social effects, have been almost equally neglectful. In an excellent review, Sears (1987) has shown that the great majority of social psychological studies since the early 1960s have relied exclusively on college students tested in the laboratory and that the most prestigious research is, if anything, more likely to have done so. He also presents evidence suggesting the possibility that such "subjects are likely to have less crystalized attitudes, less formulated senses of self, stronger cognitive skills, stronger tendencies to comply with authority, and more unstable peer group relationships than do older adults. . . ." He concludes that these peculiarities of social psychology's predominant database may have unwittingly, and perhaps misleadingly, contributed to such major substantive conclusions as that people are easily influenced, behave inconsistenly with their attitudes, do not rest their self-perceptions on introspection, and are highly egocentric. Sears also raises the possibility that this database may also contribute to the strong emphasis in contemporary social psychology upon cognitive processes.

It is my firm belief that Sears' (1987) call for greater sensitivity to the possible distorting effects of this peculiar database upon social psychology's portrait of human nature is even more applicable to cognitive psychology's portrayal of human thought. As was the case for social psychology, the very results of cognitive research demonstrate the necessity of increasing the variety and representativeness of the subjects used. A wide range of cognitive studies have shown that not only the content but the nature of thinking processes can be affected by experiences, such as training on and practice with various cognitive strategies, whose likelihood of occurrence may well be a function of the individual's place in the social structure.

Empirical cognitive research has demonstrated that many types of thinking are affected by training and/or practice. Among these are:

- *Spatial thinking*—Pellegrino, Alderton, and Regian (1984) have found that the three components of spatial ability—perceptual speed, spatial relations, and spatial visualization—as well as "the ability to establish precise and stable representations of unfamiliar stimuli" can be dramatically improved by practice. In a further study, Regian, Shute, and Pellegrino (1985) have demontrated that subjects with both high and low ability show practice effects executing the encoding, comparison, and rotation processes estimated in mental rotation tasks and that these practice effects generalize to paper-and-pencil reference ability tests.

- *Mathematical thinking*—Schoenfeld and Herrmann (1982) have demonstrated that faced with the task of classifying nonstandard math problems, able novices differ from experienced experts by classifying the problems according to surface features, whereas the experts classify them according to the general approach appropriate for the solution (e.g., analogy, induction). It appears that the novices do not have the knowledge necessary to quickly grasp which type of problem-solving strategy is most likely to be effective. When half the students are given a training course in mathematical problem solving, their approach becomes more similar to that of the experts.

- *Statistical thinking* — Fong, Krantz, and Nisbett (1986) have shown that either experimental training on the implications of the law of large numbers or training in statistics affected their subjects' thinking about everyday problems, even when the subjects are tested in situations and on topics completely outside the training context.

- *Logical thinking* — Cheng, Holyoak, Nisbett, and Oliver (1986) used a variety of experimental training procedures to test their hypothesis that people reason using abstract knowledge structures induced from ordinary life experience. The authors term these structures "pragmatic reasoning schemas" which they defined in an earlier paper (Cheng & Holyoak, 1985) as "a set of generalized context-sensitive rules which, unlike purely syntactic rules, are defined in terms of classes of goals . . . and relationships to these goals (such as cause and effect or precondition or allowable action)" (p. 395). Their experimental findings indicate that although training in purely abstract logic has almost no effect, training increases the logical level of reasoning when abstract principles are coupled with appropriate examples. Furthermore, even short periods of training in the use of pragmatic schema, as opposed to abstract logical principles markedly improve performance.

In a somewhat different approach, Denney, Jones, and Krigel (1979) have shown that either providing examples or instructing subjects on relatively abstract rules increases the logic of questioning strategy in a 20 questions game. In yet another approach, Feuerstein (1980) reports both widespread and long-lasting improvements in cognitive functioning when individuals are trained in various logical processes through his Mediated Learning Experience Model. In this technique, the mediator transforms the relevant stimuli to make them appropriate for inculcating the desired logical process; he or she then selects, transforms, and shapes the responses to the desired response. The program usually begins at an elementary level and then establishes the prerequisite knowledge and motivation to modify the trainees' cognitive processes so that they can achieve successively higher levels of logical functioning.

- *Expertise* — A variety of other studies have shown differences between novices' and experienced experts' problem-solving approaches in a wide range of fields: Larkin, McDermott, Simon, and Simon (1980) for physics problems; Voss, Tyler, and Yengo (1983) for social science problems; and Scribner (1984) for the more mundane problems arising in work at a dairy processing plant. In fact, not only has much of the recent literature in cognitive science dealt with expert performance in limited domains, but so did some ground-breaking empirical work in psychology: Bryan and Harter's (1899) studies on the acquisition of telegraphic language.

Researchers applying an experimental cognitive approach to the study of developmental and life-span issues have also found evidence of generalized training effects:

- *Children*—Among the many studies of generalized training effects in children, Stigler, Chalip, and Miller (1986) have shown that abacus training of Taiwanese children results not only in better calculating skills but in more abstract and flexible understanding of the number system. More surprisingly, abacus training leads not only to superior spatial ability but also independently to better reading.
- *The elderly*—A wide range of training effects have been demonstrated with the elderly (for a review see Willis, in press). On Piagetian tasks, levels of conservation, classification, avoidance of spatial egocentrism, and formal operations have been raised through training procedures. Concept formation and intellectual rigidity have also been modified through training, as have the psychometrically defined abilities of figural relations and inductive reasoning. Inductive reasoning, in fact, seems to be improved even by practice without feedback.

In an important methodological advance in the assessment of the nature of training generalization, Willis and Schaie (1986) have actually demonstrated that training on one indicator of a multiple indicator-based latent factor resulted in significant training effects on other indicators of that factor. Such significant training effects were found at the factor score level for both inductive reasoning and spatial orientation.

In addition to studies based directly on cognitive theory, the very findings on the effects of environmental complexity I am seeking to explain demonstrate that differences in experience, many of which are determined by social structural position, affect the nature of cognitive processes.

Jepson, Krantz, and Nisbett (1983) reach similar conclusions from the findings of their cognitive research program. They state "These facts seem consistent with the view that inductive reasoning, like other kinds of human problem solving . . . is a skill not a native ability. 'Ordinary human reasoning' does not 'set its own standards,' rather its standards are determined by culturally evolved tools, such as probability concepts" (p. 498). These are clearly not equally available to all members of a society. "Inductive reasoning . . . can be improved through education and frequent practice" (p. 496). "The results do tend to undermine . . . any normative theory of inductive reasoning that presupposes a broad competence for inductive reasoning shared by all unimpaired members of the culture" (p. 498).

COGNITIVE GENERALIZATION

The findings of both cognitive and social researchers that cognitive processes are a function of experience and that experiences in one situation affect the nature of cognitive processes in another have important implications for both social and cognitive science. Besides raising strong concerns about generalizing to "standard" human thinking from experiments carried out on college students, the findings provide strong evidence that cognitive generalization does take place. It is through learning how such generalization takes place that social scientists can learn from cognitive scientists. Before such a lesson can be learned, however, two questions raised by the cognitive evidence must be faced. For one of these we have some empirial answers; for the other, theoretical answers far exceed empirical ones.

The question for which we do have some empirical answers has to do with how generalizable cognitive training is from one type of thinking, or from one subject area, to another. As of now, the answer is not very much. Thus, Willis and Schaie (1986) found in their training studies of the elderly that there was no transfer from training on one factor (e.g., inductive reasoning) to improved performance on another (e.g., spatial orientation). This relative lack of generalizability marks many training attempts with both older and younger individuals. Similarly, many studies indicate that expert individuals do not generally show the same level of thought outside their area of expertise. Furthermore, knowledge of an area often seems to be a necesary precondition for the application of effective problem-solving techniques. Thus, Kunda and Nisbett (1986) indicate that statistically knowledgeable people were unable to recognize the existence of various statistical phenomena in data with which they were unfamiliar; and Pellegrino and Goldman find (1983) that correlational data involving both classification and analogy performance indicate higher correlations for common content domains than for common task forms.

There is also evidence that people differ in their abilities to take advantage of different types of training. For example, in a study of the effectiveness of different types of strategy training for spatial tasks, Lohman and Kyllonen (1983) found that subjects differ in the readiness with which they learn and apply various types of strategies. Subjects low in both spatial and verbal ability perform best after training that models the visualization process, whereas subjects low in spatial but high in verbal ability perform best after a treatment that models a nonvisual strategy.

Despite all this evidence, the exact nature of the limitations of cognitive generalizability remains an open question. Cognitive studies, such as those of Cheng et al. (1986) indicate that generalizable pragmatic reasoning schemas do develop. Our own research indicates that some of what is learned at work is generalized to other situations. Much more research is needed to see how the degree of generalization is affected by differences in subjects (e.g., old vs. young or those exposed to complex environment vs. those exposed to simple ones) or in subject matter (e.g., mathematical, spatial, verbal, or human relations problems).

The question for which we have more theories than facts is how does such generalization take place. Concern over the nature of the processes through which what is learned in one situation is generalized to another obviously preceded the "cognitive revolution." Reinforcement theorists from Pavlov to Hull to Skinner produced models of how this might happen through various reinforcement processes. Their work differs from that of cognitive theorists in various ways; the most important differences, perhaps, being their disregard for the conscious, mental, or even internal processes of the individual and their belief that learning does not take place from a single pairing of a set of events but rather requires some form of reinforcement history. Reinforcement and cognitive theories may not be empirically incompatible. Mishkin (1986), in summarizing his neuropsychological investigations of monkeys, makes a very strong case that Tolman and Hull may both have been right. He does this by providing evidence (Mishkin, Malamut, & Bachevalier, 1984) for the existence of two parallel learning processes, one generally following the rules of the cognitive scientists, the other of reinforcement theorists.

Cognitive theorists have described a variety of ways in which what has been learned in one situation may be applied to another. Anderson (1983) provides perhaps the most fully worked out theoretical model of how this might happen. The basic hypothesis "is that underlying human cognition is a set of condition-action pairs called productions. The condition specifies some data patterns, and if elements matching these patterns are in working memory, then the production can apply. The action specifies what to do in that state" (pp. 5–6). In dealing with the "interesting question [of] how similar productions are identified for possible generalization" (p. 244), Anderson describes how when a new production is created it is compared with existing productions. "The data-flow matching process would identify the condition that best matches the condition of this production. The overlap between the two conditions would identify the clauses that the productions have in common. . . . [However], just as it is necessary to generalize overly specific procedures, it is also necessary to restrict the range of application. . . . The discrimination process tries to restrict the range of application of a production to the appropriate circumstances" (pp. 244–245). This requires having examples of both correct and incorrect applications of the production and looking for some feature of the unsuccessful one that differs from the successful one. "The probability of choosing the right feature to discriminate . . . depends on the similarity of the successful and unsuccessful situations. The more similar they are, the fewer the distracting possibilities, the easier it is to identify the critical feature" (p. 248).

From a somewhat more inclusive perspective, I believe that the forms of learning generalization listed in Table 4.1 are among those that have been specifically hypothesized or are readily deducible from various cognitive theories. Although some alternatives in Table 4.1 are seen by their proponents as being mutually exclusive and alternate explanations of the same phenomena (Cheng, 1985b; Schneider & Shiffrin, 1985), it is quite plausible that several of these generalization mechanisms can be used either simultaneously or by different people in different situations. My immediate concern is discovering which of these, if any, underlies Mel Kohn's and my specific findings about the effects of occupational self-direction on intellectual flexibility or the similar, more general findings about the cognitive effects of environmental complexity that my literature search revealed.

MICROLEVEL CONVERGENCES AND LESSONS

Besides these dual issues of generalizability from population to population and from situation to situation, there are other ways in which cogni-

TABLE 4.1
A Listing of Some Possible Forms of Cognitive Generalization

I. Changes in memory, association, or storage of information:
   A. Experience with related stimuli leads to the development of memory structures that permit the integration of greater amounts of information and thus lead to more efficient chunking, so more information can be dealt with at one time. The prototypical exemplar of such a process would be the ability of skilled chess players to recall the position of large numbers of chess pieces if they are arranged in a meaningful pattern on the board.
   B. Similar experiences may lead to a more effective superposition of traces at time of storage, resulting in composites that are effective portrayals of what related experiences have in common (McClelland & Rumelhart, 1985).
   C. The spread of activation becomes efficiently generalized to what is common to related experiences (Anderson, 1983).
II. Changes in the way information is directly processed or linked to performance might be accomplished through:
   A. The extension of automatized performance across an increasing range of situations (Shiffrin & Schneider, 1977).
   B. Restructuring reactions to broader ranges of experiences so that they are "coordinated, integrated or reorganized into new perceptual, cognitive, or motor units, thereby allowing the procedure involving the old components to be replaced by a more efficient procedure involving the new components" (Cheng, 1985a, p. 414).
   C. The development, as a result of experience in similar situations, of better initial models with which to deal with ambiguities and uncertainties, as well as more effective ways of adjusting the models as more evidence becomes available (Einhorn & Hogarth, 1985).
III. The development of relatively context-free forms of information processing that can be used in a variety of structurally similar but substantively different situations. Among ways that this can be accomplished are:
   A. The development of generalized schemas applicable across related types of experience.
   B. The development of appropriately generalized production models (Anderson, 1983).
   C. The development of more effective executive or metacognitive controls of thinking.

tive scientists and social scientists can inform each other. Each has something to say to the other relevant both to microlevel concerns about the nature of the immediate environmental conditions affecting cognitive processing and to macrolevel concerns about the social and cultural context in which such functioning takes place.

At the microlevel, both the cognitive studies and those concerned with the relationship between social structural effects and environmental complexity share a common concern with the definition of complexity. In my rough-hewn theory about the effects of complex environments (Schooler, 1984a), the complexity of an environment "is defined by its stimulus and demand characteristics. The more diverse the stimuli, the greater the number of decisions required, the greater the number of considerations to be taken into account in making these decisions, and the more ill defined and complex the contingencies, the more complex the environment" (pp. 259-260).

Researchers studying human behavior in organizations have also faced the issue of measuring task complexity. The most formally elaborated measure (Wood, 1986) involves three elements: (a) component complexity — "the number of distinct acts that need to be executed in the performance of the task and the number of distinct information cues that must be processed in the performance of these acts" (p. 66); (b) coordinative complexity — "the nature of the relationships between task inputs and task products. The form and strength of the relationships between information cues, acts and products, as well as the sequencing of inputs, are all aspects of coordinative complexity" (p. 68); (c) dynamic complexity — the degree of "changes in the cause-effect chain or means-ends hierarchy . . . during performance of a task . . . due to changes in the states of the world, which have an effect on the relationships between task inputs and products" (p. 71).

Among cognitive researchers, Anderson (1983) defined the complexity of a stimulus pattern that has to be matched before a production can be executed in terms of the size of its structure (p. 150). The nature of environmental complexity is also an issue for decision theorists in their work on how people cope with ambiguity and uncertainty, both of which are aspects of environmental complexity. The model of such coping developed by Einhorn and Hogarth (1985) involves parameters, not only of perceived ambiguity but also of the person's attitude toward ambiguity. Furthermore, their results suggest "strong personal propensities in evaluating evidence that transcend the particular content of scenarios" (p. 457). These attitudes toward ambiguity may well be a function of social structure. We have abundant evidence that acceptance of ambiguity is a function of a variety of social-structurally determined experiences that make it likely that individuals with higher status would be more tolerant of ambiguity than ones with lower status (Kohn & Schooler, 1983).

A variety of cognitive studies point to the importance for effective cognitive functioning of another characteristic of the environment related to my definition of environmental complexity—the susceptibility of the relevant environmental stimuli to appropriate categorization. Experiments (Kunda & Nisbett, 1986; Nisbett, Krantz, Jepson, & Kunda, 1983) assessing people's ability to apply logical psychometric principles to everyday life find that people are not only unlikely to apply such principles to unfamiliar subject matter but that the events in question have to be highly codable. *Codability* is defined "as the ease with which events may be unitized and given a score characterizing them in clear and readily interpretable terms" (Kunda & Nisbett, 1986, p. 198).

Although the forms of environmental categorization most efficient for statistical manupulations are pretty well known to cognitive researchers, the nature of effective semantic categorization is still a hotly contested issue. Questions, some reminiscent of the old philosophical issue of nominalism versus realism, exist about whether categories involve prototypes and whether they are fixed, fuzzy, or dynamic. The effectiveness of categorization may also be a function of the types of features upon which the categories are based. Thus, intrinsic features—those true of an entity considered in itself—provide more clear-cut forms of categorization than do extrinsic features—those representing the relationship between two or more entities (Barr & Caplan, 1987).

It may well be that both social structural position and experience with complex environments help determine how individuals categorize phenomena and which forms of categorization are most effective for them. Certainly, the social psychological experiments of the Streuferts (1978) demonstrate that categorization processes are affected by exposure to complex environments. When processing stimulus information, individuals exposed to complex environments are more likely to place stimuli on several different dimensions, whereas those less exposed to such environments are more likely to use one dimension.

On a somewhat more general theoretical level, social psychological studies of the processing of social information do represent one area in which the investigation of social and cognitive processes have strongly influenced each other. Granted, there have been complaints that the "revolution" in psychological social psychology, which has taken place with the recent dramatic increase in concern over cognitive issues, has reduced much of social psychology to a sidestream branch of cognitive science. Nevertheless, in a recent article, Wyer and Srull (1986) have used many findings of social information-processing reasearch to develop a theory of cognitive functioning that rivals that of Anderson's (1983) in its completeness and elaboration. Wyer and Srull noted that their theory is complementary to Anderson's, possibly differing in many respects only because of the nature of the phenomena examined. They demonstrate, however, that findings on cognitive processing of social phenomena necessitate some basic changes in the tenets of cognitive theory. One change is the recognition of the importance of the role of task objectives in determining the way information is processed. Another is the development of a bin concept of information storage, according to which each bin is identified by a header that specifies the nature of its contents and determines whether it will be identified in the search for information relevant to a particular processing objective. Once a bin is identified, the remaining features of its header are searched for information relevant to the attainment of that objective. If these features are sufficient, they are used without retrieving any information from the bin itself. If the contents of a bin must be searched for more information, the search proceeds from the top (most recent) down. Wyer and Srull maintain that these and related postulates make it possible to explain findings on the cognition of social phenomena that other theories cannot comprehensively explain. Whether or not their theory ultimately proves valid, Wyer and Srull have provided valuable examples of how cognitive and social research can be combined in a way that sheds substantial light on both fields.

The work of classical sociologists is also useful in providing clues for cognitive scientists about the mechanisms through which effective cognitive functioning can develop. As early as 1902, Simmel (1950) speculated:

> The psychological basis of the metropolitan type of individual consists of the intensification of nervous stimulation which results from the swift and uninterrupted change of outer and inner stimuli. . . . Thus the metropolitan type of man . . . develops an organ protecting him against the threatening currents and discrepancies of his external environment that would uproot him. He reacts with his head instead of his heart. . . . Intellectuality is thus seen to preserve the subjective life against the overwhelming power of metropolitan life. (pp. 410-411)

Writing at about the same time Durkheim, together with Mauss (1901–02), "maintained that the genesis of the categories of thought is to be found in the group structure and relations and that the categories vary with changes in the social organization" (Merton, 1968, p. 519).

More recently, Coser (1975) has focused on the psychological effects of complex role sets. She defines a role set as "complex when several role partners are differently located in the social structure and subject to change" (p. 243). Individuals in complex role sets, faced with varied, often ambiguous and incompatible expectations of their role partners, are forced to reflect; such reflection leading to individualism and intellectual flexibility. This linking of social structural conditions with the nature of intellectual functioning has also been suggested by others. Thus, Gabennesch (1972) has maintained that environmental conditions fostering thought and initiative enlarge the individual's conceptions of reality and in doing so not only reduce authoritarianism but also the tendency toward a cognitive style involving logically inappropriate reification.

The relationship between effective cognitive functioning and an individualistic orientation is also implicated in what is perhaps the most specific hint from the sociological literature about how environmental conditions may affect cognitive functioning. This hint comes from research of our own laboratory examining the effects of self-directed work on intellectual flexibility in both school and occupational settings. In our analyses of school work (Miller, Kohn, & Schooler, 1986), we found intriguing differences between our college and secondary school respondents. For secondary school students, a large proportion of the effect of educational self-direction on intellectual flexibility is direct. On the college level, however, the effect is mainly indirect, mediated by self-directedness of orientation. The effect of self-directed work among employed workers also seems to be in large part indirect — self-directed work leading to a self-directed orientation, which in turn leads to intellectual flexibility (Kohn & Schooler, 1983).

The total pattern of findings suggests that the experience of self-direction may affect intellectual flexibility differently at different stages of educational and later occupational career. More of the effect seems to be direct at the earlier stages, when the process may be more a matter of cognitive training per se; more of the effect apparently being indirect in the later stages, when the process may become less a matter of cognitive training and more a matter of attitude and adaptability. In any case, the possibility that individuals may experience environmental complexity in some circumstances, or stages of life, that may affect their cognitive functioning indirectly by changing related, but not specifically, cognitive attitudes and orientations is something that cognitive scientists should take into consideration in formulating their theories.

MACROLEVEL CONVERGENCES AND LESSONS

As I have noted previously, cognitive scientists should also be aware of the empirical finding that various aspects of the macrosocial context affect cognitive functioning. Besides the effects of social structural conditions on cognitive functioning, which I have already discussed, two other social contexts have been demonstrated to affect cognitive processes — cohort and culture. The initial and still most complete analysis of the cognitive effects of cohorts is being carried out from the perspective of life-span psychology by Warner Schaie (1986). He has found "that there are substantial shifts in performance level for some, but not all, cognitive abilities across successive population cohorts . . . [and that] the magnitudes of such shifts are well within the range of reported age related decline and of the range of gains that can be obtained by means of cognitive intervention." This latter finding suggests that the cohort differences in cognitive functioning may well be the result of cohort differences in the degree to which they have undergone experiences similar to those represented in the training sessions.

Another example of possible cohort differences in cognitive functioning can be found in the work of Flynn (1984), whose analyses provide strong evidence "that the changing norms of every Stanford-Binet and Wechsler standardization sample from 1932 to 1978 established norms of a higher standard than its predecessor" (p. 29). Flynn notes that, not only do the combination of IQ gains and decline in performance in the Scholastic Aptitude Test (SAT) seem almost inexplicable but IQ gains of this magnitude pose a serious problem of causal explanation. Zajonc (1986), on the other hand, believes he has found an explanation for cohort changes in SAT scores in his confluence theory of the effects of birth order, family size, and sibling spacing on cognitive functioning. This theory is based on the hypothesized environmental advantage that older children have, both in terms of the average level of cognitive functioning of the other members of their households and in terms of the positive effect that older sibs experience in teaching younger ones. Zajonc applies this theory to a model based on the demographic differences between successive cohorts in family size and ordinal position that seems to predict both the downswing and more recent upswing in cohort scores (but see Galbraith, 1982; Schooler, 1972b, 1984b).

Differences in environmental complexity provide a possible explanation of the general increase in performance level of successive cohorts reported by Flynn (1984). Analyses of the social antecedents of adult psychological functioning (Schooler, 1972a) suggest that being younger, having a father with a high level of education, and being raised in an urban area, a liberal religion and a part of the country far from the South are all related to having been raised in a relatively complex environment. Each of these characteristics also independently leads to both a rejection of external constraints and a relatively high level of intellectual functioning.

A somewhat similar analysis I carried out on the psychological effects of ethnic group membership (1976) raises the issue of the effects of yet another macrosocial context — culture — on psychological functioning. In this analysis, I found that Americans from ethnic groups with a recent history of serfdom show the non-self-directed orientation and lack of intellectual flexibility characteristic of American men working under conditions limiting opportunity for self-direction. These findings hold true even when the individual's other background characteristics and own level of occupational self-direction are controlled. Although it is impossible to confirm each link in the causal chain, a model emphasizing the effects on ethnic groups' culture of historical conditions restricting the individual's autonomy seems a probable and parsimonious explanation of these ethnic differences.

A number of cognitive scientists have also examined cultural effects on cognition. Kearins (1981) found that Australian Aboriginal children perform better on visual-spatial memory tests than do Australian White children. Furthermore, there seem to be differences in stragegy. "Aboriginal children attempted visual strategies, while most White children probably attempted verbal strategies" (p. 434). On the other hand, Piagetian researchers have found in their investigation of the development of logical concepts that Australian Aboriginal children and adults remote from European contacts demonstrate such concepts, if at all, much later than Europeans usually do. Aboriginal children living in urban communities, however, perform like European children (Dasen, 1973). Somewhat similar results were obtained earlier by Luria (1976), who carried out his research in the 1930s. In an attempt to test Vygotsky's (1962, 1978; Vygotsky & Luria, 1930) hypotheses about the importance of historically determined cultural factors, Luria found that the development of various logical concepts was directly related to the amount of exposure Central Asians had to European culture. Luria saw his results as supporting Vygotsky's view that language not only helps humans control their own behavior through mediational processes but also permits them to transmit what they have learned over time through the development of cultures.[1] Other evidence of the effect of culture on cognitive processes can be found in Berry and Dasen (1973) and Cole and Scribner (1974).

Perhaps the strongest evidence of the importance of culture as a determinant of cognitive processes can be found in the work of Hacking (1975). He has convincingly demonstrated that the very concepts of statistical probability, whose prevalence Nisbett and others have used to test the cognitive competence of present-day college students, were only developed in the 17th century. Although the history of gaming is ancient, Hacking suggests that anybody with a 17th-century knowledge of probability would probably have become very rich in classical Greece. Thus, the nature of culturally available concepts clearly places strong limits on the way people can think.

The importance of the cultural context and the consequences of its neglect by cognitive scientists is also one of the major points raised by Keating (1983) in his critical review of his own and his fellow cognitive scientists' work (for a somewhat similar but less fully developed and documented discussion, see Norman, 1980). In his paper "The Emperor's

---

[1]Similar conclusions about the unique relationship between people and their cultures were also reached from the vantage point of comparative animal psychology by Schneirla (1972) in his discussion of the qualitative differences among species in levels of complexity of both neuronal and social organization (see also Schooler, 1986).

New Clothes: The 'New Look' in Intelligence Research," Keating raises a series of strong and essentially valid challenges to both the theoretical presuppositions and empirical conclusions of researchers using the three major approaches to the study of intelligence — the psychometric measurement of individual differences, the experimental testing of Piagetian developmental structuralism, and the componential analysis of the cognitive skills presumably underlying "intelligent behavior."

Keating (1983) sees the neglect of the cultural and social context in which intelligent behavior takes place as a difficulty underlying each of these approaches. He views such neglect as leading to "the consistent tendency to reduce the problem of human intelligence to an entity in the head of a person" (p. 34). As a consequence, intelligence comes to be seen as a biologically determined unfolding of a particular form of cognitive processing. This unfolding is seen to occur independently of both the nature of the demands society placed on the individual and the cognitive tools it provides. Keating sees the "new look" in cognition as comfortably fitting a belief in the existence of a single biologically fixed pattern of cognitive development and pessimistically concluded that "[t]here is much time but little metaphorical distance between brain size (Broca, 1861) and computer capacity as explanations of individual or group differences" (p. 35).

Quite possibly because I have not been in the field as long as Keating, I am somewhat more sanguine about the accomplishments of the cognitive revolution and its new look at individual intellectual functioning. I believe much has been learned and more can be. However, in order to be truly successful, cognitive psychology must be able not only to take into account, but also to explain, the mechanisms through which the social context affects the individual. It is not sufficient for Anderson (1983) to produce a program modeling the language acquisition of his two-year-old son. Cognitive psychology must also eventually answer such questions as: How does doing substantively complex work at school or on the job increase intellectual flexibility? Only if cognitive and social scientists are willing to learn from each other will we be able to understand the dynamic linkages beween social, cultural, and intellectual processes as people move through the life course.

ACKNOWLEDGMENTS

Because I have written this chapter as part of my duty as a government worker, it is not copyrighted.

I am grateful to Leslie Caplan, Morris Rosenberg, Nina Schooler, and

Jonathan Schooler for their helpful critical readings of an earlier version of this chapter.

REFERENCES

Anderson, J. R. (1983). *The architecture of cognition.* Cambridge, MA: Harvard University Press.
Barr, R. A., & Caplan, L. J. (1987). Category representations and their implications for category structure. *Memory and Cognition, 15,* 397–418.
Berry, J. W., & Dasen, P. R. (Eds.). (1973). *Culture and cognition: Readings in cross-cultural psychology.* London: Methuen.
Bryan, W. L., & Harter, N. (1899). Studies on the telegraphic language. The acquisition of a hierarchy of habits. *Psychological Review, 5,* 345–375.
Broca, P. (1890). Sur le volume et la forme du cerveau suivant les individus et suivant le races. *Bulletin de la Societe d'Anthropologie Paris, 2,* 139–207, 301–321, 444–446.
Cheng, P. W. (1985a). Restructuring versus automaticity: Alternative accounts of skill acquisition. *Psychological Review, 92,* 414–423.
Cheng, P. W. (1985b). Categorization and response competition: Two nonautomatic factors. *Psychological Review, 92,* 585–586.
Cheng, P. W., & Holyoak, K. J. (1985). Pragmatic reasoning schemas. *Cognitive Psychology, 17,* 391–416.
Cheng, P. W., Holyoak, K. J., Nisbett, R. E., & Oliver, L. M. (1986). Pragmatic versus syntactic approaches to training deductive reasoning. *Cognitive psychology, 18,* 293–328.
Cole, M., & Scribner, S. (1974). *Culture and thought.* New York: Wiley.
Coser, R. L. (1975). The complexity of roles as a seedbed of individual autonomy. In L. A. Coser (Ed.), *The idea of social structure* (pp. 237–251). New York: Harcourt Brace Jovanovich.
Dasen, P. R. (1974). The influence of ecology, culture, and European contact on cognitive development in Australian Aborigines. In J. W. Berry & P. R. Dasen (Eds.), *Culture and cognition: Readings in cross-cultural psychology* (pp. 381–408). London: Methuen.
Denney, N. W., Jones, F., & Krigel, S. (1979). Modifying the questioning strategies of young children and elderly adults. *Human Development, 22,* 23–36.
Durkheim, F., & Mauss, M. (1901-02). De quelques formes primitives de classification. *L'Année Sociologique, 6,* 1–71.
Einhorn, H. J., & Hogarth, R. M. (1985). Ambiguity and uncertainty in probabilistic inference. *Psychological Review, 92,* 433–461.
Feuerstein, R. (1980). *Instrumental enrichment: An intervention program for cognitive modifiability.* Baltimore: University Park Press.
Flynn, J. F. (1984). The mean IQ of Americans: Massive gains 1932 to 1978. *Psychological Bulletin, 95,* 29–51.
Fong, G., Krantz, D. H., & Nisbett, R. E. (1986). The effects of statistical training on thinking about everyday problems. *Cognitive Psychology, 18,* 253–292.
Gabennesch, H. (1972). Authoritarianism as world view. *American Journal of Sociology, 77,* 857–875.
Galbraith, R. C. (1982). Sibling spacing intelligence and the confluence model. *Developmental Psychology, 18,* 151–173.
Hacking, I. (1975). *The emergence of probability: A philosophical study of early ideas about probability, induction and statistical inference.* London: Cambridge University Press.
Jepson, C., Krantz, D. H., & Nisbett, R. E. (1983). Inductive reasoning: Competence or skill? *Behavioral and Brain Sciences, 3,* 494–501.

Kearins, J. A. (1981). Visual spatial memory in Australian Aboriginal children of desert regions. *Cognitive Psychology*, *13*, 434–460.

Keating, D. P. (1983). The emperor's new clothes: The 'new look' in intelligence research. In R. J. Sternberg (Ed.), *Advances in the psychology of human intelligence*, (Vol. 2, pp. 1–45). Hillsdale, NJ: Lawrence Erlbaum Associates.

Kohn, M. L., & Schooler, C. (1969). Class, occupation, and orientation. *American Sociological Review*, *34*, 659–678.

Kohn, M. L., & Schooler, C. (1983) *Work and Personality: An inquiry into the impact of social stratification*. Norwood, NJ: Ablex.

Kunda, Z., & Nisbett, R. E. (1986). The psychometrics of everyday life. *Cognitive Psychology*, *18*, 195–224.

Larkin, J. H., McDermott, J., Simon, D. P., & Simon, H. P. (1980). Expert and novice performance in solving physics problems. *Science*, *208*, 1335–1342.

Lohman, D. F., & Kyllonen, P. C. (1983). Individual differences in solution strategy on spatial tasks. In R. F. Dillon & R. R. Schmeck (Eds.), *Individual differences in cognition* (pp. 105–136). New York: Academic Press.

Luria, A. R. (1976). *Cognitive development: Its cultural and social foundations*. Cambridge, MA: Harvard University Press.

Mannheim, K. (1954). *Ideology and utopia: An introduction to the sociology of knowledge*. New York: Harcourt.

Marx, K. (1964). *Early writings* (T. B. Bottomore, Ed. & Trans.). New York: McGraw-Hill.

McClelland, J. L., & Rumelhart, D. E. (1985). Distributed memory and the representation of general and specific information. *Journal of Experimental Psychology*, *114*, 159–188.

Merton, R. (1968). *Social theory and social structure*. New York: Free Press.

Miller, K. A., & Kohn, M. L. (1983). The reciprocal effects of job conditions and the intellectuality of leisure-time activities. In M. L. Kohn & C. Schooler (Eds.), *Work and personality: An inquiry into the impact of social stratification* (pp. 217–241). Norwood, NJ: Ablex.

Miller, K. A., Kohn, M. L., & Schooler, C. (1986). Educational self-direction and personality. *American Sociological Review*, *51*, 372–390.

Mishkin, M. (1986, September). *Behaviorism, cognitivism and the brain*. Distinguished scientific contribution award address at the American Psychological Association Convention, Washington, DC.

Mishkin, M., Malamut, B., & Bachevalier, J. (1984). Memories and habits: Two neural systems. In G. Lynch, J. L. McGaugh, & N. M. Weinberger (Eds.), *Neurobiology of learning and memory* (pp. 65–77). New York: Guilford.

Nisbett, R. E., Krantz, D. H., Jepson, C., & Kunda, Z. (1983). The use of statistical heuristics in everyday inductive reasoning. *Psychological Review*, *90*, 339–363.

Norman, D. A. (1980). Twelve issues for cognitive science. *Cognitive Science*, *4*, 1–32.

Pellegrino, J. W., Alderton, D. L., & Regian, J. W. (1984, December). Components of spatial ability. Paper presented at NATO Advanced Study Institute in Cognition and Motivation, Athens, Greece.

Pellegrino, J. W., & Goldman, S. R. (1983). Differences in verbal spatial reasoning. In R. F. Dillon & R. R. Schmeck (Eds.), *Individual differences in cognition* (pp. 140–180). New York: Academic Press.

Regian, J. W., Shute, V. J., & Pellegrino, J. W. (1985, November). *The modifiability of spatial processing skills*. Paper presented at the 26th meeting of the Psychonomic Society, Boston.

Schaie, K. W. (1986, August). *Social context and cognitive performance in old age*. Paper presented at the American Sociological Association, New York.

Schneider, W., & Shiffrin, R. (1985). Categorization (restructuring) and automatization: Two separable factors. *Psychological Review*, *92*, 414–428.

Schneirla, T. C. (1972). *Selected writings*. (L. R. Aronson, E. Tobach, D. S. Lehrman, & J. S. Rosenblatt, Eds.). San Francisco: W. H. Freeman.

Schoenfeld, A. H., & Herrmann, D. J. (1982). Problem perception and knowledge structure in expert and novice mathematical problem solvers. *Journal of Experimental Psychology, 8*, 484–494.

Schooler, C. (1972a). Social antecedents of adult psychological functioning. *American Journal of Sociology, 78*, 299–322.

Schooler, C. (1972b). Birth order effects: Not here, not now! *Psychological Bulletin, 78*, 161–175.

Schooler, C. (1976). Serfdom's legacy: An ethnic continuum. *American Journal of Sociology, 81*, 1265–1286.

Schooler, C. (1984a). Psychological effects of complex environments during the life span: A review and theory. *Intelligence, 8*, 259–281.

Schooler, C. (1984b). Citation classic commentary on birth order effects: Not here, not now! *Current Contents, 16*(12), 18.

Schooler, C. (1986, August). *The perspective of a psychologist practicing sociology.* Paper presented at the American Sociological Association, New York.

Scribner, S. (1984). Studying working intelligence. In B. Rogoff & J. Lave (Eds.), *Everyday cognition: Its development in social context* (pp. 9–40). Cambridge, MA: Harvard University Press.

Sears, D. O. (1987). Implications of the life-span approach for research on attitudes of social cognition. In R. P. Abeles (Ed.), *Life-span perspectives and social psychology.* Hillsdale, NJ: Erlbaum.

Shiffrin, R. M., & Schneider, W. (1977). Control and automatic human information processing: II. Perceptual learning, automatic attending, and a general theory. *Psychological Review, 84*, 127–190.

Simmel, G. (1950). The metropolis and mental life. Lecture, 1902–03. In K. H. Wolff (Ed. & Trans.), *The sociology of Georg Simmel.* Glencoe, IL: Free Press.

Stigler, J. E., Chalip, L., & Miller, K. F. (1986). Consequences of skill: The case of abacus training in Taiwan. *American Journal of Education, 94*, 447–479.

Streufert, S., & Streufert, S. C. (1978). *Behavior in the complex environment.* New York: Wiley.

Voss, J. F., Tyler, S. W., & Yengo, L. A. (1983). Individual differences in the solving of social science problems. In R. F. Dillon & R. R. Schmeck (Eds.), *Individual differences in cognition* (pp. 205–232). New York: Acadamic Press.

Vygotsky, L. S. (1962). *Thought and language.* Cambridge, MA: MIT Press.

Vygotsky, L. S. (1978). *Mind and society.* Cambridge, MA: Harvard University Press.

Vygotsky, L. S., & Luria, A. R. (1930). *Essays in the history of behavior.* Moscow-Leningrad: State Publishing House.

Willis, S. L. (in press). Cognitive training in later adulthood: Remediation vs. new learning. In L. Poon & B. Wilson (Eds.), *Everyday cognition in adult and late life.* Cambridge: Cambridge University Press.

Willis, S. L., & Schaie, K. W. (1986). Training the elderly on the ability factors of spatial orientation and inductive reasoning. *Psychology and Aging, 1*, 239–247.

Wood, R. E. (1986). Task complexity: Definition of the construct. *Organizational Behavior and Human Decision Processes, 37*, 60–82.

Wyer, R. S., & Srull, T. K. (1986). Human cognition in its social context. *Psychological Review, 93*, 322–359.

Zajonc, R. B. (1986). The decline and rise of scholastic aptitude scores—A prediction derived from the confluence model. *American Psychologist, 41*, 862–867.

Social Structure as a Determinant of Environmental Experience

Ronald P. Abeles
Behavioral and Social Research
National Institute on Aging

In considering Dr. Schooler's chapter, I would like to amplify and comment upon two of his points: (a) social structure as a determinant of the kinds of environments that people experience and (b) the nature of the bridge between social structure and cognitive functioning.

Dr. Schooler distinguishes between *microlevel* "concerns about the nature of the immediate environmental conditions affecting cognitive processes" and *macrolevel* "concerns about the social and cultural context in which such functioning takes place." At the microlevel, he identifies complexity as the environmental component that influences cognitive functioning. Moreover, he offers a mechanism for converting environmental complexity into cognitive functioning, a point that I explore later on.

MICROLEVEL PROCESSES

As a social psychologist, I find Dr. Schooler's emphasis on the immediate social environment, as the locus of social structural features influencing inter- and intraindividual differences, to be highly reasonable (Abeles and Riley, 1987). We know that there is great variation in the nature of the immediate social environment to which different people are exposed, and this variation could be a source of interindividual differences in cognitive functioning, as is demonstrated in Kohn and Schooler's research (1978, 1981, 1982).

In contrast, we know relatively little about *intra*individual differences in environmental complexity. What is the degree of consistency in level of complexity across the various social environments in which a person

149

lives out his or her daily life? For example, are there equivalent degrees of complexity in both the work and the family environments? Similarly, we know little about the consistency in exposure to social environmental complexity as the person ages and moves through a succession of different environments. Such questions lead naturally to the question of what are the consequences (for cognitive functioning) of consistency or inconsistency in levels of complexity across environments and over time? For instance, a change in complexity levels is implicit in hypotheses about the detrimental psychological consequences of retirement.

MACROLEVEL PROCESSES

Dr. Schooler discusses the concepts of cohort and culture as macrolevel social structural processes affecting cognitive functioning. Another major means—and in some instances a specification of the other two—by which macrolevel social processes affect cognitive functioning is in the allocation of people to particular social roles and hence to particular microlevel social environments. In this manner, macrolevel social structures and processes do not influence cognitive functioning directly, but they are essential components in a "two-step flow" of influence (to borrow a term from communications research). At the macrolevel, social structure influences both the kinds and the patterning of experiences to which people are exposed as a result of roles that they occupy over their lives.

This influence is most readily demonstrated in terms of the impact of an individual's socioeconomic status (SES), viewed as the individual's position in the larger society. Socioeconomic status is a strong determinant of the quality and quantity of education and of the subsequent nature of work in which people engage during their lifetime. Thus, it affects the likelihood of being exposed to microlevel environments and processes that foster or inhibit particular kinds of intellectual and cognitive functioning. Besides affecting the individual's probability of having particular experiences or of being exposed to particular social environments, SES affects *when* significant life experiences are likely to occur within the individual (Abeles, Steel, & Wise, 1980; Hagestad & Neugarten, 1985; Hogan, 1981). Similarly, the sequencing of life experiences is influenced by SES. For example, lower SES women are more likely to become unmarried teenage mothers, which is an "off-time" life event with long-enduring and mostly negative consequences for subsequent educational and occupational careers (Card, Steel, & Abeles, 1982; Presser, 1974).

After being associated with Matilda Riley for almost 15 years, it is difficult not to have learned that *age* itself is also a component of social structure, which operates in a fashion similar to SES in allocating and recruiting people to roles and in evaluating their performance in those roles (Riley, Johnson, & Foner, 1972). Chronological age (or some indicant of age) is a feature not only of individuals and populations but also of role structures through which people move as they grow older. Like social class, age is a determinant of the kinds of social environments in which people spend their daily lives. Age affects which roles are open or closed to an individual (e.g., pupil, worker, spouse), and which social networks and cultural norms will offer which opportunities or impose which demands. Age is built into the changing organization of institutions and roles through formal or informal criteria for entry and exit, through expectations of how roles are to be performed, and through sanctions for role performance. There are social rules, some with the force of norms, that govern the age at which people are expected and/or allowed to engage in particular activities.

This view of macrolevel processes implies that such processes are more likely to account for differences in cognitive functioning between groups or aggregates of people than for differences between particular individuals. Thus, they are useful for comprehending cohort, cross-national, and ethnic group differences in cognitive functioning, such as those discussed by Dr. Schooler. For example, the impact of social change on people is dependent on their location in a social system, such as the age-stratification system. Consider the case of the industrial revolution in Germany, which did not impact upon all age groups equally. Not all farmers, regardless of their age, traded their plows for steam-driven hammers in the factories of the Ruhr. Rather, in each successive cohort, greater and greater proportions of young workers moved into nontraditional occupations at the time they entered the labor force (e.g., see Mueller, Willms-Herget, & Handl, 1983). Once workers entered into an occupational area, they were unlikely to move into other domains as they aged. That is, despite the opening up of new occupations through Germany's industrialization, older workers did not move into the new occupations.

In sum, it appears that the more fruitful and powerful social structural influence on cognitive functioning is to be found at the microlevel, if one is interested in explaining inter- and intraindividual differences. Macrolevel structures and processes as well as changes therein are probably too gradual and remote to have a significant impact on the life of a given individual. Moreover, when it appears that they do, it is difficult to specify how this impact is direct and not mediated through exposure to particular microlevel environments.

BRIDGING SOCIAL STRUCTURE
AND COGNITIVE FUNCTIONING

In his chapter in this book and elsewhere (Schooler, 1984), Dr. Schooler has identified environmental complexity as a critical aspect of the immediate social environment having an impact upon cognitive functioning. He does not stop at this point, but goes on to pose the central question of this book: How is a social level variable (or process) translated into an individual level outcome? How is the gap between the social and the psychological bridged? He offers the concept of generalization as the psychological process connecting these two levels.

Although I do not deny that generalization plays a role, it seems to me that some process is needed prior to generalization. By invoking the concept of generalization, one is assuming that something has already been learned, and then that it is transfered or applied in another situation or behavioral domain. But, this leaves open the question of how or why does environmental complexity result in a particular kind of learning (i.e., improved performance on standard tests of cognitive functioning). Perhaps an answer to this question can be found in the concepts and research of Daniel Berlyne (1960).

Berlyne developed a motivational theory based upon the notion that organisms require and strive toward some optimal level of physiological, specifically nervous system, arousal. Both too much and too little stimulation, hence arousal, are states that are avoided. Arousal is achieved through controlling the amount and kind of stimulation received from internal and external environments. For example, arousal can be heightened through exploring an environment. Moreover, the reinforcing value of environmental stimuli are a function of their ability to produce momentary increases in arousal level (so-called *arousal-jag*).

Berlyne postulated that stimuli (or environments) characterized by novelty, complexity, conflict, and uncertainty have the capability of producing arousal and thereby have intrinsic reinforcement qualities. He employed these concepts to explain why animals and humans explore their environments and acquire knowledge in the absence of extrinsic reinforcements (i.e., out of curiosity as opposed to a search for food or water).

It is interesting to note that Dr. Schooler's definition of environmental complexity (i.e., number of elements, ambiguity, diversity of stimuli, and change in stimulation over time) has the same characteristics that Berlyne associated with novelty, complexity, conflict, and uncertainty. This leads me to suggest that the missing link in Dr. Schooler's formulation (i.e., why does more learning take place in complex environments) can be found in a Berlyne-like model of learning. That is, environmental complexity (within limits) is sought out by individuals, and dealing with complexity is intrinsically rewarding for them, which leads, in turn, to learning and improved cognitive functioning. Moreover, such a conceptualization adds to Dr. Schooler's formulation, for instance, by helping us understand why routinization (i.e., performing the same, unchanging task or role) over long periods of time, regardless of the level of complexity of the task, might have negative psychological consequences. Although still complex, the task loses its novelty and its ability to produce a reinforcing *arousal-jag*.

Obviously, a Berlyne-like model is not without its difficulties in operationalization. But, it appears to be a route toward understanding why social environmental complexity might lead to changes in cognitive functioning over the life of an individual, thus providing a link between social structural and psychological processes.

REFERENCES

Abeles, R. P., & Riley, M. W. (1987). Longevity, social structure, and cognitive aging. In C. Schooler & K. W. Schaie (Eds.), *Cognitive functioning and social structure over the life course* (pp. 161–175). Norwood, NJ: Ablex.

Abeles, R. P., Steel, L., & Wise, L. L. (1980). Patterns and implications of life-course organization. In P. B. Baltes & O. G. Brim, Jr. (Eds.), *Life-span development and behavior* (Vol. 3, pp. 307–337). New York: Academic Press.

Berlyne, D. E. (1960). *Conflict, arousal, and curiosity.* New York: McGraw-Hill.

Card, J. J., Steel, L., & Abeles, R. P. (1982). Sex differences in the patterning of adult roles as a determinant of sex differences in occupational achievement. *Sex Roles, 8*(9), 1009–1024.

Hagestad, G. O., & Neugarten, B. L. (1985). Age and life course. In R. H. Binstock & E. Shanas (Eds.), *Handbook of aging and the social sciences* (2nd ed., pp. 35–91). New York: Van Nostrand Reinhold.

Hogan, D. P. (1981). *Transition and social change: The early lives of American men.* New York: Academic Press.

Kohn, M. L., & Schooler, C. (1978). The reciprocal effects of the substantive complexity of work and intellectual flexibility: A longitudinal assessment. *American Journal of Sociology, 84,* 24–52.

Kohn, M. L., & Schooler, C. (1981). Job conditions and intellectual flexibility: A longitudinal assessment of their reciprocal effects. In D. J. Jackson & E. F. Borgatta (Eds.), *Factor analysis and measurement in sociological research: A multi-dimension perspective* (pp. 281–313). London: Sage.

Kohn, M. L., & Schooler, C. (1982). Job conditions and personality: A longitudinal assessment of their reciprocal effects. *American Journal of Sociology, 87,* 1257–1286.

Mueller, W., Willms-Herget, A., & Handl, J. (1983). *Strukturwandel der Frauenarbeit, 1880–1980.* Frankfurt am Main: Campus Verlag.

Presser, H. (1974). Early motherhood: Ignorance or bliss? *Family Planning Perspectives, 6,* 8–14.

Riley, M. W., Johnson, M. J., & Foner, A. (1972). *Aging and society. Vol. 3: A sociology of age stratification* (pp. 3–26). New York: Russell Sage Foundation.

Schooler, C. (1984). Psychological effects of complex environments during the life span: A review and theory. *Intelligence, 8,* 259–281.

Cognitive Socialization Across the Life Span:
Comments on Schooler's Chapter

Daniel P. Keating
Ontario Institute for Studies in Education

In several respects, I find myself in an awkward position in responding to the analyses put forth by Schooler. From his study of social and cognitive science perspectives on aging processes, he examines the lessons from which we can draw in our understanding of cognitive aging. Most important among my occasions of awkwardness is the fact that I am in nearly total agreement with the thrust of the analyses. As a consequence, my options in commentary are somewhat limited. One solution is to offer a hearty endorsement and to reiterate the main points. Another is to find some minor points of disagreement and to elevate them to a status of more fundamental importance. The former course does not advance the discussion, and the latter is no more than an academic version of the "dog in the manger." Instead, I seek to accomplish a third option: to emphasize the importance of the major points, perhaps elaborate on them slightly, and to propose some issues that strike me as being the most difficult to deal with as we pursue a conjoint cognitive and social science analysis.

A second source of awkwardness for me in giving my commentary is Schooler's perception of "pessimism" in my earlier critique of contemporary cognitive science's approaches to explain individual and developmental differences in intellectual performance (Keating, 1984). As Schooler notes, I have criticized the recurrent tendency of researchers to seek explanations for variability in cognitive functioning "in the head of the person," rather than to recognize and deal with the inherently *systemic* nature of such differences. This tendency seems apparent to me in the applications of each of the currently dominant research traditions—psychometric, Piagetian, and information processing—even when there is an avowed desire to avoid "closed structure" or reified models.

Perhaps Schooler has detected a note of despair in my earlier comments, as it has become apparent to me that novel attempts to understand the cognitive processing underlying real-world cognitive activity—such as the current "cognitive revolution"—tend to be rapidly absorbed into the persistent fabric of purely "mentalist" accounts. For example, it is clear that for many researchers the only change in their analyses is the use of reaction times as the basic "scores" instead of total scores on paper-and-pencil tests. These reaction times are often employed in such a way as to suggest little or no connection between the cognitive analyses that gave rise to the tasks and their use in developmental or individual differences analyses. Thus, *any* reaction time—global reaction time, movement reaction time, residual reaction time—can be entered into factor analyses or, increasingly, latent trait analyses, with no evident concern as to their intended or analyzed *meaning* (Keating & MacLean, 1987). This strikes me as an almost certain guarantee that the unproductive wheel-spinning within psychometric theory—how many ability factors are there *really*?—will be recreated, with predictable analyses in 10 years as to why the effort was misguided from the start! Rather than restate those arguments here, I refer readers to the more detailed analyses of the validity requirements for such investigations that I have proposed elsewhere (Keating, 1984; Keating & MacLean, 1987).

As I noted in my earlier paper cited by Schooler, these critical analyses do represent something of a promissory note. It is insufficient for making progress on these questions to note merely where contemporary approaches are off the mark. Although I regard this as an important task, there is no self-evident positive agenda that arises from such critiques. Fortunately, I think that a positive agenda *does* arise from the analyses proposed by Schooler; and that agenda, I believe, is complementary to one that Darla MacLean and I have recently advanced (Keating & MacLean, 1988). The most obvious point of agreement is on the importance of studying cognitive socialization in a much more specific fashion than we have heretofore. I briefly summarize the major points of that agenda for the primary purpose of emphasizing the major points of agreement with Schooler's analyses. From that basis, some difficult—although I think not intractable—problems clearly arise in our attempts to implement this research agenda. I briefly summarize several key difficulties, in the hope that like-minded researchers may be induced to tackle and, perhaps, resolve them.

COGNITIVE SOCIALIZATION
IN A POSTSTRUCTURALIST AGENDA

As cognitive science has coalesced and matured over the past quarter century or so, its roots in fundamental, and unresolved, epistemological issues have become apparent (Keating & MacLean, 1988). As with its predecessors in the Western empirical psychological tradition — psychometric analyses of mental ability structures and Piagetian theories of the structures of logical operations — contemporary cognitive science has principally sought to address the ways in which our underlying cognitive structure or architecture prescribe how we come to know the world we live in. Based on a rather straightforward computer-processing analogy (Neisser, 1976), cognitive scientists have tried to explain the *mechanisms* of "knowing." Although each of these major traditions of empirical research — psychometric, Piagetian, and information processing — differ among themselves in important features, each rests upon a fundamental epistemological assumption, whether explicitly or implicitly. The assumption is that the *internal structure* of the knowing organism has priority for explaining the processes and outcomes of cognitive activity. This is of course a long tradition, one that predates any of the contemporary empirical manifestations, from Platonic "idealism" to the preeminence of logical reasoning, as the road to "truth" in our current adherence to scientific "methodism" (Feyerabend, 1975; Keating, in press).

The difficulty with the assumption is that its epistemological priority is precisely that, an assumption. Two major alternative epistemological assumptions can be used to undermine our confidence in internal subjective explanations of the nature of human cognitive activity (Dreyfus & Rabinow, 1982). The first is a set of assumptions embedded in a notion of *phenomenology*. From this perspective, the problem of how information in the real world is "processed" — veridically or not — is a nonproblem. That is, the subjectivity of the organism and the objectivity of the material world are not independent aspects that require the positing of a set of processing mechanisms or a cognitive architecture for accurate "interpretation." Rather, they are inherently attuned to one another at a level of direct meaning. This notion is articulated in the theoretical epistemology of Merleau-Ponty (1962), and perhaps more familiarly serves as the epistemic basis for J. J. Gibson's (1979) notion of direct perception; that is, perception that does not require the "mediation" of an internal cognitive structure. This perspective has raised fundamental challenges to some structuralist assumptions of cognitive scientists, some of which have been detailed by Neisser (1976).

The second major alternative epistemological assumption is that which assigns the veridical knowledge of the world to the "correct" interpretations or readings of *objective reality* rather than to the validity of internal cognitive mechanisms. This is sometimes referred to as a hermeneutic perspective, in that the primary search for the basis of valid knowledge rests on the accuracy of the interpretation of objective social forces. The most elaborated theory of cognitive activity derived from this set of assumptions is that advanced by Vygotsky in the 1930s, although available in English translation substantially later (Vygotsky, 1962, 1978). From this perspective, our understanding of the nature of cognitive activity rests principally upon our understanding of how culture and society have evolved historically and how the nature of *social* relationships guides our knowledge of the world.

Before addressing the implications of these analyses for a productive research agenda in cognitive and social science, let me note briefly that these epistemological assumptions for priority in explaining cognitive activity—internal mental structure, objective social reality, or their phenomenological indivisibility—represent fundamentally unresolvable counterclaims. Thus, attempts to *explain* the nature and validity of cognitive activity from any of these a priori bases are open to (successful) challenges from either of the other two perspectives. This is decidedly unsettling, as many of the deconstructionists have been noting at length, either joyfully or menacingly. If the validity of our understanding of the world can not successfully be attributed to *some* explanation of our cognitive activity, then are we not mired in an uncomfortable position of total relativism or even nihilism? Certainly this seems to be the necessary outcome of two centuries of epistemological investigation framed by Kant's critiques, which can be said to have ushered in the modern era (Dreyfus & Rabinow, 1982).

I contend that this dilemma is a false one. It rests upon the belief— deeply rooted in our Western philosophical and scientific tradition—that the validity of knowledge rests upon the form of knowing. For the dominant explanations of cognitive psychology, these "forms of knowing" are preeminently the accuracy of the processes, especially logical reasoning (Keating, in press). But, there is an alternative basis for judging the validity of our knowledge. This criterion is the *practical success* of the outcomes of cognitive activity. Of course, this criterion is easier to state than to apply.

In the domains of the natural sciences, it can be relatively straightforward. Our applications of physical principles typically have self-evident successful or unsuccessful outcomes: Bridges stand or fall, planes fly or crash; hence, our greater confidence and notion of progress in physics, chemistry, and biology. It is worth noting here that for even the "purest" of the sciences, mathematics, a strong case can be made for the criterion of practical success to evaluate the validity of mathematical reasoning (Kline, 1980).

In the domains of the human sciences, the criterion is much harder to apply, though just as appropriate. This is because the criterion of practical success is inevitably a value-laden estimation. Imagine a study in which we demonstrated that authoritarian classroom discipline increased achievement test scores significantly. If the practical criterion of "improved achievement" is used, clearly this style of discipline is superior. But, is it the most important criterion relative to other possible criteria, such as student self-esteem or eventual student self-discipline? Selecting the most important criterion is a value judgment, which ultimately rests on the individual's judgments of what is *desirable*. In this analysis, it is clear that the role of social power—which selects the criteria of success—is *central* to our understanding of the nature of the cognitive activity that gives rise to "good" solutions.

At this point, the points of overlap with Schooler's analysis are probably apparent. Understanding the nature of human cognitive activity can not proceed validly in the absence of an understanding of how the social setting shapes that activity. This is not to gainsay the importance of understanding the internal structure of human cognitive activity. Rather, it is to recognize that these structures are not independent, even at the most basic levels, of the social system in which they develop. In fact, we have proposed a rough model in which these various perspectives can potentially be integrated (Keating & MacLean, 1988). In this model—a theoretical and research agenda—it becomes crucial to understand (a) the "phenomenological priors" of the organism, which are likely to be primarily perceptual; (b) how these guide or constrain the construction of the individual's *schemes* (or structures) for interpreting the information in the world; *and* (c) how the nature of the information available, including its socially given content, is incorporated into the individual's cognitive constructions. Clearly, a life-span developmental notion is critical to this research agenda, because cognitive activity can only be understood ontogenetically. Further, it argues for a much greater role of *cognitive socialization* in that cognitive structures are neither given nor unfolding but inherently inseparable from the physical and social system in which the organism develops. In order for this part of our "poststructuralist" agenda to be pursued, a deeper understanding of the social settings of cognitive activity is fundamental.

SOME DIFFICULT ISSUES
IN PURSUING THE AGENDA

As I noted earlier, pursuing this analysis raises some quite difficult issues. I suspect that this may partly account for the relative scarcity of such approaches in empirical work, for surely the ideas are not entirely novel (for a historical account, cf. Dixon & Nesselroade, 1983). I do not intend this to be an exhaustive list of known concerns, much less those that might emerge as we pursue this path. The three issues I briefly examine are the problems of matching levels of analysis between and within cognitive and social science accounts, the nature of cognitive generalization, and the problem of value-laden criteria of effective cognitive functioning.

Levels of Analysis

A recurrent problem in the analysis of human cognitive activity from a cognitive science perspective has been the identification and separation of theoretically different levels of that cognitive activity. Many early researchers aimed at identifying rather "pure" processing accounts of elementary information processes (Neisser, 1967). Thus, a principal initial goal for many researchers was to isolate the operation of such activities as short-term memory scanning, mental rotation of spatial imagery, and access and retrieval from long-term or semantic memory. It soon became clear that these processes would be quite difficult to isolate from other features of cognitive activity. The role of procedural knowledge, or "control" processes, was soon recognized as crucial to any complete account. This quite naturally led to an examination of the role of content knowledge and its influence on both elementary and control processes.

Finally, given these multiple influences, two further inferences were unavoidable. First, the hope that, for simplicity's sake, these various elements might be potentially *separable* features of the cognitive system seems to have given way to a recognition of their fundamental interdependence. One consequence of this recognition is the current popularity of models of "expertise," as Schooler notes, and the notion of more flexible application of the various features of the cognitive system by the individual as he or she confronts some complex cognitive task. Second, this more elaborated understanding requires the posing of yet another level of the cognitive system, which we may call an executive monitor, that is responsible for selecting among the various ways of approaching a given complex task. This more complicated system—elementary processes, procedural knowledge, content knowledge, and an executive monitor—fits nicely with models of expertise, but poses some significant difficulties for more general production system models. Especially the reintroduction of the "cognitive actor" in the role of an executive monitor makes simple, mechanical modeling of the entire system difficult.

In contrast to the rather careful attention being given to levels of analysis *within* the cognitive system, there is much less focus on the levels of analysis of the social system as they impinge on the development of cognitive activity. Indeed, the work of Schooler and his associates represents one of a handful of exceptions to this generalization. Most work relating social and other environmental factors to cognitive functioning have employed what Bronfenbrenner and Crouter (1983) have termed "social address" models; that is, demographic indices or other global variables that are surrogates of such indices. As Bronfenbrenner and Crouter noted, developmentalists have in general been remiss in refining their characterizations of "environmental" influences. As Schooler argues, it is necessary to consider both microlevel and macrolevel analyses of the contexts in which cognitive activity both develops and takes place.

Drawing appropriate connections between the levels of analysis of the cognitive system and of the social setting is surely not an easy task. It is, however, a necessary one for any reasonably complete account of cognitive activity. In so doing, the possibilities for inferential errors are many, and they are especially likely to occur when comparisons among the cognitive functioning of different groups — culturally or developmentally — are the goal (Cole & Means, 1981). One example considered in some detail by us (Keating & MacLean, 1988) and others (e.g., Olson, 1986) is whether the age differences in "fluid intelligence" really represent differences in nonacculturated, incidental learning; or do they perhaps represent differences owing to the highly specific formal acculturation associated with schooling? We have argued that the latter interpretation is at least as plausible as the former. We contend further that the resolution of this issue is not to be found solely in the more detailed analyses of test-covariance matrices but rather in the integration of cognitive science and social science analyses, which take rigorous account of the various important levels of analysis within and between these approaches.

Cognitive Generalization

As Schooler rightly notes, one key and persistent issue in the study of cognitive functioning is the role of generalization. Indeed, it is precisely the ability to generalize to relatively novel situations that has been one main argument in favor of cognitive or mentalist models and against purely associationist models. As a key theoretical claim underlying each of the major empirical traditions investigating human cognition, and as a matter of considerable practical importance as well, it deserves this special attention. In addition, the recognition that generalization to novel situations is a frequent cognitive activity serves as a counterbalance to the strong trend toward highly domain-specific models of expertise. The social structures and settings that encourage or discourage such activity is also of special importance. The findings that Schooler cites regarding the connection between demanding, complex work environments and intellectual flexibility illustrate this connection clearly.

The problem of *appropriate* generalization remains a difficult one. Schooler notes several categorization systems to encompass types of generalization and offers a rather comprehensive list. At the risk of engaging in an abstract parlor game, let me propose yet another way of categorizing types of cognitive generalization. In defense of the proposal, I think it has the virtue of simplicity ("trinity" models have a long history in human cognition and mythology!), and it permits me to reemphasize a point I raised earlier.

The three types of cognitive generalization that I propose and believe are open to empirical investigation are:

1. Generalization *within* a well-identified knowledge base. These are largely *algorithmic* applications, and the most obvious examples are perhaps from mathematics. In these cases, the generalization is likely to be correct, as long as the nature of the knowledge base is in fact the same. The major developmental function here is some form of *automaticity*, including chunking and less effortful processing, and perhaps even a transition from a production system to a retrieval system for highly overlearned material (Miller, Perlmutter, & Keating, 1984). The advantages for cognitive functioning are readily apparent, especially in the attentional resources available for allocation elsewhere. There is some good evidence that this is an important developmental function (e.g., Manis, Keating, & Morrison, 1980).

2. Generalization through the use of *analogy*. Analogical reasoning is of course the basis for much research in the several empirical research traditions, and histories of scientific progress have highlited the importance of recognizing previously overlooked connections among different disciplines or approaches. At a more mundane level, we would typically expect at least this level of generalization in order to accord the term *conceptual* understanding. In a recent study, Lynda Crane and I (Crane & Keating, 1986) presented college students, each of whom had been prescreened with a paper-and-pencil test of performance on problems involving ratios, fractions, and proportions, with a simple concrete problem set requiring the *same* proportional reasoning: Judge the relative proportions removed from two geometrically regular wooden objects of different shapes and sizes. Nearly half the subjects, 45%, made a significant number of errors on the "real" problems, even though all had displayed mastery on the same proportional comparisons in the paper-and-pencil test. Clearly, these subjects had the ability to generalize algorithmically but apparently not analogously. They did not recognize the concrete problem as one in which ratios and proportions were the keys to a simple, even trivial, solution strategy.

One caveat with respect to thinking by analogy, and one that is too often overlooked, is worth noting. Thinking by analogy is often wrong. Generating analogies is relatively easy; generating appropriate analogies is more difficult. As cognitive researchers, I think we are often struck more forcibly by failures to generalize—as in the example I have just noted— and tend to be more forgiving of errors of overgeneralization. Perhaps this is because analogies are our stock in trade ("The mind is like a computer; semantic organization is like a branching tree"). What bears repetition here is that the value of any analogy — as with any cognitive solution strategy — is against the criterion of practical success. For both social and cognitive scientists, the limitations of analogy should never be far from mind. The salient example of "social Darwinism" from the last century and its contemporary descendants might serve as a useful reminder.

3. Generalizations that incorporate previously different knowledge systems through *analysis of principles*. This form of generalization is evident both in ontogenesis and at the cultural level in the development of knowledge systems. Numerous examples of the latter in the history of mathematics are documented by Kline (1980). In individual cognitive activity, the best examples are perhaps those from the emerging literatures on expertise cited by Schooler. In many of these cases, a key distinction between novice and expert is that the expert immediately recognizes the *formal* identity or similarity among superficially dissimilar problem spaces, whereas the novice is misled by the superficial dissimilarity, presumably due to the absence of principled understanding. Again, we need to be skeptical when such formal identities are proposed beyond rather narrow domain-knowledge boundaries. Gilligan (1982) and others have, for example, been critical of asserted formal identities between propositional and moral logics. But a search for common principles is a powerful form of cognitive generalization. In passing, it is worth noting that this is precisely the level of cognitive generalization that many have lamented as being increasingly rare in secondary and postsecondary education in the United States (Keating, 1986).

These three forms of cognitive generalization — algorithmic application, analogy, and analysis of principles — are likely to have different developmental histories, as well as support or hindrance from different aspects of the process of cognitive socialization. In some cases, socialization for one type of generalization may inhibit the development of another, and an important task for both cognitive and social scientists is to understand this acquisition process in much greater detail. The development of automaticity for algorithmic applications may be an important step in making sufficient cognitive resources available for more sophisticated forms of generalization. Encouraging excessive reliance on algorithms, however, may reduce our possibility of understanding their underlying principles. A further complication is that this developmental process seems likely to be different across different domains of knowledge; but our recent experiences in this regard should lead us to accept this complication. The nature and role of cognitive generalization may well fail to generalize across knowledge domains!

Social Values and the Criteria
of Effective Cognitive Functioning

My final concern has been anticipated by many of the earlier comments and thus can be briefly articulated. Simply put, we need to eschew the belief that we can identify and measure *generally effective* cognitive functioning. It strikes me as reasonable to assume that most individuals are cognitively well adapted to their social setting. Those social settings of course vary in their breadth, indexed perhaps by the variety of social roles they incorporate; in their desirability, indexed by the level of prestige or social power associated with them; and in their complexity, indexed, as Schooler indicates, by the variety of cognitive challenges they pose. Although it seems self-evident, even "second nature," to us that effective cognitive functioning covaries closely with such variables, we should be wary of such assumptions.

Consider, for example, our Western preference of semantic categorical thinking as opposed to functionally based categorical thinking. The former has clearly proved its effectiveness in the research and applications — that is, the *practices* of the natural sciences. We are nevertheless *not* entitled to assume the validity of such thinking as it applies to the cognitive or social sciences. This is a good example of reasoning by analogy: its success remains to be demonstrated in practice. Our wariness should not inhibit empirical investigation; quite the opposite. It should lead us to be specific about the range of effectiveness that we ascribe to specific forms of cognitive functioning; and we should include in those specifications both the domains in which we have examined the cognitive activity and the criteria by which we have judged it to be effective.

REFERENCES

Bronfenbrenner, U., & Crouter, A. C. (1983). The evolution of environmental models in developmental research. In P. Mussen (Ed.), *Handbook of child psychology.* (Vol. 1, pp. 357–414). New York: Wiley.

Cole, M., & Means, B. (1981). *Comparative studies of how people think.* Cambridge, MA: Harvard University Press.

Crane, L., & Keating, D. P. (1986, March). *The limits of reasoning: Within domain constraints.* Paper presented at the annual meeting of the Society for Research in Adolescence, Madison, WI.

Dixon, R. A., & Nesselroade, J. R. (1983). Pluralism and correlational analysis in developmental psychology: Historical commonalities. In R. M. Lerner (Ed.), *Developmental psychology: Historical and philosophical perspectives* (pp. 113–145). Hillsdale, NJ: Lawrence Erlbaum Associates.

Dreyfus, H. L., & Rabinow, P. (1982). *Michel Foucault: Beyond structuralism and hermeneutics.* Chicago: University of Chicago Press.

Feyerabend, P. (1975). *Against method*. London: New Left Books.

Gibson, J. J. (1979). *The perception of the visual world*. Boston: Houghton-Mifflin.

Gilligan, C. (1982). *In a different voice*. Cambridge, MA: Harvard University Press.

Keating, D. P. (1984). The emperor's new clothes: The "new look" in intelligence research. In R. J. Sternberg (Ed.), *Advances in the psychology of human intelligence* (Vol. 2, pp. 1–45). Hillsdale, NJ: Lawrence Erlbaum Associates.

Keating, D. P. (1986). *Higher order thinking in high school: Developmental and educational constraints*. Unpublished manuscript, University of Maryland, Baltimore.

Keating, D. P. (in press). Structuralism, deconstruction, reconstruction: The limits of reasoning. In W. F. Overton (Ed.), *Reasoning, necessity, and logic: Developmental perspectives*. Hillsdale, NJ: Lawrence Erlbaum Associates.

Keating, D. P., & MacLean, D. J. (1987). Cognitive ability, cognitive processing, and development: A reconsideration. In P. A. Vernon (Ed.), *Speed of information-processing and intelligence* (pp 239–270). Norwood, NJ: Ablex.

Keating, D. P., & MacLean, D. J. (1988). Reconstruction in cognitive development: A post-structuralist agenda. In P. B. Baltes, D. L. Featherman, & R. M. Lerner (Eds.), *Life-span development and behavior* (Vol. 8, pp. 283–317). Hillsdale, NJ: Lawrence Erlbaum Associates.

Kline, M. (1980). *Mathematics: The loss of certainty*. New York: Oxford University Press.

Manis, F. R., Keating, D. P., & Morrison, F. J. (1980). Developmental differences in the allocation of processing capacity. *Journal of Experimental Child Psychology, 29,* 156–169.

Merleau-Ponty, M. (1962). *The phenomenology of perception*. London: Routledge & Kegan Paul.

Miller, K., Perlmutter, M., & Keating, D. P. (1984). Cognitive arithmetic: Comparison of operations. *Journal of Experimental Psychology: Learning, Memory, and Cognition, 10,* 46–60.

Neisser, U. (1967). *Cognitive psychology*. New York: Appleton-Century-Crofts.

Neisser, U. (1976). *Cognition and reality*. San Francisco: W. H. Freeman.

Olson, D. R. (1986). Intelligence and literacy: The relationships between intelligence and the technologies of representation and communication. In R. J. Sternberg & R. K. Wagner (Eds.), *Practical intelligence* (pp. 338–360). Cambridge: Cambridge University Press.

Vygotsky, L. S. (1962). *Thought and language*. Cambridge, MA: MIT Press.

Vygotsky, L. S. (1978). *Mind in society*. Cambridge, MA: Harvard University Press.

5

Personality and Aging at the Crossroads:
Beyond Stability Versus Change

Margie E. Lachman
Brandeis University

The field of personality and aging appears to be at a critical juncture, not unlike the one we witnessed in the general field of personality in the late 1960s and early 1970s (Bowers, 1973; Mischel, 1973). The preoccupation with stability versus change in the personality and aging field is analogous to the heated debate over person versus situation in the personality field.

In response to Mischel's (1968) challenge to trait psychology, a great debate emerged about the contribution of the person versus the situation to behavioral outcomes. Mischel had criticized the fundamentals of trait psychology by arguing that behavior shows little consistency across situations and that correlations between traits and behaviors rarely exceeded .30. This person versus situation debate led to the interactionist movement in personality and the now famous book by Magnusson and Endler (1977): *Personality at the Crossroads*. Today, there are very few who would deny that behavior is determined by both the person and the situation. My decision to borrow from this title was, in part, based on my assessment that the time is right for a comparable revolution in the field of personality and aging, in which both stability and change will be universally acknowledged. I noticed, however, that Magnussen and Endler were not the only ones to use a crossroads title before me. In the *Journal of Irreproducible Results* in an article called "The Crowded Crossroads" (Martin, 1975), I found 31 citations for articles with crossroads in the title (for example: "Education at the Crossroads," "Group Relations at the Crossroads," and "Crossroads in Cooking").

The second part of this chapter title suggests that we can move *beyond stability versus change.* In the field of personality and aging, the predominant focus for the last decade has been, "Is there stability or is there change?" An important lesson can be learned from the person versus situation debate in our parent field and from earlier debates involving dichotomies, such as nature versus nurture. Although such debates are useful for stimulating research, there comes a point when it is more fruitful to acknowledge that the two extremes are not necessarily mutually exclusive and that an interaction of the two positions is a more realistic view. It is really not a question of "which one" or "how much of each," as Anastasi (1958) told us about the role of heredity and environment in the intellectual domain. Anastasi's recommendation was not to abandon the debate, but rather to ask different questions. Instead of asking "which" or "how much," she recommended we ask "how?" This advice also seems appropriate in the case of stability and change. Rather than focus on which, it seems that the time is right to turn our attention to other questions such as: Under what conditions does personality show stability and change? What are the antecedents and consequences of stable and changing personalities during the aging process?

At this juncture, I take a road that has not been heavily traveled by researchers in the field of personality and aging. I am grateful for the opportunity, provided by the editors of this volume, to think and learn about personality and aging in relation to social structures, for I believe it is a road that will help to move us beyond the current preoccupation with stability versus change.

In going this route, that is, in considering social structure in relation to personality and aging, one cannot abandon issues of stability and change. Rather, information about stability and change provides an important foundation for such an analysis.

First, I present a preview of the points I wish to highlight in this chapter: (a) some personality dimensions are largely stable and unchangeable and others are subject to change in adulthood and old age; (b) social structures can be examined both as antecedents and consequences of personality change and stability; (c) the subjective interpretations of outcomes, especially control beliefs and causal attributions, are crucial for understanding the mechanisms that link social structures and personality; (d) successful aging can be characterized as a match between the characteristics of the individual and the nature of the environment and social structures. The analysis of social structures and personality can be useful for predicting and modifying outcomes to optimize well-being in aging.

These four themes appear throughout the chapter, which is organized in four sections: (a) a conceptual overview of personality; (b) a summary of the past and the current state of affairs in the field of personality and aging, with a focus on which dimensions are stable and which show change;

(c) a description of the traditional focus of the field of personality and social structure; (d) an examination of the interpersonal and psychological mechanisms that may be involved in linking personality and social structure in aging. My hope is that this discussion will stimulate further exploration of the antecedents and consequences of stability and change in personality across the life span.

CONCEPTIONS OF PERSONALITY

I agree with Elder's analysis in his 1973 paper "On Linking Social Structure and Personality": We need a clear definition of both personality and social structure before we can examine the links between these domains. A number of other chapters in this volume provide useful conceptions of social structure. As a representative of the personality domain, my plan is to provide an overview of conceptual and empirical approaches to personality. There are, of course, multiple ways to conceptualize personality; I try to present a conceptual view of personality that is useful for examining social structure and aging.

If there is consistency and agreement on anything in the field of personality, it is that the field is in a state of confusion and disarray. We often see the written body of work on personality characterized as "litter-ature" (Block, 1977). There are a myriad of theories and definitions of personality. I give you a few sample definitions. According to Mischel (1986), personality is: "The distinctive patterns of behavior (including thoughts and emotions) that characterize each individual's adaptation to the situations of his or her life" (p. 4). Pervin's (1980) definition is: "Personality represents those characteristics of the person or of people generally that account for consistent patterns of response to situations" (p. 6). And Cattell (1965) defined personality as: "That which tells what a man will do when placed in a given situation" (p. 25). These and other definitions of personality vary in their emphasis on enduring dispositions or more malleable characteristics and in their focus on overt behaviors or covert processes.

There are numerous ways one can summarize and organize the different approaches to personality (Matarazzo & Garner, 1985). The traditional textbook approach is to group individual theories into categories such as: psychodynamic (Freud, Jung, Erikson, Horney); humanistic (Rogers, Maslow); existential (Frankl, May); individual differences (Cattell, Allport, Eysenck); cognitive (Kelly); social learning (Rotter, Bandura, Mischel); and behavioral (Skinner).

For purposes of studying personality in adulthood and old age, these textbook approaches are typically not very useful. Within categories, there are differing views across theories regarding the nature of personality sta-bility and changes in adulthood. In the psychodynamic category, for ex-ample, the Freudian view is that there is no change in adulthood, except perhaps with psychoanalysis; and the Jungian view is that there is a natural course of maturation and change throughout life. Even within theories, some aspects of the person are postulated to change and others are ex-pected to remain stable. Thus, rather than organizing personality as a func-tion of theories for the purposes of examining personality and aging, I find it more useful to identify patterns of stability and change for specif-ic personality dimensions. Are there consistent findings in the literature that indicate which aspects of personality are stable and which are malle-able? For an answer, let us turn to the field of personality and aging, where this question has been of primary concern.

PERSONALITY AND AGING

Historical View

The field of personality and aging is relatively young. This may not be surprising when one considers that the predominant personality theory for many years was the psychoanalytic view of Freud. Freud, of course, held that personality was set in plaster by adolescence and there was no way to break the mold, except perhaps with psychoanalysis. When the trait view came into favor in the 1940s and 1950s, the view of a stable person-ality in adulthood was further engrained. Even when the trait view was challenged, it was not the long-term stability that was challenged but the consistency across situations without regard to time. Nothing was special about personality in aging, except for the possibility of senility.

There are at least two sets of circumstances that could have provided the impetus for those interested in aging to study personality. The first is the number of longitudinal studies, like the Berkeley and Fels studies, which had the appropriate data to look at long-term personality stability and change. Studies by Kagan and Moss (1962), Kelly (1955), Maas and Kuypers (1974), and others showed that there was a great deal of stability, but they also found some hints of change. The second circumstance is that personality was, somewhat accidentally, found to play an important mediating role in the aging process (Neugarten, Havighurst, & Tobin, 1968; Reichard, Livson, & Peterson, 1962). Even if personality was stable, the course of aging was seen to vary as a function of personality characteris-tics. For some, happiness in old age was tied to being active, and for others happiness was associated with an inactive lifestyle. These findings

challenged the disengagement and activity theories and led to the formulation of the continuity theory, which implied that there were stable individual differences in personality. In contrast to the disengagement or
activity theories, continuity theory held that successful aging involves the
maintenance of a lifestyle consistent with life-long dispositions. Even if
forced to retire, the older person who is suited to an active lifestyle could
find alternative ways of remaining active.

Another emphasis in the early work on personality and aging was the
study of intrapsychic dimensions inspired by the neo-Freudians (e.g., Jung,
Erikson, Bühler) who postulated lifelong growth. Using projective techniques and in-depth clinical interviews, Neugarten and her colleagues
(Neugarten, 1968; Neugarten & Guttman, 1968) found evidence for intrapsychic changes in later life. For example, they found changes from
active to passive to magical mastery, greater introspection, and a crossover
of sex role behaviors in later life. Butler's (1968) life review was postulated as a universal stage, which could facilitate resolution of intrapsychic
conflicts prior to death. Unfortunately, much of this work was cross-
sectional and has not been replicated.

There have been a number of reviews of the personality and aging field.
The earliest reviews focused on theoretical issues, most likely because there
was little data to discuss (e.g., Havighurst, 1973; Looft, 1973; Neugarten,
1973; Riegel, 1959). It was not until Neugarten's (1977) chapter in the first
volume of the *Handbook of the Psychology of Aging* that we began to see summaries of empirical work in personality and aging. Neugarten began by
saying: "For the reader who comes fresh to the topic of this review, the
first questions are likely to be these: Does aging affect personality? And
does personality affect aging? At a common sense level, the answer to both
of these questions is obviously yes. . . . The problem is that while psychologists 'know' the answers to both these questions, they cannot demonstrate
those answers satisfactorily" (p. 626).

Eight years later in the second edition of the *Handbook of the Psychology
and Aging*, there were several chapters relevant to personality. The one
written by Bengtson, Reedy, and Gordon (1985) corresponds most closely with the topics of Neugarten's chapter. This chapter started with the
following questions: "Does personality change with aging? To what extent
is selfhood 'fixed' by the time individuals reach adulthood? Does negative self-evaluation increase with old age? Whether there are characteristic changes in personality over the life course remains one of the most
enduring puzzles in the social psychology of aging" (p. 544).

So where have we come in eight years? There is evidence for great stability in our research agenda, but there is also some indication of change.
Whereas Neugarten ends with a plea for more research on stability and
change, Bengtson et al. provide a summary of findings on stability and

change from a wide range of studies, and they end with a proposed agenda for clarifying patterns of stability and change. This information can help us to move on beyond the stability-change debate.

Relevance of Stability and Change

Before I summarize what is known about stability and change in personality during adulthood, it is important for us to consider why this information is important for developing theory and research about social structure and personality in aging. The fact that some aspects of the personality are stable in adulthood should not imply that social structure cannot influence the adult personality, but rather that the influences occur early in life and are pervasive throughout the life span. In addition, those aspects of the personality subject to change may be influenced by social structure in later life. It is also useful for us to consider that stable personality dimensions will influence the selection and perception of social environments throughout the life span, and the formation of attitudes. Of course, one reason why some aspects of personality may be stable is because we have chosen and constructed social structures that reinforce or nuture these traits (Costa, & McCrae, 1980; Featherman, 1980).

At this point in time, I hope you are convinced that there is both stability and change in personality and that this has relevance to the study of social structures. Now let us consider the major findings.

Summary of Findings on Stability and Change.   The findings reported in this chapter have been derived from the reviews by Neugarten (1977) and Bengtson et al. (1985). Those dimensions that are largely stable in adulthood are presented in Table 5.1. Because the findings may vary as a function of the type of design, measurement instrument, or change indicator, this information is also presented.

The five major personality traits, identified by Costa and McCrae (1986) — neuroticism, extraversion, openness to experience, conscientiousness, agreeableness — have been studied both cross-sectionally and longitudinally with self-report items. Ratings by significant others have also been gathered for validational purposes. Stability has been found it terms of retest correlations, means, and structure. Other stable dimensions are cognitive style (field dependence) and generalized attitudes toward the self, such as locus of control beliefs.

In contrast, there is evidence of change on a number of dimensions. These are shown in Table 5.2. Intrapsychic variables, domain-specific attitudes, and self-esteem all show evidence of change. For example, in my own work I have found that generalized control beliefs do not show age

TABLE 5.1
Stable Dimensions of the Adult Personality

Dimension	Design[a]	Measure	Change Indicator
Temperament/Traits			
Extraversion, sociability, outgoingness	C-S long. C-S	questionnaire, behavioral questionnaire,	mean, correlational, structural
Neuroticism, adjustment, anxiety	long.	behavioral	mean, correlational, structural
Openness to experience	C-S long.	questionnaire	correlational
Achievement, conscientiousness	C-S long.	questionnaire	mean, correlational
Agreeableness, amiability	C-S long.	questionnaire	mean, correlational
Generalized attitudes toward the self			
Locus of control	C-S long.	questionnaire	mean, correlational
Self-confidence, perceived competence, personal efficacy	C-S long.	questionnaire	mean, correlational
Cognitive style	C-S	ratings, experimental, behavioral	mean, correlational

[a]C-S = cross-sectional; long = longitudinal

differences but that domain-specific forms of control do reflect age differences (Lachman, 1986). Also, the findings do vary somewhat as a function of the design, so longitudinal studies are more likely to show stability and cross-sectional studies are more likely to show age or cohort differences. Moreover, self-report questionnaires are more likely to show stability than projective or open-ended interview techniques. Research on personality stability and change has been largely conducted with cross-sectional designs; thus more longitudinal work is needed.

THE FOCUS OF EXPLANATORY PERSONALITY RESEARCH

To move beyond descriptive studies of stability and change in personality, we need to examine the antecedents and consequences. Kluckhohn and Murray's (1948) classic statement, "Every man is in certain respects like all other men, like some other men, like no other man," (p. 35) sets an agenda for the study of personality in relation to other variables. This goal is to describe and explain the commonalities and uniqueness in individuals.

TABLE 5.2
Dimensions of Personality Subject to Change in Adulthood

Dimension	Design[a]	Measure	Change Indicator
Domain-specific attitudes about the self			
Intellectual control	C-S	questionnaire	mean
Health control	C-S	questionnaire	mean
Intrapsychic variables			
Mastery style	C-S	projective techniques, clinical interviews	mean
Introspection	C-S	projective techniques, clinical interviews	mean
Coping Styles	C-S	questionnaires, clinical interviews	mean
Defenses	C-S	questionnaires, clinical interviews	mean
Values	C-S	questionnaires, clinical interviews	mean
Self-concept	C-S	semantic differential, questionnaire	mean
Masculinity/femininity, sex roles	C-S	projective techniques, open-ended interviews	mean
Self-esteem	C-S	Q-sort, questionnaire	mean
Achievement motivation, aspirations	C-S	questionnaire	mean
Affective variables			
Anxiety	C-S	questionnaire	mean
Depression	C-S	questionnaire	mean
Fatigue	C-S	questionnaire	mean
Well-being	C-S	questionnaire	mean
Life satisfaction	C-S	questionnaire	mean

[a]C-S = cross-sectional

We are all alike in some ways because all members of our species share common biological and environmental factors. We all have the same basic needs and we all experience birth, aging, and death. Some stage theorists, like Erikson (1963), Vaillant (1977), and Levinson (1986), argue that the life-course structure and organization is similar for everyone regardless of social class or culture, although they acknowledge that the specific content and outcomes of lives will vary.

A central focus for the study of social structure and personality is the ways in which we are like some others. We can identify subgroups of people who have similar characteristics and who differ from those in other groups. Academicians are different from corporate executives; Americans differ from Europeans on some dimensions; and the elderly as a group have common features that differentiate them from the young. In addition to a comparison between groups, however, it is also of interest to look for differences within groups. For example, academicians who are psychologists are in some ways different from those who are sociologists or chemists; Americans who are New Yorkers differ from those who are Bostonians — and even their respective sports teams have distinctive characters, as several newscasters pointed out during the 1986 World Series.

Identifying the unique aspects of the individual falls into the realm of clinical psychology. This entails detailed case studies and idiographic work, which can provide rich data about the social-cultural influences on behavior. However, it is difficult to make generalizations from such individualized work. Thus, for our purposes, we focus on the commonalities and differences between and within groups.

Determinants of Personality. Kluckhohn and Murray (1948) delineated four classes of determinants of personality: constitutional, group membership, roles, and situational. These four influences operate both separately and interactively. The first involves the genetic and physiological makeup of the person. There is strong evidence, for example, that temperament has a large genetic component. Sheldon's somatotype theory is a good example of one that emphasizes the constitutional determinants of personality. The latter three influences are particularly relevant to the analysis of social structure.

Members of a group have common personalities because of their similarities in both heredity and environmental factors. Members of the same group are more likely than outsiders to have similar socialization experiences.

All group members also have roles. Individuals conform to the cultural definition of roles such as parent, grandparent, or department chair. We see only the person's public behavior or persona based on the way that person interprets his or her role. The fact that we see behavioral differences across roles should not imply that personality is changing. It is adaptive to behave differently across situations, and roles provide the settings for various expressions of our personality.

Finally, situational influences are occurrences in life that have a profound effect in molding the personality. They may be accidental or non-normative (Baltes, Reese, & Lipsitt, 1980), yet they have a decisive effect. Events such as divorce of one's parents, absence of a father, or death of a mother are situational influences; and their timing in the life span is a crucial element when we assess their impact.

PERSONALITY AND SOCIAL STRUCTURE

There is a long tradition of theory and research on personality and social structure (DiRenzo, 1977). This work has traditionally been carried out by sociologists (e.g., Elder, 1973; House, 1977, 1981; Inkeles, 1971, 1983; Kohn & Schooler, 1983; Smelser & Smelser, 1963). House (1977) identified the area of personality and social structure as one of the three faces of social psychology. A related field is the study of personality and culture or national character, which has primarily been the focus of anthropologists (e.g., Inkeles & Levinson, 1954; LeVine, 1982; Wallace, 1970).

The study of social structure and personality is focused on the relationship of macrosocial variables (e.g., societies, organizations, social class, racial groups); microsocial environments (e.g., job conditions, physical environment, family constellation); and processes (e.g., industrialization, modernization, urbanization, social mobility) to dimensions of the individual personality (values, attitudes, traits, behaviors, motives, needs, feelings, and beliefs). The emphasis is on the identification and definition of social structure variables and the impact these have on personality.

There are a number of classic topics that have been studied in this field. For example, Easterlin (1980) has examined the relationship between size of birth cohort and economic conditions, marital timing, fertility, and sense of well-being. He has contended that those born in a large cohort, such as the baby boomers of the 1940s through the 1960s, are likely to experience more depression and mental illness than those born in a small cohort. Rosenberg and Pearlin (1978) have examined the relationship between social class and self-esteem. Kohn and Schooler (1983) have studied how conditions on the job, such as the self-directedness of one's work, are related to personality variables, such as intellectual flexibility and self-confidence. Inkeles (1983) has studied modernization and its effects on personal adjustment.

There is neither the space nor the need to review this large body of work here. Rather, I would like to raise several issues about the field as a whole. I focus on identifying the mechanisms likely to be involved in linking personality and social structure, especially in aging.

MECHANISMS LINKING PERSONALITY
AND SOCIAL STRUCTURE

There are three issues I would like to raise about the typical approaches to identifying mechanisms in research on social structure and personality: (a) there is little attention given to psychological processes, (b) there is typically a unidirectional focus, and (c) the conceptions are largely static.

Of course, exceptions to these points do exist, and the work of several contributors to this volume (e.g., House, Kohn, Schooler, Featherman, and Riley) qualify as notable exceptions (Featherman, 1983; Riley, 1986).

Universality and Specificity of Social Structure Influences.

A major consideration when identifying underlying mechanisms is to what extent social structures have universal or generalized effects across persons. In contrast, we could ask what role does the individual play in mediating the effects of social structure on personality? Indeed, according to Mortimer, Lorence, and Kumka (1986) the central question for the area of social structure and personality is : "Do environmental conditions, associated with positions in social structure, generally have the same impacts on the individual, or do their effects differ, depending on particular features of the person?" (p. 197). Again, I caution against posing this as an "either-or" question. I argue, first, that the answer depends on the nature of the social conditions we are talking about, and, second, that individuals play an active role in negotiating the effects of social structure.

It is difficult to demonstrate whether any one social structure has a universal effect because individuals exist in multiple social structures simultaneously. Clearly there may be some structures that have a more salient role in determining personality, but their effects are subject to modification as a function of the constellation of structures in an individual's life; therefore, after we get through partialling certain influences, any one may not account for a large amount of variance.

If I use the example of social class, the interesting question for me is not whether or how all people in the lower class are similar to each other and different from those in the middle class, but why some in the lower class manage to move up and defy the odds. In aging, there are numerous findings that show the elderly are, on the average, not as well off as the young. What I find more interesting is to identify those factors that distinguish the elderly who appear like the young from those who show decrements.

To look at homogeneity and variability in the effects of social structure, we need to make both between-group and within-group comparisons. Elder's (1979) work on cohort differences in the timing of the Great Depression, in conjunction with comparisons of males and females and lower- and middle-class people within cohorts, is a good example of this approach. Differences clearly exist between cohorts, but there are many factors that can account for these differences. Also, cohort distributions will show some overlap, and explaining the within-group variability is a useful strategy for pinpointing social structural influences. Because everyone is involved in a constellation of social structures, within-group comparisons help to examine the multiplicity of influences. This serves, in a sense, to hold constant one important factor and to look for other sources of variance.

Strong and Weak Social Structures

What factors will determine the strength of social structure effects and whether they result in universal or variable outcomes? It may be useful to draw a parallel with the principle of strong versus weak situations from interactional psychology (Mischel, 1977; Snyder & Ickes, 1985). When situational cues are strong, there is conformity in behavior. For example, most people will stop at a red light (it is difficult to use this example in Boston; any one who has driven there will understand why). When the role expectations are clear, most everyone conforms to the rules, and we can virtually ignore personality in predicting behavior. In weak situations in which there is less normative information, individual differences will play a major role in determining behavior. For instance, at a yellow light we begin to see more variability; the cautious stop and the daring go through. It is this reasoning that is behind the use of projective techniques in personality assessment. The projective stimulus, an inkblot or TAT card, for example, is vague and ambiguous, so personality will be revealed by the person imposing meaning and structure on the stimuli. There are some common responses, even to ambiguous stimuli (e.g., many people see a bat in the fifth Rorschach card), yet there is enough variability to warrant consideration of individual factors in explaining responses.

What characteristics of social structure are analogous to strong situations? I propose that social structures are strong to the extent that they have clear-cut norms or prescriptions for how to behave. If the guidelines are vague, then individual differences will play a major role in determining behavior.

It is unclear to what extent there are strong social structures, which lead to conformity, in aging. The nursing home is one possible example. Margret Baltes and her colleagues (Barton, Baltes, & Orzech, 1980) found that the staff created strong and clear contingencies in support of dependent behavior, and the frequency of dependent behavior was high. Even if there are such strong situational influences, we can not ignore that social structures (group memberships, roles, and situational influences) interact. An older person born in a large birth cohort is also a member of a social class, lives in a particular type of environment (e.g., community or nursing home; rural or urban setting), has a certain family size, had a certain kind of job experience, may have had a parent die at a young age, may have an ill spouse, and so on. Thus, it is difficult to trace the origins of personality changes to one isolated social structure variable. If we again consider the nursing home, it is important to ask who enters the nursing home in the first place? Do some people foster nurturant behavior more than others? Social psychologist Leslie McArthur (McArthur & Apatow, 1983–84) has found that regardless of actual age, those with babyish faces are judged to be weaker, more submissive, and more dependent than those with more mature faces. Baby-faced elderly adults, then, may elicit more caretaking behavior from others.

Consideration of *how* social structure variables influence personality may shed light on the nature of the effects. Two classes of mediational influences have received attention: (a) interpersonal and (b) psychological or interpretational (Elder, 1973).

Interpersonal Mechanisms

The influences of social structures are channeled through our interactions with others in the same social structure. Kluckhohn and Murray (1948) captured this theme well: "The individual is never directly affected by the group as a physical totality. Rather his personality is molded by the particular members of the group with whom he has personal contact and by his conceptions of the group as a whole" (p. 42). Such a framework acknowledges that there will be individual differences in the effects of social structure. Our identity is tied to our experiences with certain representatives of a group. A tremendous body of work demonstrates that attitudes and stereotypes about groups are formulated on the basis of generalizing from one's limited experience with a subset of the group.

Parents and teachers are the major source of value and attitude transmission in childhood. Attitudes toward the elderly and toward one's own aging, for example, are likely to be formed in childhood. Those children who have more direct contact with older adults may develop more positive attitudes toward the elderly.

Interpretational Mechanisms

Even if we can objectively characterize the social structures in an individual's life, it may not tell us the entire story because individuals vary in the way they interpret their experiences. What for one person may seem like a fortune, for another seems like poverty. Keep in mind W. I. Thomas's (cited in Elder, 1985) dictum: "If men define situations as real, they are real in their consequences." There are a number of psychological positions in which the salience of perceptions and the self-construction of one's life is acknowledged (Ryff, 1984; Thomae, 1970; Whitbourne, 1985).

It is possible to define and to assess characteristics of one's social milieu objectively and reliably. However, any attempt to predict behaviors from environmental characteristics will be limited without also considering individual differences in the interpretation of and reaction to situations. Perceptions are influenced by personality variables including needs, values, goals, motivations, and attitudes. Maslow gave the example of the bakery that we walk by every day and never see until the day we are hungry. I have chosen to focus on two such psychological mechanisms: control beliefs and attributional processes. There is a great deal of research that shows these variables to have behavioral and affective implications for effort, choice, depression, and self-esteem.

Control Beliefs.   Although it may be possible to reach a consensus about which situations and social structures are more controllable than others, we see evidence that individuals vary in the extent to which they believe they can exert control in a given situation, regardless of the true state of affairs. Even when the outcome of a situation appears to be beyond one's control, such as a lottery game, individuals may behave as if they have some control (Langer, 1975). There appear to be strong motivational forces operating to create the belief that we are in control. Because one's beliefs in his or her abilities to control situations have implications for behavior, it is adaptive to know when one does and does not have control, otherwise one may engage in fruitless actions or fail to act when required. The elderly appear to be as accurate and perhaps more realistic in assessments of control than the young. Thus, although we can achieve some degree of accuracy in our predictions about behavior and personal reactions by knowing the objective account of controllability, we are likely to make more accurate predictions about behavior change if we focus on individuals' perceptions of control.

Given that we are motivated to control our destinies, most people are ill-affected by a lack of control. However, some people are able to adjust better to a lack of control than others. It is consistently found that social classes differ in their beliefs about their abilities to control situations (Gurin & Gurin, 1976). Melvin Kohn (1977) has captured this: "The essence of higher class position is the expectation that one's decisions and actions can be consequential; the essence of lower class position is the belief that one is at the mercy of forces and people beyond one's control" (p. 198). Nevertheless, within classes, there are some who respond to this lack of control as a challenge and others who are debilitated by it. Elder (Seligman & Elder, 1986) found that lower-class women from the Berkeley studies were more likely to be debilitated than middle-class women who experienced economic losses in the Great Depression. In the middle class, those who suffered the greatest losses had the highest levels of adaptation in later life. This was not true for the lower class, and Elder suggested that the middle-class women were more likely to rebound because they had more resources available to cope with the losses.

Aging and Control. It has been postulated that control beliefs in later life should diminish due to the numerous constraints and losses that the elderly experience. For example, there is mandatory retirement, death of loved ones, nearness to one's own death, shrinking social network, low status, and lack of respect. However, not everyone responds in the same way to such uncontrollable situations. There are some individuals who cope well with adversity. There are some elderly who despair and give up, and others who accept things the way they are and make the best of it. It is unclear to what extent this attitude or coping style is a lifelong characteristic.

One of the major tasks of late adulthood is to come to grips with the uncontrollable losses. These losses occur both in the person and in the environment. If a person-related loss is uncontrollable, then we must do something to the environment to compensate (Skinner, 1983). Likewise, if something in the environment or social structure is uncontrollable (e.g., mandatory retirement), then the individual must make some changes (e.g., change attitudes about leisure or find substitute activities). As described previously, some people are more prepared than others to cope with a lack of control, and these differences are, in part, due to social structural influences.

One possible definition of successful aging is the ability to achieve a balance between the loss and maintenance of control (Schulz, 1986). Some have argued that it is adaptive to give up some control (Brim, 1974). One way an individual can give up control, while still maintaining a sense of personal efficacy, is to delegate responsibility to others (Lachman, 1986). There is evidence that the elderly may also compensate for a loss of control by readjusting their standards. Thus, the elderly appear to maintain a higher level of personal efficacy; that is, they report being better able to carry out plans and get things done, relative to middle-aged groups. They do so, however, by readjusting, typically by lowering, their level of aspirations (Lachman, 1985).

R. Schulz (1986) and J. Weisz (1986) presented a two-component model of primary and secondary control. Primary control involves the modification of external realities to be consistent with the self. In contrast, secondary control involves changing the self to fit external realities. The older adult may be forced to give up primary control yet can maintain secondary control. If adaptation is a match between person and environment, secondary control is one means of achieving this. As mentioned earlier, Barton et al. (1980) found that nursing home staff members foster dependence and helplessness in their patients and do not reward independence. It is not surprising, then, that among nursing home residents, the happiest are those with an external sense of control (Felton & Kahana, 1974).

Control and Competence.   As mentioned earlier, personality traits guide people to select situations. Internally controlled individuals are more likely to choose situations involving skill, whereas externals prefer situations in which luck determines the outcomes (Phares, 1976). This is likely because internals are more likely to have high performance expectancies in skill situations, and we tend to choose situations in which we expect to succeed (Bandura, 1977). To the extent that situations are seen as under our control, they are likely to have different effects on personality. Rosenberg and Pearlin (1978) suggested that social class has an effect on self-esteem in adulthood but not in childhood because social class is achieved in adulthood but ascribed in childhood. In the work domain, House (1981) has said: "It seems likely that where individuals perceived their occupational conditions as resulting from their own choice, or at least their own responsibility, they are more likely to learn and generalize from those conditions than if they perceived these conditions as having been imposed against their will or efforts" (p. 552). This is in accordance with Bandura's theory, which states that performance outcomes will affect self-efficacy only if they are perceived as within one's control.

Age Differences in Control Beliefs.   There is evidence that the elderly, relative to the young, have a more external control orientation. However, two points need qualification. First, if we take a multidimensional approach to control, we see that externality increases for some, but not for all, dimensions. Second, it is beliefs about control in specific domains and not the generalized sense of control that changes (Lachman, 1986; Rodin, Timko, & Harris, 1985).

Specifically, the elderly believe that they are less in control over their health and their intellectual functioning than the young (Lachman, 1986). These differences are found on external control dimensions (chance, powerful others) but not on internal dimensions (personal efficacy). The age differences in perceptions most likely are consistent with reality. Nevertheless, there are individual differences in control beliefs among the elderly; and greater internal control and lower external control are associated with higher levels of functioning in a wide variety of domains. Thus, control beliefs seem to play an adaptive role for the elderly as they do for younger adults.

Attributional Processes.   The study of attributions is concerned with how we explain outcomes (for a recent review, see Ross & Fletcher, 1985). Control beliefs are related to attributions in that those who have strong internal control beliefs are more likely to make internal attributions. However, the adaptive value of internal attributions differs as a function of whether the outcome is a success or a failure. Making internal attributions for success will increase self-efficacy, whereas making internal attributions for failure will decrease self-efficacy. In addition to the internal–external locus dimension, other components of attributions have been identified: (a) stable–unstable—is the cause permanent or can it be modified? and (b) global–specific—is this cause present in all situations or only in this specific one? (Abramson, Seligman, & Teasdale, 1978; Weiner, 1986). A stable, global, internal attribution for failure, such as lack of ability, can have debilitating consequences; whereas an unstable, specific, internal attribution for failure, such as lack of effort, can have adaptive value.

There is evidence that people engage in a causal analysis of outcomes in the course of their everyday experiences. We are most likely to make causal attributions when the outcome is unexpected or undesirable. For the young, failure is usually unexpected, but for the elderly, failures are often expected whereas successes are not. Thus, making adaptive attributions for success may be critical for the elderly. The attributions we make have consequences for subsequent performance, emotional reactions, and self-concept (Weiner, 1986).

Seligman contended that there is a stable attributional style reflected in a characteristic pattern of explanations for outcomes across situations and time (Seligman & Elder, 1986). A maladaptive or helpless attributional style is one in which failures are attributed to internal, stable, and global causes. In contrast, it is adaptive to attribute successes to such causes. Seligman believed these styles to be formed in response to experiences in early life. In Dweck's (Dweck & Wortman, 1982) studies of children, she identified the helpless types who respond to failure by giving up and the mastery-oriented types who rebound and try harder after failure. Parents and teachers influence our attributional style by the explanations they give us for our successes and failures.

Also, the outcomes associated with uncontrollable events in childhood will tend to influence attributional style in later life. Seligman and Elder (1986) suggested that those who learn to cope with trauma in early life will be immunized against stress; that is, they will be better equipped to handle stressful events later in life. On the other hand, those who fail to cope with trauma in early life will be more susceptible to a helpless explanatory style in later life. To the extent that members of the lower class experience more uncontrollable events in early childhood, they are more prone to develop a helpless attributional style. As to the elderly, they are

likely to experience more uncontrollable events than the young, and therefore, those who have developed a helpless attributional style earlier in
life will be more at risk for depression and other side effects of a helpless
attributional style (e.g., increased health risk, cognitive deficits).

Seligman and Elder (1986) presented convincing data to show that attributional style is predictive of adaption in a variety of domains, including school performance, job success, and health, across the life span. For
example, Seligman and Schulman (1986) found that insurance agents with
an adaptive explanatory style were less likely to quit and more likely to
achieve greater productivity than those with a helpless explanatory style.
These findings point to the important mediating effects of attributions.
All the insurance agents had chosen the same job and had similar job conditions, yet some made it and others did not. It appears that the way in
which these agents construe the causes of their successes and failures has
a major impact on the ultimate outcome.

Age Differences in Attributions.   There is evidence that the elderly, when
compared to the young, are more likely to attribute failure to internal
and stable factors, a characteristic of a helpless style (Blank, 1982; Lachman & McArthur, 1986). However, it is important to keep in mind that
the elderly also make adaptive attributions for successes, which are often
unexpected. In fact, they make stronger internal stable attributions for
success than they do for failure (Lachman & McArthur, 1986). Thus, it
should not be assumed that if one makes internal stable attributions for
failures, one will not also do so for successes. On balance then, the elderly acknowledge their weaknesses but they also take credit for their successes. This is in contrast to younger adults who use an egotistical style
by which they attribute failure externally and successes internally.

As discussed earlier, it is important not only to compare between groups
(young vs. elderly) but also to look within groups. Individual differences
in attributional responses within the elderly group appear to have implications for performance and emotional well-being. The findings of a recent study (Lachman, Steinberg, & Trotter, in press) showed that those
elderly who made more internal, stable, and global attributions for a successful memory performance maintained, and even slightly increased, their
performance over two trials. In contrast, those who made more external,
unstable, and specific attributions for their good memory performance
showed decreases in performance across trials and higher levels of depression. These findings suggest that not taking credit for success can be as
detrimental as blaming oneself for failure.

Not seeing a connection between successful outcomes and one's own
actions is related to the perception of noncontingent reinforcement. If
one does not see a connection between one's efforts or ability and a successful outcome, the motivation to work hard on a task will diminish and

performance will ultimately deteriorate. Skinner (1983) pointed out that we often give noncontingent reinforcement to the elderly by praising them regardless of how well they have performed, and this will inevitably result in lower standards. There is potential danger in creating social structures and environments that make it too "easy" for the older person to succeed without taking an active role. Rather, the elderly should have opportunities for mastery experiences, which show clear contingencies between behaviors and outcomes. In short, we need to facilitate internal, stable attributions for success.

CONCLUSION

Personality in adulthood and old age shows evidence of both stability and change. I have suggested that social structures can be treated as both antecedents and consequences of personality stability and change, and that control beliefs and attributions mediate this relationship.

What attributions are likely to be triggered by the social structures in aging? Which social structures are controllable and which are not? What are the distal and proximal influences on personality in aging? How do stable traits affect the course of aging and the choice of social structures? These are some questions that will require attention in future research, if we are to articulate further the relationship between personality and social structures in aging.

In aging, changing roles, such as becoming a grandparent, may influence personality variables, such as nurturance. And personality variables, such as achievement motivation or self-esteem, may affect the individual's decision to undergo a role change, such as retirement, when there is a choice. When there is some choice involved in a role change, such as retirement, some persons will make internal attributions (e.g., I am no longer a competent worker), and others will make external attributions (e.g., it is to make way for younger workers). These differing attributions are likely to result in different experiences and have different consequences for personality, even though the same event occurs in both cases.

In summary, the central message of this chapter is the need for us to consider both the objective aspects of the social structure and the person's subjective interpretations in tandem. Typically, we study one or the other. I propose that optimal aging entails achievement of a balance between a person's characteristics and the nature of the environment in which he or she exists. Modifications may be required in the actual environment, in the person's way of viewing the self or the environment, or in both, in order for the person to achieve this.

It is often said that sociologists focus on the *what* and psychologists focus on the *how* of human behavior. If we take to heart one of the central messages of this volume—the need for interdisciplinary collaboration— we will be more likely to advance our understanding of both the what and the how of personality and social structures in aging.

REFERENCES

Abramson, L. Y., Seligman, M. E. P., & Teasdale, J. D. (1978). Learned helplessness: Critique and reformulation. *Journal of Abnormal Psychology, 87,* 49–74.
Anastasi, A. (1958). Heredity, environment, and the question "how"? *Psychological Review, 65,* 197–208.
Baltes, P. B., Reese, H. W., & Lipsitt, L. P. (1980). Life-span developmental psychology. *Annual Review of Psychology, 31,* 65–110.
Bandura, A. (1977). Self-efficacy: Toward a unifying theory of behavioral change. *Psychological Review, 84,* 191–215.
Barton, E. M., Baltes, M. M., & Orzech, M. (1980). Etiology of dependence in older nursing home residents during morning care: The role of staff behavior. *Journal of Personality and Social Psychology, 38,* 423–431.
Bengston, V. L., Reedy, M. N., & Gordon, C. (1985). Aging and self-conceptions: Personality processes and social contexts. In J. E. Birren & K. W. Schaie (Eds.), *Handbook of the psychology of aging* (2nd ed., pp. 544–593). New York: Van Nostrand Reinhold.
Blank, T. O. (1982). *A social psychology of developing adults.* New York: Wiley.
Block, J. (1977). Advancing the psychology of personality: Paradigmatic shift or improving the quality of research. In D. Magnusson & N. S. Endler (Eds.), *Personality at the crossroads: Current issues in interactional psychology* (pp. 37–63). Hillsdale, NJ: Lawrence Erlbaum Associates.
Bowers, K. S. (1973). Situationism in psychology: An analysis and a critique. *Psychological Review, 80,* 307–336.
Brim, O. G., Jr. (1974, September). *The sense of personal control over one's life.* Paper presented at the 82nd annual convention of the American Psychological Association, New Orleans.
Butler, R. (1968). The life review: An interpretation of reminiscence in the aged. In B. L. Neugarten (Ed.), *Middle age and aging.* (pp. 486–496). Chicago: University of Chicago Press.
Cattell, R. R. (1965). *The scientific analysis of personality.* Baltimore, MD:
Costa, P. T., Jr., & McCrae, R. R. (1980). Still stable after all these years: Personality as a key to some issues in adulthood and old age. In P. B. Baltes & O. G. Brim, Jr., (Eds.), *Life-span development and behavior* (Vol. 3, pp. 65–102). New York: Academic Press.
Costa, P. T., Jr., & McCrae, R. R. (1986). *The NEO Personality Inventory manual.* Odessa, FL: Psychological Assessment Resources.
DiRenzo, G. J. (1977). Socialization, personality, and social systems. *Annual Review of Sociology, 3,* 261–295.
Dweck, C. S., & Wortman, C. B. (1982). Learned helplessness, anxiety, and achievement motivation: Neglected parallels in cognitive, affective, and coping responses. In H. W. Krohne & L. Laux (Eds.), *Achievement, stress, and anxiety* (pp. 93–125). Washington, DC: Hemisphere.
Easterlin, R. A. (1980). *Birth and fortune: The impact of numbers on personal welfare.* New York: Basic Books.
Elder, G. H., Jr. (1973). On linking social structure and personality. *American Behavioral Scientist, 16,* 785–800.
Elder, G. H., Jr. (1979). Historical change in life patterns and personality. In P. B. Baltes

& O. G. Brim, Jr. (Eds.), *Life-span development and behavior* (Vol 2, pp. 117–159). New York: Academic Press.

Elder, G. H., Jr. (Ed.). (1985). *Life course dynamics: Trajectories and transitions, 1968-1980.* Ithaca, NY: Cornell University Press.

Erikson, E. (1963). *Childhood and society* (2nd ed.). New York: Norton.

Featherman, D. L. (1980). Schooling and occupational careers: Constancy and change in worldly success. In O. G. Brim, Jr., & J. Kagan (Eds.), *Constancy and change in human development* (pp. 675–738). Cambridge, MA: Harvard University Press.

Featherman, D. L. (1983). The life-span perspective in social science research. In P. B. Baltes & O. G. Brim, Jr. (Eds.), *Life-span development and behavior* (Vol. 5, pp. 1–57). New York: Academic Press.

Felton, B., & Kahana, E. (1974). Adjustment and situationally-bound locus of control among institutionalized aged. *Journal of Gerontology, 29,* 295–301.

Gurin, G., & Gurin, P. (1976). Personal efficacy and the ideology of individual responsibility. In B. Strumpel (Ed.), *Economic means for human needs* (pp. 131–157). Ann Arbor, MI: Institute for Social Research.

House, J. S. (1977). The three faces of social psychology. *Sociometry, 40,* 161–177.

House, J. S. (1981). Social structure and personality. In M. Rosenberg & R. H. Turner (Eds.), *Social psychology: Sociological perspectives* (pp. 525–561). New York: Basic Books.

Havighurst, R. J. (1973). History of developmental psychology: Socialization and personality development through the life span. In P. B. Baltes & K. W. Schaie (Eds.), *Life-span developmental psychology: Personality and socialization* (pp. 3–24). New York: Academic Press.

Inkeles, A. (1971). Continuity and change in the interaction of the personal and sociocultural systems. In B. Barber & A. Inkeles (Eds.), *Stability and social change* (pp. 265–281). Boston: Little, Brown.

Inkeles, A. (1983). *Exploring individual modernity.* New York: Columbia University Press.

Inkeles, A., & Levinson, D. J. (1954). National character: The study of modal personality and sociocultural systems. In G. Lindzey (Ed.), *Handbook of social psychology* (Vol. II, pp. 977–1020). Reading, MA: Addison-Wesley.

Kagan, J., & Moss, H. A. (1962). *Birth to maturity.* New York: Wiley.

Kelly, E. L. (1955). Consistency of the adult personality. *American Psychologist, 10,* 659–681.

Kluckhohn, C., & Murray, H. A. (1948). Personality formation: The determinants. In C. Kluckhohn & H. A. Murray (Eds.), *Personality in nature, society, and culture* (pp. 35–48). New York: Knopf.

Kohn, M. L. (1977). *Class and conformity.* Chicago: University of Chicago Press.

Kohn, M. L., & Schooler, C. (1983). *Work and personality: An inquiry into the impact of social stratification.* Norwood, NJ: Ablex.

Lachman, M. E. (1985). Personal efficacy in middle and old age: Differential and normative patterns of change. In G. H. Elder (Ed.), *Life-course dynamics: Trajectories and transitions, 1968-1980* (pp. 188–213). Ithaca, NY: Cornell University Press.

Lachman, M. E. (1986). Locus of control in aging research: A case for multidimensional and domain-specific assessment. *Psychology and Aging, 1,* 34–40.

Lachman, M. E., & McArthur, L. (1986). Adulthood age differences in causal attributions for cognitive, social, and physical performance. *Psychology and Aging, 1,* 127–132.

Lachman, M. E., Steinberg, E. S., & Trotter, S. D. (in press). The effects of control beliefs and attributions on memory self-assessments and performance. *Psychology and Aging.*

Langer, E. J. (1975). The illusion of control. *Journal of Personality and Social Psychology, 32,* 311–328.

LeVine, R. A. (1982). *Culture, behavior, and personality* (2nd ed.). New York: Aldine.

Levinson, D. J. (1986). A conception of adult development. *American Psychologist, 41,* 3–13.

Looft, W. R. (1973). Socialization and personality throughout the life span: An examination of contemporary psychological approaches. In P. B. Baltes & K. W. Schaie (Eds.), *Life-span developmental psychology: Personality and socialization* (pp. 25–52). New York: Academic Press.

Maas, H. S., & Kuypers, J. A. (1974). *From thirty to seventy*. San Francisco: Jossey-Bass.

Magnusson, D., & Endler, N. S. (1977). Interactional psychology: Present status and future prospects. In D. Magnusson & N. S. Endler (Eds.), *Personality at the crossroads: Current issues in interactional psychology* (pp. 3–35). Hillsdale, NJ: Lawrence Erlbaum Associates.

Martin, J. B. (1975). The crowded crossroads. In J. Ertel (Ed.), *The Journal of irreproducible results: Selected papers*. Chicago: J.I.R. Publishers.

Matarazzo, R. G., & Garner, A. M. (1985). Approaches to personality theory. In G. A. Kimble & K. Schlesinger (Eds.), *Topics in the history of psychology* (pp. 331–369). Hillsdale, NJ: Lawrence Erlbaum Associates.

McArthur, L. Z., & Apatow, K. (1983-84). Impressions of baby-faced adults. *Social Cognition, 2*, 315–342.

Mischel, W. (1968). *Personality and assessment*. New York: Wiley.

Mischel, W. (1973). Toward a cognitive social learning reconceptualization of personality. *Psychological Review 80*, 252–283.

Mischel, W. (1977). The interaction of person and situation. In D. Magnusson & N..S. Endler (Eds.), *Personality at the crossroads: Current issues in interactional psychology* (pp. 333–352). Hillsdale, NJ: Lawrence Erlbaum Associates.

Mischel, W. (1986). *Introduction to personality: A new look* (4th ed.). New York: Holt, Rinehart & Winston.

Mortimer, J. T., Lorence, J., & Kumka, D. S. (1986) *Work, family, and personality: Transition to adulthood*. Norwood, NJ: Ablex.

Neugarten, B. L. (Ed.). (1968). *Middle age and aging*. Chicago: University of Chicago Press.

Neugarten, B. L. (1973). Personality changes in late life: A developmental perspective. In C. Eisdorfer & M. P. Lawton (Eds.), *The psychology of adult development and aging*. Washington, DC: American Psychological Association.

Neugarten, B. L. (1977). Personality and aging. In J. E. Birren and K. W. Schaie (Eds.), *Handbook of the psychology of aging* (pp. 626–649). New York: Van Nostrand Reinhold.

Neugarten, B. L., & Gutmann, D. L. (1968). Age-sex roles and personality in middle age: A Thematic Apperception Study. In B. L. Neugarten (Ed.), *Middle age and aging* (pp. 58–71). Chicago: University of Chicago Press.

Neugarten, B. L., Havighurst, R. J., & Tobin, S. S. (1968). Personality and patterns of aging. In B. L. Neugarten (Ed.), *Middle age and aging* (pp. 173–177). Chicago: University of Chicago Press.

Pervin, L. A. (1980). *Personality: Theory, assessment and research*. New York: Wiley.

Phares, E. J. (1976). *Locus of control in personality*. Morristown, NJ: General Learning Press.

Reichard, S., Livson, F., & Petersen, P. G. (1962). *Aging and personality*. New York: Wiley.

Riegel, K. F. (1959). Personality theory and aging. In J. E. Birren (Ed.), *Handbook of aging and the individual* (pp. 797–851). Chicago: University of Chicago Press.

Riley, M. W. (1986). Overview and highlights of a sociological perspective. In A. B. Sorenson, F. E. Weinert, & L. R. Sherrod (Eds.), *Human development and the life course: Multidisciplinary perspectives* (pp. 153–176). Hillsdale, NJ: Lawrence Erlbaum Associates.

Rodin, J., Timko, C., & Harris, S. (1985). The construct of control: Biological and psychological correlates. In C. Eisdorfer, M. P. Lawton, & G. L. Maddox (Eds.), *Annual review of gerontology and geriatrics* (Vol. 5, pp. 3–55). New York: Springer.

Rosenberg, M., & Pearlin, L. I. (1978). Social class and self-esteem among children and adults. *American Journal of Sociology, 84*, 53–77.

Ross, M., & Fletcher, G. J. O. (1985). Attribution and social perception. In G. Lindzey & E. Aronson (Eds.), *The handbook of social psychology* (3rd ed., Vol. II, pp. 883–947). New York: Random House.

Ryff, C. D. (1984). Personality development from the inside: The subjective experience of change in adulthood and aging. In P. B. Baltes & O. G. Brim, Jr. (Eds.), *Life-span development and behavior* (pp. 1979–1985). New York: Academic Press.

Schulz, R. (1986). Successful aging: Balancing primary and secondary control. In J. Karuza, Jr. (Ed.), Psychosocial issues in successful aging: A change in focus. *American Psychological Association Newsletter, 13*, 2–3.

Seligman, M. E. P., & Elder, G. H., Jr. (1986). Learned helplessness and life-span development. In A. B. Sorenson, F. E. Weinert, & L. R. Sterrod (Eds.), *Human development and the life course: Multidisciplinary perspectives* (pp. 377–428). Hillsdale, NJ: Lawrence Erlbaum Associates.

Seligman, M. E. P., & Schulman, P. (1986). Explanatory style as a predictor of productivity and quitting among life insurance sale agents. *Journal of Personality and Social Psychology, 50*, 832–838.

Skinner, B. F. (1983). Intellectual self-management in old age. *American Psychologist, 38*, 238–244.

Smelser, N. J., & Smelser, W. T. (Eds.). (1963). *Personality and social systems*. New York: Wiley.

Snyder, M., & Ickes, W. (1985). Personality and social behavior. In G. Lindzey & E. Aronson (Eds.), *The handbook of social psychology* (3rd ed., Vol. II, pp. 883–947). New York: Random House.

Thomae, H. (1970). Theory of aging and cognitive theory of personality. *Human Development, 13*, 1–16.

Vaillant, G. E. (1977). *Adaptation to life*. Boston: Little, Brown.

Wallace, A. F. C. (1970). *Culture and personality* (2nd ed.). New York: Random House.

Weiner, B. (1986). Attribution, emotion, and action. In R. M. Sorrentino & E. T. Higgins (Eds.), *Handbook of motivation and cognition* (pp. 281–312). New York: Guilford.

Weisz, J. R. (1986). Understanding the developing understanding of control. In M. Perlmutter (Ed.), *Cognitive perspectives on children's social and behavioral development. The Minnesota Symposium on Child Psychology* (Vol. 18, pp. 219–278). Hillsdale, NJ: Lawrence Erlbaum Associates.

Whitbourne, S. K. (1985). The psychological construction of the life span. In J. Birren & K. W. Schaie (Eds.), *Handbook of the psychology of aging* (2nd ed., pp. 594–618). New York: Van Nostrand.

Comments on Lachman's "Personality and Aging at the Crossroads"

Susan Krauss Whitbourne
University of Massachusetts at Amherst

Dr. Lachman's chapter provides us with an intriguing set of ideas concerning the interface between personality and social structure in adulthood. She responds to the challenge facing the personality and aging literature with insightful suggestions about how the issue of stability versus change in adult personality can be more profitably addressed. I have chosen to direct my comments on Dr. Lachman's chapter to the implicit model of the personality–social structure interaction that she has proposed. Specifically, I suggest that the individual's interpretational processes emerge from the "core identity," the underlying layers of the individual's conscious experience of the self. I attempt to show how the core identity forms the primary source of the interpretational processes that Dr. Lachman has convinced us are so critical for determining the individual's adaptation to the aging process.

The model of the personality–social structure interaction in adulthood, as described by Dr. Lachman, can be characterized according to the diagram presented in Fig. 1.

This model portrays interpretational processes as the product of the joint contribution of the individual's personality, health, and social environment. The interpretational processes are beliefs about control and attributions about causality. Dr. Lachman has shown how these processes are influenced by the individual's personality, particularly by the individual's stable dispositions and values. The changeable features of the individual's personality, such as specific attitudes and self-esteem, are in turn influenced by the outcome of the individual's interpretations of given events and circumstances. Dr. Lachman also quite accurately includes health as a factor that interacts with personality and social structure in

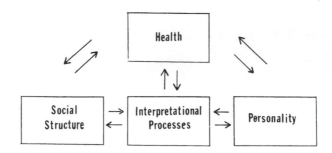

FIG. 1 Lachman's model of the interaction between personality and social structure

adulthood. This factor becomes particularly important in cases when the individual must cope with deleterious age changes in physiological functioning in addition to the losses associated with chronic physical illness. The individual's strategies for coping with these limitations are influenced by personality as well as by available social resources. The physical health of the older person may, in turn, be influenced by the particular compensatory strategies that he or she has chosen to follow. Finally, the social structure serves to define the limits of the individual's attempts to cope with the aging process. However, as Dr. Lachman has pointed out, the effects of the social structure on personality are mediated by the individual's interpretations of that structure and by the role or roles upon which the individual chooses to focus.

I find this transactional kind of model to be a useful way of approaching the complex feedback loops that characterize the relationships between the aging individual and the social structure. It is particularly valuable when seen in the fourth dimension; that is, as a process that occurs over time. I would like to add to Dr. Lachman's portrayal of the relationship between the individual and society by elaborating on her ideas regarding the distinction between stable and changing dimensions within the adult personality. I think that this is indeed a crucial distinction, and an understanding of its implications can clarify further the relationship of adults to the in social contexts.

The direction I pursue in following the change-stability distinction is given impetus by Dr. Lachman's observations about the inadequacy of psychodynamic theory in defining the adult personality. Like many life-span developmental psychologists, Dr. Lachman has criticized the psychodynamic model because it is focused so exclusively on early personality development. Dr. Lachman is quite correct in asserting that Freudian and neo-Freudian psychoanalytic theory regard personality as essentially fixed by the end of childhood, if not before. However, I am not so sure that this position is all that different from the contemporary views about stability in personality from childhood to adulthood (Moss & Sussman, 1980) and across adulthood (Conley, 1985; Costa, McCrae, & Arenberg, 1983). As Dr. Lachman points out in her summary of research on personality develop-ment, basic dispositions, temperament, and values are relatively stable from childhod, through adolescence, and even well into adulthood. The empirical data, then, actually bear out quite well what Freud and his fol-lowers had speculated from their clinical cases.

An even stronger argument can be made if we consider the "data" of contemporary psychoanalytic theory regarding adult personality develop-ment. Although there is no one accepted model within this discipline, there seems to be general agreement (e.g., Eagle, 1984) that basic attitudes toward the self and the world are formed within the first few months of life. Many modern analytic thinkers no longer regard the Oedipal complex as the basic paradigm for personality development. The versions of Freudian theory as they have evolved today place far less emphasis on instinctual drives and instead focus on the child's relationships with significant others, what psychoanalysts call "objects." On this basis, current psychoanalytic theory lays out a reasonably coherent framework from which we can un-derstand the origins of personality structure in early childhood, which has clear implications for adult development.

In its most general form, object relations theory proposes a sequence of steps in the child's relationships to parents through which the child develops a psychological self as well as an understanding of "reality" in the outside world. One requirement for healthy personality functioning that emerges from this process is that the individual sees himself or her-self as separate from the other people in his or her environment. The second requirement is that the individual develops an inner self-repre-sentation that captures his or her unique constellation of personal attrib-utes. Thirdly, the self must be cohesive enough to give the person a sense of continuity over time. Because the child's ideas about the self develop-ment in the context of object relationships, the self always has within it an interpersonal element. Images of the parents within the child's inner world are the starting point for the components of the self.

In developing his psychoanalytic self-psychology, Heinz Kohut (1971, 1977) has probably given the greatest attention among object relations theorists to the manifestations in the adult personality of early events in the development of the self. According to Kohut (1977), it is critical that the individual emerge from adolescence with a cohesive self in order to have the inner strength and integrity to withstand the vicissitudes of adult life experiences and the aging process. The child's parents mirror back to the child his or her intrinsic competence, lovingness, and goodness, which forges the child's cohesive self.

In proposing that we look to psychoanalytic theory for ideas about nor-mal adult development, I realize that I run the risk of overgeneralizing from clinical cases selected by proponents of the theory to bolster their

own positions. However, I believe that this theory offers a set of reasonable hypotheses about why some features of adult personality have stability over time. These hypotheses can then be tested as to their applicability
to the population of "normal" adults. Without such a test, we on the normal personality side of the issue are just as narrow-minded as we claim
the psychoanalysts to be in their position.

Given this caveat, I would like to examine the overlap between object
relations theory and research on life-span personality development. There
is a striking similarity between the orientations to the world thought to
be acquired through object relationships and the enduring dimensions
of personality identified in follow-up research on attachment in infancy
(Thompson & Lamb, 1986); on infant temperament (Thomas & Chess,
1984); and on adult neuroticism, extraversion, and experiential openness
(Costa & McCrae, 1980). These are the stable dimensions that Dr. Lachman suggests underly the adult's experiences in the social environment.
Object relations theory suggests a set of processes that would account for
the persistence over life of a disposition that is either confident and optimistic, or insecure and pessimistic. The attitude of parents toward the
child would, according to this theory, be translated into the individual's
relationship to the self as an object (Bollas, 1982). The child with harshly
critical parents will be overly demanding of himself or herself as an adult.
The child whose parents temper their demands with the child's ability to
meet them will be self-accepting. Creativity and spontaneity would characterize the adult whose parents encouraged him or her to develop unique
talents and ideas about life.

What object relations theory adds to the view of personality adopted
in the field of adult personality development is the possibility of an underlying layer of the individual's experience of the self. This is what I believe is missing from feedback models such as that proposed by Dr.
Lachman, although its existence appears to be implied in her notions of
personality stability. The individual's interpretations of social structure,
health, and his or her own behavior have to originate from somewhere.
Otherwise, the model is totally recursive, revolving around an endless series of person–environment interactions. Because we are studying a temporal process, I believe it is safe to make some assumptions about the
direction of causality in development. That is what I propose to do in
the remainder of my comments.

The point of origin for understanding the relationship between the
individual and the social structure over the course of adulthood is what
I call the "core identity." This identity is the abstract distillation of the
individual's early experiences with parenting figures. It contains the individual's central or pivotal feelings and ideas about the self. These components are analogous to core "hypotheses" (Epstein, 1973) or "schemata"
(Markus, 1983) that others have identified in the self-concept. In my model,

identity is the crucial psychological variable. Identity conveys the notion of continuity, individuality, and cohesiveness; attributes that are not necessarily implied in the definition of self-concept. Identity is thus a more appropriate construct to use before examining developmental processes in the individual's self-representations.

The psychoanalytic perspective has provided me with the beginning of answers to the questions raised in my own research on adult identity (Whitbourne, 1986). I have been struck by the extent to which normal mentally healthy adults use what clinicians would call defense mechanisms; what I have called "identity assimilation processes." That is, adults will go to almost any length, no matter how illogical, to preserve the impression that they are competent at work, loving toward family, and faithful in adhering to a solid code of ethics. However, they are not aware of using these assimilation processes. The existence of these processes can only be inferred in a manner analogous to the clinician's use of the "third ear." Kohut's (1971, 1977) theory suggests a motivation behind the adult's use of identity assimilation processes. To admit to weaknesses in any of these features of adult identity is tantamount to blowing apart the very foundations upon which the individual's entire approach to life has been constructed. The position that adults strive to maintain as cohesive an identity as possible over time also tells us that the individual's relationships to society is based upon interpretation processes.

Thus, normal nondepressed adults will attempt to preserve a stable, positive, and cohesive identity throughout the vicissitudes of bodily changes and life experiences in adulthood. Depessed adults will engage in the opposite set of processes, using identity assimilation to maintain their negative identities (Pietromonaco & Markus, 1985). However, it is also critical for adults to be able to adjust their identities when counterevidence regarding their identities based on experiences too incongruous for them to assimilate. For normal adults, these experiences would highlight their weaknesses, failures, and inadequacies. I have called this process of adjustment "identity accommodation." Feelings of well-being and adjustment will accompany the state of balance between identity processes only when the individual is neither overly assimilating nor overly accommodating to the experiences of adult life.

Reframing Dr. Lachman's ideas about personality and social structure in these terms leads to the model illustrated in Fig. 2. The presumed origin of the core identity is in the interaction among the unique qualities of the individual present at birth, particularly the interaction between temperament and responsiveness (Thomas & Chess, 1984). The parents respond to these qualities of the infant and also introduce their own needs and ideas about the child into the situation. At this point in life, the individual's position in the social structure can influence personality development inasmush as the parents have resources, expectations about

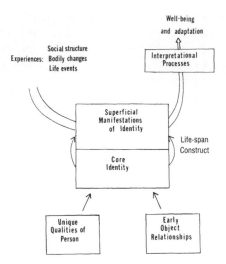

FIG. 2 Model of interpretational processes as embedded in the matrix of identity

the child, and knowledge about parenting, all of which are specific to their social class. However, after the core identity is formed, it becomes an underpinning of the individual's personality that is relatively impermeable to social structure, or any other experiences for that matter. The only experiences that can permeate the core identity would be severely traumatic ones (Janoff-Bulman & Frieze, 1983) or intensive psychotherapy (Kohut, 1982).

The influence of the core identity on the adult's conscious awareness about the self is exerted indirectly in the translation of the core constructs about the self into more ephemeral, transient ideas about the individual's specific competencies in various realms of adult life. It is in this surface manifestation of identity that experiences pass to exert their influence on the individual. These experiences include social structural variables, such as income, education, ethnicity, family life transitions, and random life events. As these pass through identity, their interpretation is influenced by the individual's assimilative processes. However, the individual's superficial layer of identity can change as a result of identity accommodation if this is necessary to maintain a realistic relationship to the environment.

In Fig. 2, I have proposed that the translation from core identity into superficial manifestations of identity is accomplished via the individual's ideas about his or her life span as a totality. The "life-span construct" is the concept I have used (Whitbourne, 1985) to describe the adult's projections about the future and recollection about the past. These goals for the future and memories of the past are hypothesized to be formulated in terms of identity. Thus, the young person constructs a "scenario" of life whose form and content is based on the expectations derived from his or her identity. The young person sets goals that fit his or her ideas; these ideas are consistent with the parts of identity that he or she would like to implement. The older adult weaves a "life story" that involves reconstructions of the past tailored to fit his or her identity, emphasizing those features that he or she regards as desirable and downplaying others that would have unfavorable connotations. As I am conceptualizing identity now in terms of a core that underlies a set of superficial manifestations, the life-span construct provides a crucial bridge. It is through this construct that the individual's most central feelings and ideas about the self achieve their expression in directly observable features of adult identity as it is played out in everyday life. Adults who were made to feel loving by their own parents have a solid and cohesive conception of themselves, which becomes translated into a life-span construct organized around family. As young people, they project a scenario that incorporates this identity, and when they are old they retell their life stories in terms of their spouses, children, and grandchildren.

Now I have arrived at the point in the model where the specific interpretational mechanisms proposed by Dr. Lachman come into play. As you can see from Fig. 2, I characterize the individual's feelings of control and attributions about the causes of significant life events as a joint product of identity and experiences. The kinds of experiences that stimulate these mechanisms can involve social phenomena and changes in the body's functioning due to aging and/or illness. However, it is the interpretations that individuals make of these experiences that determine the impact of the experiences on well-being and adaptation. An individual whose core identity is secure and cohesive will take a more sanguine attitude toward the potential threats of aging than an individual whose core identity has major areas of weakness. The secure core identity will allow the individual to make negative attributions about the self in a nondefensive fashion. The weak core identity requires defensive protection above all other costs. The well-being of such an individual is predicated on maintenance of the belief that bad events in important life areas are outside the realm of control and good events result from personal effort.

The model I am presenting in this discussion suggests that developmental processes are built into the very foundation of identity, and this core identity is what allows the individual to feel continuous over time and across situations. The concept of life-span development is also built into the transformation of the "deep structure" of identity into its "surface structure," to borrow a metaphor from Chomsky. I hope that my attempt to integrate psychoanalytic theory into concepts of life-span development involving the individuals' relationship to experience adds a useful perspective to Dr. Lachman's concepts of interpretative mechanisms as mediators of personality and social structure. The application of psychodynamic theory to processes of life-span development represented here is consistent with what seems to be a revitalized focus in psychoanalytic theory upon questions regarding the self, continuity over time, and existential issues involved in aging (e.g., Mann, 1985; Shenfield, 1984–1985). Perhaps attention to these issues can help move the personality and aging field to a point where the stability versus change issue is finally transcended and we can focus our attention upon the lifelong processes of the growth of the self.

REFERENCES

Bollas, C. (1982). On the relation to the self as an object. *International Journal of Psychoanalysis, 63,* 347–359.

Conley, J. J. (1985). Longitudinal stability of personality traits: A multitrait-multimethod-multioccasion analysis. *Journal of Personality and Social Psychology, 49,* 1266–1282.

Costa, P. T. Jr., & McCrae, R. R. (1980). Still stable after all these years: Personality as a key to some issues in adulthood and old age. In P. B. Baltes (Ed.), *Life-span development and behavior* (Vol. 3, pp. 65–102). New York: Academic Press.

Costa, P. T. Jr., McCrae, R. R., & Arenberg, D. (1983). Recent longitudinal research on personality and aging. In K. W. Schaie (Ed.), *Longitudinal studies of adult psychological development* (pp. 222–265). New York: Guilford.

Eagle, M. N. (1984). *Recent developments in psychoanalytic theory.* New York: McGraw-Hill.

Epstein, S. (1973). The self-concept revisited: Or a theory of a theory. *American Psychologist, 28,* 404–416.

Janoff-Bulman, R., & Frieze, I. H. (1983). A theoretical perspective for understanding reactions to victimization. *Journal of Social Issues, 39,* 1–17.

Kohut, H. (1971). *The analysis of the self.* New York: International Universities Press.

Kohut, H. (1977). *The reconstruction of the self.* New York: International Universities Press.

Kohut, H. (1982). *How does analysis cure?* Chicago: University of Chicago Press.

Mann, C. H. (1985). Aging—a developmental reality ignored by psychoanalytic theory. *Journal of the American Academy of Psychoanalysis, 13,* 481–487.

Moss, H. A., & Susman, E. J. (1980). Longitudinal study of personality development. In J. Kagan & O. G. Brim, Jr. (Eds.), *Constancy and change in development* (pp. 530–595). Cambridge, MA: Harvard University Press.

Markus, H. (1983). Self-knowledge: An expanded view. *Journal of Personality, 51,* 543–565.

Pietromonaco, P. R., & Markus, H. (1985). The nature of negative thoughts in depression. *Journal of Personality and Social Psychology, 48,* 799–807.

Shenfield, M. E. (1984–85). The developmental course of defense mechanisms in later life. *International Journal of Aging and Human Development, 19,* 55–71.

Thomas, A., & Chess, S. (1984). Genesis and evolution of behavioral disorders from infancy to early life. *American Journal of Psychiatry, 141,* 1–9.

Thompson, R. A., & Lamb, M. E. (1986). Infant–mother attachment: New directions for theory and research. In P. B. Baltes, D. L. Featherman, & R. M. Lerner (Eds.), *Life-span development and behavior* (Vol. 7, pp. 1–41). Hillsdale, NJ: Lawrence Erlbaum Associates.

Whitbourne, S. K. (1985). The life-span construct as a model of adaptation in adulthood. In J. E. Birren & K. W. Schaie (Eds.), *Handbook of the psychology of aging* (2nd ed.). New York: Van Nostrand Reinhold.

Whitbourne, S. K. (1986). *The me I know: A study of adult identity.* New York: Springer-Verlag.

Comments on Lachman's "Personality and Aging at the Crossroads"

Melvin L. Kohn
The Johns Hopkins University

Early in her chapter, Margie Lachman states that there are four themes she wishes to highlight. My commentary is in the form of a dialogue with her, addressed to these four themes.

THEME 1: SOME PERSONALITY DIMENSIONS ARE LARGELY STABLE AND UNCHANGEABLE AND OTHERS ARE SUBJECT TO CHANGE IN ADULTHOOD AND OLD AGE

Stable versus changing personality dimensions is an important point, and Dr. Lachman develops the theme well. Still, there is a serious flaw in the formulation.

Before dealing with this flaw head on, I want to take you a short way down the garden path by noting that most studies seriously understate the stability of personality, because they do not take unreliability of measurement into account. This necessarily means that they do not take into account that errors of measurement are correlated in repeated measurement of the same dimensions of personality. Thus, to take the prime example from Carmi Schooler's and my research (Kohn & Schooler 1978), the 10-year overtime correlation of adult men's ideational flexibility, conventionally measured by ordinary factor analysis, is 0.57; but when unreliability of measurement is taken into account, the 10-year overtime correlation of ideational flexibility turns out to be 0.93. More generally, most dimensions of personality are much more stable than the research literature, which has only recently begun to take measurement error seriously, would lead you to believe.

I would therefore seem to be arguing the "stable and unchangeable" side of Lachman's formulation. No such thing! I told you I would lead you a little way down the garden path. I believe that equating "stable" and "unchangeable" is a profoundly erroneous formulation of the problem. Equally erroneous is the second part of Lachman's statement: "The fact that some aspects of the personality are stable in adulthood should not imply that social structure cannot influence the adult personality [which is correct thus far], but rather that the influences occur early in life and are pervasive throughout the life span." Stability of personality in adult life says *nothing* about whether the influences occurred "early in life" or later; Lachman is right, though, in her concluding phrase about the influences being "pervasive throughout the life span" or, more precisely, throughout that portion of the life span actually studied in the research, I say this with some vehemence because it took me nearly a decade of struggling with the problem before I realized what now seems to me to be a self-evident truth.

In 1978 when Schooler and I published our first longitudinal analysis of job conditions and personality, we realized that unless our longitudinal measurement models, *both* of job conditions *and* of personality, took measurement error into account, our causal analyses would be altogether misleading. If, for example, we assessed the impact of the substantive complexity of work on ideational flexibility, using 0.57 as our estimate of the overtime correlation of ideational flexibility when that correlation really is 0.93, most of the causal influence we would be attributing to the complexity of work would really reflect, not the impact of work on personality but noise in our measurement of personality.

But then we faltered. Having recognized the importance of correctly assessing the overtime correlation of ideational flexibility, we misformulated the causal question, as follows: "The question for causal analysis is whether, despite this overall stability, there has been enough individual change for job conditions to have had much of an effect" (Kohn & Schooler 1978, p. 39). We assumed that job conditions — which I use in this discussion as illustrative of all social structural conditions — matter only for explaining change in personality. A fundamental error! Social structure can explain not only *change* but also *stability* or *maintenance* of personality. Put more generally: Because some facet of personality is highly stable over time doesn't mean that it's built into the wiring system, or that it's set, once and for all, in childhood or adolescence. Stability doesn't mean "unproblematic" and, absent experimental evidence, it certainly doesn't mean "unchangeable." To say that some facet of personality is highly stable does not answer the question of whether this facet of personality is affected by social structure. It only poses the question: *Why* is this facet of personality so stable?

In the case of ideational flexibility, Schooler's and my analyses demonstrated *part* of the answer: The substantive complexity of men's work has a profound influence on their ideational flexibility—and the substantive complexity of people's jobs tends not to change very much once people get established in their occupational careers. More generally, our analyses (Kohn & Schooler 1982) demonstrate that job conditions affect many facets of personality; that job conditions tend to be stable; and that this is part of the reason why personality tends to be stable. More generally still, the issue of the relationship between social structure and personality is not answered—it isn't even properly addressed—by our learning how stable is personality. Accurate assessments of the stability of personality are essential, not for answering questions, but for tooling up before one can even begin to address the real questions.

THEME 2: SOCIAL STRUCTURES CAN BE EXAMINED BOTH AS ANTECEDENTS AND CONSEQUENCES OF PERSONALITY CHANGE AND STABILITY

I am in wholehearted agreement with the spirit of this theme. In fact, if I were to make a single overarching empirical generalization from what Schooler and I have found (Kohn & Schooler 1983) in 20 years of research, it is that the relationship between work and personality is quintessentially reciprocal.

Yet, I have difficulty with the precise statement of the theme. If by social structure Lachman means, as her text implies, the larger structures of the society—class, stratification, occupational structure, the major institutions of the society—then "personality" can hardly affect social structure, except in the vague sense that social structures can be affected by the average or "modal" personalities of the members of the society. I don't think she means that. And I hope she doesn't mean that large-scale social structures, for example, the class structure of the society, really can be modified by any single individual's personality. I think and hope she means not that personality affects social structure but that the individual's personality affects his or her *position in* that social structure. If so, I not only agree, but Schooler and I have presented solid evidence to demonstrate that this is indeed the case.

THEME 3: SUBJECTIVE INTERPRETATIONS OF OUTCOMES (ESPECIALLY CONTROL BELIEFS AND CAUSAL ATTRIBUTIONS) ARE CRUCIAL FOR UNDERSTANDING THE MECHANISMS THAT LINK SOCIAL STRUCTURES AND PERSONALITY

Subjective interpretations of outcomes coupled with linking mechanisms is a very interesting idea. I'm certain that at a sufficiently high level of abstraction it must be true that "interpretations of outcomes" play an important part in the social psychology of social structure. Lachman quotes an earlier statement of mine about the relevance of "control beliefs" (her term, not mine) in understanding the effects of social class on values and orientations; I still believe what I then wrote.

Unfortunately, however, this says nothing about *mechanisms*. When it comes to discussing the actual mechanisms by which social structure affects personality, Lachman talks mainly about interpersonal relations, as is the wont of social psychologists. She states it baldly: "The influences of social structures are channeled through interactions with others in the same social structure." She even quotes the social psychological bible, by Kluckhohn and Murray (1948), to the effect that, "The individual personality is never directly affected by the group as a physical totality. Rather his personality is molded by the particular members of the group with whom he has personal contact and by his conceptions of the group as a whole" (p. 42). Applied to face-to-face groups, this statement may well be true. Applied to larger social structures, this statement is decidedly questionable. I do not see the evidence for the primacy of face-to-face "interactions with others" as an explanation of the relationship between social structure and personality. Rather, I see Lachman's formulation as nine-tenths disciplinary faith, a faith shared by psychologists and sociologists, and one-tenth empirical evidence, most of which turns out to be ephemeral when closely examined. I overstate my argument deliberately, because it is so difficult to shake social psychologists out of the misconception that "social psychology" and "face-to-face interactions" are equivalent ways of saying the same thing. It is only a hypothesis, not a received truth, that the mechanisms by which social structure affect personality are primarily "interpersonal" or "interactional" or "face to face."

By contrast, I place my money on an alternative hypothesis—that social structures are more than small groups writ large. I see considerable evidence for other mechanisms that link social structure to personality, mechanisms that Lachman totally ignores. From Schooler's and my research on work and personality, I would extrapolate:

1. Social structure matters for personality—for cognitive functioning, for values, for self-conceptions, for social orientations—mainly because position in the larger social structure greatly affects more proximate conditions of life. As I put it a quarter of a century ago in talking about social class: "Members of different social classes, by virtue of enjoying (or suffering) different conditions of life, come to see the world differently—to de-

velop different conceptions of social reality, different aspirations and hopes and fears, different conceptions of the desirable" (Kohn 1963, p. 471). I focus on conditions of life, not on standards of comparison, feelings of status, or interpersonal relationships. These may matter too, but I put the emphasis on the concrete realities of life, the conditions under which people live, the experiences that shape their thoughts and feelings. Some of these experiences are interpersonal, "face to face"; many are not.

2. The principal reason why these proximate conditions of life affect personality—I hesitate to say it out loud, it's so obvious—is because people *learn* from their experiences and *generalize* the lessons learned in one realm of life to other realms as well.

Let me put it in terms of what we know about the effects of job conditions on adult personality (Kohn & Schooler 1983). There is accumulating evidence to show that job conditions affect adult personality mainly through a direct process of learning and generalization—learning from the job and generalizing what has been learned to other realms of life. Although such indirect processes as compensation and reaction-formation may also contribute to the effects of work on adult personality, the learning–generalization process is of predominant importance. Thus, people who do intellectually demanding work come to exercise their intellectual prowess not only on the job but also in their nonoccupational lives; they even seek out intellectually demanding activities in their leisure time pursuits. More generally, people who do self-directed work come to value self-direction more highly, both for themselves and for their children, and to have self-conceptions and social orientations consonant with such values. In short, the lessons of work are directly carried over to nonoccupational realms. All these findings are consistent with the theoretical expectation that "transfer of learning" extends to a wide spectrum of psychological functioning. The findings also are consistent with the fundamental sociological premise that experience in so central a domain of life as work must affect orientations to and behavior in other domains as well.

I must quickly acknowledge that we know very little about this learning–generalization process. It's a black box. But at least we have good, solid evidence that it's the right black box. Probably not the only black box, but an important one—important enough to study, and study hard. I would much rather invest my research energies here than go on endlessly believing as a matter of faith that the key to the relationship of social structure and personality must lie, somehow, in face-to-face interpersonal relationships.

THEME 4: SUCCESSFUL AGING CAN BE
CHARACTERIZED AS A MATCH BETWEEN
THE CHARACTERISTICS OF THE INDIVIDUAL
AND THE NATURE OF THE ENVIRONMENT
AND SOCIAL STRUCTURES

Maybe successful aging does come down to a match. On this, I'm no expert. Moreover, I'm not sure what "successful" aging really means. In any case, I don't see the evidence. And similar formulations in other realms, for example, the so-called "fit" hypothesis, which posits that job conditions affect personality differentially, depending on the fit (or match) of those job conditions with the needs, values, and capacities of the individual, turn out, in my judgment, to have more a priori plausibility than empirical support. But still, maybe.

What puzzles me here, however, is that this fourth theme does not address what I see as the crucial "aging" issue in the relationship of social structure and personality: Does social structure have similar or dissimilar impact on personality at different ages, or stages of life course, or stages of career? Joanne Miller, Kazimierz Slomczynski, and I (1985) posed the issue as follows:

> Recent work in developmental and social psychology suggests that learning, particularly as represented in 'crystallized' (or synthesized) intelligence, continues throughout the life span. In principle, since 'transfer of learning' is 'an essential characteristic of the learning process,' not only initial learning but also the generalization of what has been learned should continue as [people] grow older. It is nevertheless possible that learning–generalization does not occur at the same rate or to the same extent at all ages. The process may be especially pronounced in younger [people], who are at early stages of their occupational careers, before they are preoccupied with family responsibilities, but may diminish as [people] grow older, advance in their careers, and have changing family responsibilities. It is also possible that either learning or generalization diminishes as [people] grow older, simply because of biological decrements. To see whether learning and the generalization of learning continue unabated throughout adult life requires an analysis of how [social structural] conditions affect the psychological functioning of [people] at different ages, or stages of career, or stages of life course. (p. 594)

We did one such analysis, a cross-national analysis for Poland and the United States, on the impact of job conditions on intellective process for younger, middle-aged, and older men. The main conclusion of this research was that job conditions affect intellective process of older men just as much as that of younger men. In particular, job conditions facilitative of the exercise of self-direction in work continue to enhance ideational flexibility and an open-minded, nonauthoritarian orientation, even in the oldest segment of the work force; that is, among men aged 46 to 65, in both the United States and Poland. In fact, we found a notable continuity not only in the effects of job conditions on intellective process but also in the effects of intellective process on job conditions.

I think that our findings argue strongly for the continuity of the learning–generalization process, regardless of the age of the worker and, by extrapolation, regardless of stage of career and stage of life course. Still, one analysis, even when done comparatively for the United States and Poland, is hardly definitive, particularly because we could not differentiate age groups from cohorts defined on the basis of stage of career or of life course. My argument is not that we have definitively resolved the issue but that we have at least addressed the right issue. That issue, to put it in a nutshell, is whether conditions of life impinge differently on personality at different stages of the life course. If they do, then of course there is the further question: *Why* do they impinge differently? And through what mechanisms? which of course brings us right back to the core questions of this book.

REFERENCES

Kluckhohn, C., & Murrary, H. A. (1948). Personality formation: The determinants. In C. Kluckhohn & H. A. Murrary (Eds.), *Personality in nature, society, and culture* (pp. 35–48). New York: Knopf.

Kohn, M. L. (1963). Social class and parent–child relationships: An interpretation. *American Journal of Sociology, 68*, 471–480.

Kohn, M. L., & Schooler, C. (1978). The reciprocal effects of the substantive complexity of work and intellectual flexibility: A longitudinal assessment. *American Journal of Sociology, 84*, 24–52.

Kohn, M. L., & Schooler, C. (1982). Job conditions and personality: A longitudinal assessment of their reciprocal effects. *American Journal of Sociology, 87*, 1257–1286.

Kohn, M. L., & Schooler, C. (1983). *Work and personality: An inquiry into the impact of social stratification.* Norwood, NJ: Ablex.

Miller, J., Slomczynski, K. M., & Kohn, M. L. (1985). Continuity of learning-generalization: The effect of job on men's intellective process in the United States and Poland. *American Journal of Sociology, 91*, 593–615.

A Life-Course Approach to Gender, Aging, and Intergenerational Relations

Alice S. Rossi
Social and Demographic Research Institute,
University of Massachusetts (Amherst)

INTRODUCTION

The topic I was charged to address—the impact of social structures on interpersonal relations—is so broad in scope, my first task is to narrow and specify the focus of this chapter. *Which* social structures impacting on *which* interpersonal relations can one deal with, when combined with the further charge to speculate about the relevance of the topic to our understanding of aging and adult development? In seeking some clarification of my responsibility, I asked Warner Schaie, who suggested that I dip into my own current research data and also examine "possible paradigms that would allow the specification of propositions that could be tested by studies of individual development in adulthood" (personal communication, March 14, 1986). Alas! I have failed to meet this charge, for I have not developed any innovative paradigms and no elegant and testable propositions. Indeed, I believe it is premature and not necessarily useful in 1988 to formulate paradigms of any formal variety that link individual and institutional factors relevant to aging and adult development.

My plan in this chapter is: first, to offer a few observations on recent developments in life-span developmental psychology and life-course sociology, in particular their positions vis-à-vis each other; second, to discuss the methodological desiderata that one finds in the sociological literature on life-course analysis, an important topic because I think these criteria widen the gulf between sociology and psychology rather than narrow it; third, to counter some of the desiderata with examples from my current research to illustrate how one can infuse cross-sectional data with

a sensitivity to cohort differences, historical influences, and the micro-
structure of family and lineage that are of interest to life-course sociologists, while using concepts of equal interest to psychologists concerned
with individual adult development and biosocial components of aging.

The research project in question is a study of parent–adult child relationships in three generations. Hence the "social structures" I have been
investigating are the microstructures of kinship, families of origin and
procreation, and lineage generations; and the "interpersonal relations"
are those between parents and adult children. The study aimed to illuminate the extent to which these relationships are structured by gender
and how they vary over the life course, across the generations in a lineage, and in relation to the aging of parents. The study also included a
number of measures on age and life stage satisfaction. To interest both
psychologists and sociologists, I dip into some research findings bearing
on life satisfaction as well as on gender and intergenerational relations.

LIFE-SPAN PSYCHOLOGY
AND LIFE-COURSE SOCIOLOGY

A comparison of recent literature on life-span development with what one
finds in sociological work on the life course easily leads to the expectation I held when I began to write this chapter (i.e., that the participants
at the social structure and aging conference would quickly find themselves
at loggerheads before the first session ended). I also expected the "aggressive critics" in such an exchange to be the sociologists. For 20 years now,
life-span psychologists have conceded the significance of social structure,
social situations, ecological settings or niches, and so on for psychological understanding of individual motivation, personal traits, adult development, and aging. Sociologists have not been nearly so gracious in response
to life-span psychology. One reads that many psychological variables
on adult development are epiphenomena (Dannefer, 1984; Featherman,
1986); that the life course is now so thoroughly institutionalized even such
psychological traits as self-esteem, efficacy, initiative, achievement orientation are themselves institutionalized (Meyer, 1986); that the causal origins of adult development cannot be ascertained by a personological
approach (Featherman, 1986). At the American Sociological Association
meetings in 1986, one sociological theorist argued that "emotional energy" was not a biopsychological variable but a positional sociological variable (Collins, 1986). And in his Presidential Address to the National Council on Family Relations, Ira Reiss (1986) even argued a purely sociological model to explain sexual initiation and sexual behavior in adolescence.

But if we are to further the integration of life-course sociology and life-span psychology, disciplinary turf defensiveness should be avoided. Indeed, were we further along than we are, we would no longer be linking life-course analysis to sociology and life-span to psychology. In both disciplines, we might restrict the usage of "life span" literally to time length or span of life and use the more general "life-course" concept in both fields, when we are charting either institutional patterns affecting the timing, duration, and sequencing of statuses along the life line or the processes of individual developmental change. I use life course in this generalized sense. I further assume that by "development" no one will infer any fixed, hierarchical, immutable sequence of growth nor that "aging" necessarily means senescence and decline. Rather, I assume a transactional model of development (Sherrod & Brim, 1986) that allows for individual proactive initiative, the potential for considerable plasticity and interindividual variability, along with socially and biologically constrained behavior (Lerner, 1984).

That said, however, one can still note that the life-course approach in the past several years continues to be marked by more heuristic statements of noble goals and purely theoretical exegeses than demonstrations of empirical linkages between biological, psychological, and institutional domains. *We may be interdisciplinary in our aspirations, but we remain largely multidisciplinary in practice.* With life-course sociologists emphasizing cohort and period effects and with many adult development psychologists debating and testing the limits of plasticity or "reserve capacity" in one or another domain of human behavior, "aging" as a maturational phenomenon is being left to the biomedical specialties. To read the sociological literature on the life course, one would think the human organism, like the one-horse shay, is so beautifully constructed that it only collapses at the point of demise! And to read some developmental psychology, one is tempted to fantasize about becoming an Olympic winner at 70! Perhaps, as Lonnie Sherrod and Bert Brim (1986, p. 575) have suggested, we are in a period of overreacting to earlier deterministic models of adult development and of aging as programmed senescence; hence, by taking an optimistic view of the human organism and our developmental potential, we are trying to throw the burden of proof to those with more pessimistic, static, and deterministic views.

We must also admit, however, to small progress when efforts to synthesize our work result in biology, psychology, and sociology appearing in three different *volumes* in the series on aging in 1981 under James March's editorship (Fogel, Hatfield, Kiesler, & Shanas, 1981; Kiesler, Morgan, & Oppenheimer, 1981; McGaugh & Kiesler, 1981), and separate *chapters* in one volume in the recent publication under the editorship of Aage Sørensen, Franz Weinert, and Lonnie Sherrod (1986).

METHODOLOGICAL DESIDERATA
IN LIFE-COURSE RESEARCH

Sociologists claim to be eclectic in their tolerance and respect for a diversity of research methods in their discipline, yet a review of the leading disciplinary journals suggests that prestige is far from equitably distributed across methodologies. Hence, life-course researchers in sociology are not unique in urging a particular set of preferred criteria for life-course studies; they are also reflecting some prejudices of the discipline. I sketch six such desiderata and discuss the consequences several are having on the direction in which life-course analyses have been going in recent years.

1. The larger the sample, the better.
2. National probability samples are preferred over regional or metropolitan samples.
3. Longitudinal or cohort-sequential samples are "in," and cross-sectional studies are downgraded to a "second best" status.
4. Existing public-use samples are preferred over newly gathered large data sets.
5. Standardized measures of variables, or at least replicated measures, are preferred over new and untried measures.
6. Complex multivariate statistical analysis is preferred over qualitative or descriptive analysis.

Such criteria make for greater intellectual congeniality among sociology, economics, and demography than between sociology and psychology. Although generalizability increases as these criteria are adhered to in sociological research on the life course, there is no assurance that we have added to our interpretive understanding or explanation of historical change, because the data sets used to establish cohort differences preclude such explanations. Hence, by calling for larger data sets, greater reliance on public-use samples, more "add-ons" to ongoing longitudinal studies rather than new studies, we may be paying a high price: a gain of increased generalizability, to be sure, but a loss of theory-driven "thick" descriptions (Geertz, 1972) and empirically grounded "explanations." I am frank to admit that this is too high a price to pay in my judgment.

My point is important, so let me be more explicit. There are a growing number of life-course studies that use large data sets for the purpose of describing social change through cohort analysis. In the current focus on the sequencing of life events and transitions, recourse has similarly been made to census or census-type archival data. Sometimes one reads a criticism of developmental psychology for being only "descriptive" in a paper

that then proceeds to do nothing more than give a similarly descriptive
sketch of cohort changes in the timing of transitions in early adulthood.
It is rare to find any built-in explanatory variables to interpret cohort or
period effects, no matter how large the sample or how long the time period spanned in a longitudinal study. Simply meeting the criterion of a
cohort-sequential design is no assurance that meaningful interpretations
will result. As Bernice Neugarten (1985) has observed:

> The method of cross-sequential analysis has often outweighed the significance
> of the substantive problem . . . In demonstrating . . . that a cohort differ-
> ence outweighs an age difference in adult performance on a particular psy-
> chometric test of intelligence . . . or that it is the calendar year in which
> a particular political or social attitude has been measured that outweighs
> age or cohort—the indices of age, cohort, and period remain "empty" as
> explanatory variables. (p. 296)

The major reason why explanatory variables are *not* built into such
studies is that social scientists have simply not been prescient enough to
anticipate the direction of demographic change or the occurrence of some
critical political event, economic crisis or upturn. *In the absence of such fore-
knowledge, studies do not contain appropriate measures to ground interpretation
in measured explanatory variables.* Hence it remains an unintended, fortui-
tous circumstance of earlier data collection that occasionally permits empirically based explanations. Thus, for example, it was Glen Elder's post
hoc inventiveness, not the economic forecasting genius of the psychologists who initiated the Oakland and Berkeley growth studies, that permitted him to embark on the life-course analysis he has been doing for the
past decade (e.g., Elder, 1974, 1982; Elder, Liker, & Jaworski, 1984; Elder
& Rockwell, 1978; Liker & Elder, 1983). The original investigators had
merely routinely collected income data at each contact with the parents
of the children in the study; and it remained to Elder to classify the families by whether they retained their socioeconomic status during the Great
Depression or underwent significant downward mobility, then to trace
the consequences of stable versus declining economic status for the life
choices and personal characteristics of the parents and the children who
were subjects from the 1920s birth cohort over the ensuing decades.

Sociologists have an understandable attraction to the study of "cohorts,"
because this provides a convenient handle for the study of social change
that can be related to macroeconomic and demographic trends. The
danger, however, is this: *All one has is a highly elaborated independent variable
that is not then used to explain anything.* A good deal of the energy of historical demographers and life-course sociologists has gone into establishing
the fact that between the late 19th century and the 1960s, both the proportion of the life course and the actual number of years involved in cohorts

making the transition from dependent adolescence to independent adulthood has declined and become more tightly age graded (Hareven, 1981;
Hareven & Adams, 1982; Modell, Furstenberg, & Hershberg, 1978; Modell
& Hareven, 1978; Winsborough, 1979). David Featherman, Dennis Hogan, and Aage Sørensen have elaborated the study of status transitions
in adolescence and early adulthood (Featherman, 1983; Featherman, Hogan & Sørensen, 1984; Featherman & Sørensen, 1983). More recently,
Featherman has developed the concepts of "duration dependence" and
aging as a "population process" (Featherman, 1986; Featherman & Lerner, 1985).

What remains unclear is where one goes from there, for it is not clear
whether and how one can link the phenomenon of variance in early life
transitions to subsequent development or to late life transitions. Dennis
Hogan's work (1980, 1981) remains a unique exception because he shows,
for example, that *when* an individual marries relative to when he or she
finishes school influences lifetime earnings, thus demonstrating that the
timing of education in relation to marriage is important not just the length
and quality of schooling. But so long as sociologists provide us only with
statistical histories of cohorts rather than with analyses of lives, it is difficult
to envisage a fruitful relationship, much less theoretical integration, between life-course studies in sociology and psychology.

Furthermore, most sociological research on intercohort change is historical, and any extrapolation of historical trends into the future is complex.
Social science achievement in forecasting is very poor indeed. There is
now a good deal of evidence to indicate that a shift has taken place during the past five years in the timing pattern among younger cohorts: more
births at very young ages as well as more first births at older ages; a rise
in the childlessness rate; later marriage and a downturn in the marriage
rate; postponed or erratic labor force entry due to high unemployment
rates; and a reversal of the trend toward independent residence among
young unmarried adults (Bengtson & Dannefer, 1986). Life-span psychologists who try to inform their studies of individual adult development
with sensitivity to macrosocial structural characteristics and trends will
be hard pressed to find life-course cohort analysis of use to them unless
they inspect contemporary data to check whether trends are stable, changing, or reversing. Although cohort analysis is by definition *historical* analysis, psychologists want to understand *contemporary* lives, which further adds
to the unresolved issue of how to link individual and institutional contributions to the life course.

An interesting and important exception to these observations concerns
recent analyses of "disordered cohort flows." The size of a cohort is determined by fertility rates, which remain a constant through the lifetimes
of cohort members. Hence this structural variable is as readily identifia-
ble by developmental psychologists concerned with a particular age group

as by sociologists concerned with intercohort variability. A number of sociologists and economists have been exploring the potential impact of the large baby-boom cohort now approaching middle age in the context of fundamental changes now taking place in the American economy (e.g., Bengtson & Dannefer, 1986; Carey, 1981; Easterlin, 1980). Because the baby-boom cohorts were preceded (and followed) by dramatically smaller cohorts, they have exerted enormous pressure on the capacity of schools, the job market, and even the prisons over the past 20 years to accommodate them. The much publicized affluence and lifestyle of Yuppies is misleading because they represent at most about 5% of their cohort. The majority of the baby-boom cohort will be impacted by the de-skilling and de-professionalization taking place in the economy. By "de-skilling," sociologists refer to occupations undergoing a decline in craft as a consequence of increased automation and decreased autonomy in job tasks. The growth sectors of the economy are in low skill service occupations (e.g., janitors, nurses' aides, orderlies, sales clerks, fast-food workers), which means lower paying and less intrinsically rewarding work for the younger of the baby-boom cohort and an even larger proportion of their children as they move into the labor force. Publicity to the contrary, microelectronics, although undergoing a rapid *rate* of growth at the moment, is not expected to create more than 500,000 jobs over the 12-year period from 1978 to 1990 (Carey, 1981). Then too, the word processor craze is leading many academics, managers, and other professionals to perform their own secretarial work, with as yet unknown consequences for female employment opportunities.

With the streamlining of corporate bureaucracies under the pressure of international competition, middle-aged baby boomers face restricted opportunities for promotion and wage increases when they enter their 40s and 50s. Hence even Yuppy managers and executives may reach an earlier plateau and a lower level of peak earnings than their parents experienced. Combined with the fact that they have been more effectively schooled in consumption than in saving, they may well approach old age with less personal savings than today's cohort of elderly have shown. Extrapolating from the findings of Melvin Kohn and Carmi Schooler (1983), future cohorts of adults will engage in less complex work with less on-the-job autonomy, hence some reduction in intellectual flexibility. As a result, Bengtson and Dannefer (1986) suggested that the upcoming cohorts of the elderly may enter retirement not only with fewer material resources but with fewer psychological resources as well. Guillemard's study of French retirees suggested two lifestyles rooted in the kind of work the retirees engaged in prior to retirement: a passive, disengagement style linked to a history of jobs with low stimulus and an active, goal-directed style linked to a history of enriching jobs with high stimulus (cited in Bengtson & Dannefer, 1986, p. 12). Such changes in the character of cohorts (both size and change in work experience) may lead to "reduced levels of resources, of coping and adaptive strategies for later life, and of physical and mental activity" (Bengtson & Dannefer 1986, p. 13).

The baby-boom cohort has more siblings than today's elderly but fewer children to fulfill their own primary social support and care-giving needs, and like their grandparents' cohort, one in five will have no children. These economic and social psychological trends, coupled with sharply varying size in the flow of cohorts through the age-stratification system, clearly have implications for psychologists concerned with identifying important social structural variables that impact on individual adult development and aging in the second half of life.

Another consequence of the emerging methodological desiderata in life-course sociology, concerns the phenomenon of "add-ons" to longitudinal panel studies, or the identification of earlier data sets that do not preclude later contact with respondents and therefore hold the potential of being transformed from an original cross-sectional survey into a longitudinal study. Contemporary, ongoing longitudinal projects, like bureaucracies, tend to be self-perpetuating. They entail large expenditures to initiate them and large personnel cadres to maintain and supplement them. This makes it tempting for both principal investigators and funding agencies to perpetuate and supplement ongoing projects on the assumption that adding new topics to ongoing panels is more cost-effective than gathering new sets of data.

A current example is the University of Michigan Panel Study of Income Dynamics (PSID). Begun as a relatively atheoretical project to trace income stability and change across time with particular attention to movement in and out of poverty, PSID has taken on many additional foci over the years: For example, additional information was gathered from wives concerning their employment, marital, and fertility history in 1976; presently, medical and health information is being gathered about family members; and in the planning stage now, the addition of "kin relations" is a new topic for the 1988 wave of this ongoing project.

However, the core of any annual interview in the PSID must go to the repeat questions on income, employment, and household composition change, with the result that new topics can only be covered in a 10-minute segment of the periodic telephone interview, unless a funding agency is willing to invest some $300,000 to $400,000 to support a longer, supplementary interview. Hence an "add-on" segment can provide very little elaboration and few new variables on a new topic.

Furthermore, if these new topics are not tapped in subsequent waves of the longitudinal study with identical, repeat questions, no individual change analysis is possible on the new variables, with the net result that there is only a modest advantage to a single-wave "add-on" in longitudinal studies compared to a full-scale independent survey. Unless health measures or kin relations measures are repeated in more than one survey, they may illuminate analysis of shifts in economic well-being that become apparent in subsequent panel waves, but the economic indicators can not be analyzed as factors influencing change in health status or kin relations.

The limitations I am stressing to the methodological criteria subscribed to by many sociologists conducting life-course studies have reference only to one issue of this book — the relations and aspirations for more integration between developmental psychology and sociology in life-course studies. Maximizing the utility of public-use surveys or tracing historical changes in the timing and duration of life-course transitions are useful in their own right. Rather, I question their utility from the perspective of understanding individual development and aging: I am not persuaded that adult development can be *explained* in terms of population processes or intercohort trends or the internalization of institutional norms, or that biographic analysis can only "illustrate" social structure. Broad structural factors clearly have theoretical relevance to sociologists, but whether they have any relevance to understanding the lives of individuals can only be determined by the study of individual lives. The evidence is simply not in hand to sustain the view that psychological studies of aging are necessarily purely *descriptive* whereas life-course analysis of cohorts is *explanatory*.

Additional comments on the consequences of the methodological criteria upheld by many life-course researchers are incorporated into the discussion of my current research.

FAMILY AND INTERGENERATIONAL RESEARCH

To place my current research in some context, I think it may be useful to give a brief historical sketch of the emergence of three-generation studies in recent years. Such studies build on the results of earlier work in family sociology, which dispelled the notion that the family in industrial societies is adequately described as an isolated nuclear household. The work of Marvin Sussman (Sussman & Burchinal, 1962), Bert Adams (1968, 1970), Eugene Litwak (1960a, 1960b, 1969), to name just a few, showed a significant degree of interhousehold social interaction, affective closeness, and help exchange among parents and their adult married children and young grandchildren. However, these studies were based on samples of married couples with young children, typically with the young married woman being the sole respondent concerning the family ties maintained with her parents and in-laws. Further, they provided only a static profile of the then contemporary intergenerational ties.

In the 1960s and 1970s, interest arose in following the family life cycle, typically defined in terms of the age of the youngest child, with an elaboration of family cycle stages from childless early marriage, to the passage of children through the school system, until the last child left home and the parents settled into the "postparental" or "empty nest" stage of the family cycle. A typical study, however, was restricted to White, native born, intact families with at least one dependent child, and the focus was on the marital pair rather than on intergenerational relations.

During these same decades, social gerontologists conducted studies of elderly adults and their relationship to middle-aged children, demonstrating that the parents maintained close and frequent contact with at least one child, 70% of whom have seen a child within the preceding week (e.g., Shanas, 1980; Shanas, Townsend, Friis, Milhoj, & Stehouwer, 1968).

Most family cycle studies were conducted with small budgets and local samples; appropriate cases of married female respondents were screened for study. Distrust of retrospective data even of major life events, combined with small budgets, had the effect of restricting analysis to current family relations, and hence to comparing different cohorts of adults across the family cycle. This limitation was not recognized at the time because family sociologists assumed far greater stability to family patterns in the 1960s and 1970s than they do today. That limitation could have been partially surmounted were there a strong tradition in family sociology for conducting replication studies that tested for actual cohort differences. But this has not been the case, and indeed, when one examined the measures used for family relationships in the earlier studies, there was little attraction to replicate them even if funds were available to do so. I abandoned any effort at such measurement replication after reviewing such measures and finding most inadequate to my purposes, in part because I needed questions and items appropriate to both structured personal interviews and telephone interviews. (cf. the three volumes on *Research Instruments in Social Gerontology* edited by David Mangen & Warren Peterson, 1982, 1983, 1984).

Three-generation studies have emerged against the knowledge that intergenerational ties persist beyond the departure of children from the parental home. Most of these studies, however, were not primarily guided by a life-course perspective. Other concerns predominated in these studies. Awareness of changing values and lifestyles among the young in the 1970s, and their potential implications for intergenerational harmony or conflict, was one motivation guiding such studies. Yet another concern was to understand the implications of greatly increased longevity for relations between the generations. Marriages in our era, if not terminated by divorce, may persist for a longer period of time after child rearing is over than they do during the child rearing years. Indeed, with a small family of two closely spaced children, parents can expect to relate to *adult* children for two and a half times the years they spend rearing those children to the age of 18.

So there is great diversity in the primary concerns of three-generation studies. Vern Bengtson's three-generation study in California (Bengtson, Mangen, & Landry, 1984; Mangen, Bengtson & Landry, 1988) focuses on the different values held by the generations and whether they have any impact on the affective quality, interaction, and exchange of help between the generations in a family. Bernice Neugarten and Gunhild Hagestad's three-generation study in the midwest (Hagestad, 1982b, 1986) is tracing *reciprocal influences* between members of proximate generations and the impact of divorce on the mother-daughter relationship (Hagestad, 1982a; Hagestad & Smyer, 1982). Other researchers, among them Andrew Cherlin and Frank Furstenberg, undertook studies of the relations between alternate generations in the family (i.e., between grandparents and grandchildren), with an eye to what happens to the relationship between them when the linking generation of parents is divorced (Cherlin & Furstenberg, 1986; Bengtson & Robertson, 1985). Two other three-generation studies focus on Black families (Jackson, 1979; Jackson & Hatchett, 1986; Taylor, 1986) and Mexican-American families (Markides, Bolt, & Ray, 1986).

All three-generation studies mentioned are still being analyzed, hence their results are not fully known at this time. They share certain design characteristics that should be noted however. For one, inclusion in a three-generation sample frame is usually decided by means of a screening interview to establish the existence of living members in three generations, typically within the same city or within a particular geographic radius of an interviewing team. Cooperation is sought from the three selected respondents before any interviewing takes place. If all three respondents must come from the same lineage and the youngest generation member is to be an adult, generational replacement time assures a built-in cohort selection factor: grandparents, or the G1 generation as we refer to the oldest in such studies, will be in their 60s, G2 parents in their 40s, G3 adult children in their early 20s.

There are several difficulties with this method of studying intergenerational relations. One is the selection bias imposed when data are obtained only after all three-generational members agree to cooperate. The second is some unknown bias inherent in the requirement that all three generations reside in relatively close proximity to each other (either in the same city or within a 50-mile radius). Third, there are limitations that restrict the utility of such studies to life-course analysts in either sociology or psychology: By definition, unmarried childless adults are excluded from the two older generations; most of the youngest G3 respondents are still unmarried, and because of their youth, many are still residing with their parents; there is no "normal" distribution of chronological ages in any of the three generations and little overlap in age across the generations, which limits the possibilities for tracing life-course changes in the variables included in such studies. Lastly, with the exception of the Michigan study of three-generation Black families, none of the analysts ground their studies in a probability sample of respondents because they obtain data only when the existence and access criteria are met.

ROSSI BOSTON STUDY

In designing my own study, I attempted to minimize these problems by several sampling decisions. Because the life course was itself a major focus of the study, my first decision was to secure a random probability sample of adults 18 years of age or older, so that respondents would vary normally in age and could be studied as both adult children in relationship to living parents, if they had them, and as parents of children who could also vary in age from infancy to late middle age. This also assured the inclusion of unmarried and childless adults. This "main sample" was supplemented with two additional spinoff samples: one of living parents of main survey respondents, the other of adult children of main survey respondents. Because access to blood relatives of respondents would depend on the latter's cooperation and knowledge of their kin's whereabouts, I opted to seek access only to proximate ascendant and descendant kin. That is to say, I reasoned that parents and adult children had much easier access to and knowledge of each other's addresses and telephone numbers than older G1 respondents had to their adult grandchildren's or G3 respondents had to their grandparents'.

To hold the budget within reasonable bounds and because our approach to an intergenerational study was a first of its kind, the original random sample was confined to the Greater Boston Metropolitan area, where personal interviews were conducted with 1,393 adults. This sample reported a total of roughly 600 living fathers, 835 living mothers, 550 adult sons, and 530 adult daughters. Because a key question of the study was the extent to which gender structured intergenerational relations, a selection was made from the pool of parents and adult children to assure as equitable a distribution of same-sex and cross-sex pairs as possible for the four parent–child dyads. This procedure yielded subsamples of 323 parents and 278 adult children. Telephone interviews were conducted with these two spinoff samples. No restriction was placed on their geographic distance from Boston except that the parents and children resided in the continental United States or Canada.

A major advantage and unique characteristic of this design is the fact that respondents in the spinoff samples of parents and of adult children can be compared with *nonrespondents* in these two generations, because we asked a wide array of questions concerning each parent and each child of the main sample respondents. Table 6.1 shows the case distributions involved here. Note that data on the major variables in the study were gathered *about* and *from* each child and parent. For example, 835 respondents gave ratings of affective closeness to their mothers, and 194 of these mothers who were interviewed also rated their affective closeness to the child in our main sample. Second, we can test whether there was any tendency to bias in the spinoff samples by comparing *respondent* parents with *nonrespondent* parents on their personal characteristics and on the same measures of family relationships reported by their adult children in the main sample. Note that there were two points at which a refusal could be made: by the respondent when asked for access to a parent (18% of the respondents refused access), and by the parent when we approached them by letter and phone calls (14% of the parents refused or were not reachable after a dozen or so attempted telephone interviews). Interviewers reported numerous comments by respondents when access was refused, to the effect that a parent was very ill or convalescing, hard of hearing, or understood English poorly, suggesting a protective stance on the part of these adult children to spare their parents stress or embarrassment.

An analysis of the respondent parents compared to the nonrespondent parents showed a few consistent but nonproblematic differences: Respon-

TABLE 6.1
Case Distribution of Respondents in Three Samples,
and Nonrespondents in G1 and G3 Generations

Generation	Respondents	# Reported by G2	# of Respondents		# of Nonrespondents
G1 (Parents)	323	599 Living Fathers	129 Fathers	←---→	470 Fathers
		835 Living Mothers	194 Mothers ↑↓	←---→	641 Mothers
G2 (Main Sample Respondents)	1393		588 men		
			805 Women ↑↓		
G3 (Adult Children)	278	550 Sons	136 Sons	←---→	414 Sons
		531 Daughters	142 Daughters	←---→	389 Daughters

Note: ↑ Information ABOUT a parent (or child).
        ↓ Information FROM a parent (or child).
        ←---→ Comparisons to test for selection bias.

dent parents were on average 2 years younger than nonrespondent parents, better educated but with a mean difference of only 1 year of schooling, in slightly better health, seen somewhat less often, and involved in help exchange to a slightly lesser degree. No differences were found between the two groups on affective closeness, degree to which they shared common values, or level of family cohesion during the child-rearing years.

An analysis of the correlates of geographic distance separating the two generations suggests more significant effects if inclusion in a three-generation sample depends on geographic proximity. This is illustrated in Table 6.2, which shows the correlation coefficients between mileage distance between respondents and their fathers and mothers and a variety of relationship indicators.

Obviously, interaction through visiting is the most significant correlation — the greater the distance the lower the frequency of visiting each other. A restricted visiting pattern is only modestly compensated by telephone contact: Although correlations are lower, they are still negative because the most frequent phoning takes place among those living in the same city, typically several times a week to daily, which would be too expensive a pattern when long distances separate parents and children. The extent of help exchanged is also significantly reduced by greater mileage separating the generations, although mileage distance reduces the help adult children *give* to their parents more than it does the help they *receive* from their parents. This is largely due to the fact that adult children give more proximity-dependent help to their parents (doing daily chores, shopping, help during illness, fixing an appliance) whereas parents give more help that is not proximity dependent (advice and comfort during a crisis, which can be done by phone, special gifts, money, or loans). But distance is *not* correlated with the subjective ratings on affective closeness in the parent–child relationship nor is the degree to which parents and children

TABLE 6.2
Correlation Coefficients between Geographic Distance between
Respondents and their Parents and Selected Solidarity Indices

Solidarity Indices	Fathers	Mothers
Value consensus	.00	−.04
Affective closeness	−.02	−.05
Phoning frequency	−.14*	−.26**
Extent get help from parent	−.18*	−.25**
Extent give help to parent	−.28**	−.33**
Visiting frequency	−.71***	−.83***

  * $p < .05$
 ** $p < .01$
*** $p < .001$

share similar or different values on politics, religion, or general outlook on life.

Not shown in Table 6.2 is an important correlate of geographic distance between respondents and their parents: a correlation of .33 between the educational attainment level of respondents and mileage distance from their parents, reflecting the larger regional and national labor market children with better education enter compared to those with less education. This suggests that three-generation studies that are restricted to lineage members who reside in the same city or within a narrow radius of say 50 miles may include families with much less sharp educational and socioeconomic differences beween the generations than our Boston study does.

There are several advantages to a sampling design that provides a normal age distribution of adults. As noted, three-generation studies tend to have a narrow age range within each of the three generations; the respondents in the three generations are therefore from widely separated birth cohorts. By contrast, the Boston main survey has a wide age distribution in all three generations. There is a difference of approximately 20 years in the average age of G1 parents (63), G2 respondents (45), and G3 children (23), but as Fig. 6.1 shows, there is also great overlap. In fact, some "children" of older G2 respondents are older than some "parents" of younger G2 respondents.

Because we obtained data from each respondent on several identical variables concerning their families of origin as well as their families of procreation, it is not only possible to analyze the extent of cross-generational transmission of affect, behavior patterns, and values, but we

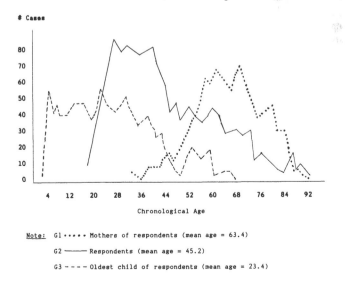

Note: G1 • • • • • Mothers of respondents (mean age = 63.4)

       G2 ———— Respondents (mean age = 45.2)

       G3 – – – – Oldest child of respondents (mean age = 23.4)

FIG. 6.1. Age distribution of main sample respondents, their mothers, and their oldest child

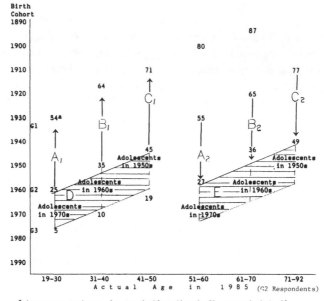

FIG 6.2.   Parent–child dyads in families of origin and procreation at childrearing stage in same historical eras

can compare families of origin and families of procreation who were in the child-rearing phases during the same historical period. Figure 6.2 shows the potential comparisons in graphic form.

Using a six-decade age distribution of main sample respondents (in their 20s, 30s, 40s, etc.), I show the mean ages of these G2 respondents along with the mean ages of their mothers and of their oldest child. These triads are plotted against the birth cohorts of the average age of persons in the six age groups in each of the three generations. The arrows joining G2 to G1 identify parent–child dyads in which the respondent is the *adult child*, whereas the arrows joining G2 to G3 identify the parent–child dyads in which the respondent is the *parent*. The shaded areas below each pair refer to the historical period in which the respondent spent childhood and adolescence in their families of origin (the first three columns), or the historical period in which the respondent's family of procreation had an oldest child in childhood and adolescence (the last three columns in Fig. 6.2). The pairs identified as A, B, and C, therefore, refer to families of origin and procreation at the same child-rearing stage during the same historical period. For example, A_1 and A_2 are families in the child-rearing years during the 1960s (childhood) and 1970s (adolescence), differ-ing in that respondents in A_1 were the children and in A_2 the parents.

By charting the age of respondents, their parents, and their children in this manner, we can infuse cross-sectional data with a historical dimen-sion and pose a variety of questions concerning whether rearing children in one era as opposed to another makes any difference in some dimen-sion of family life and whether any consequences flow from this later in life. I illustrate this in two ways. The first builds on Fig. 6.2. We ask if rearing adolescents in the "troubling" 1960s and 1970s created problems in families of a different order than if rearing adolescents in the "calmer" era of the 1950s. Our data suggests this to be so because the type of fami-ly troubles and the frequency with which they are cited reflect the social-historical eras during which respondents were either growing up them-selves or rearing their own children.

The data I am using for this analysis come from a battery of 15 "family troubles" presented to respondents on a printed card, so they had only to call out numbers for the items that characterized their family of origin or their family of procreation. The battery included such items as prolonged illness, unemployment, or death of a family member; drink-ing or drug problems; a family member in trouble with the police or school authorities; frequent quarreling among children, with relatives, or between spouses; physical or sexual abuse; exhausting jobs; one or more rebellious children; a family member who got into the "wrong crowd," and so forth.

If I were to say that younger respondents were eight times more likely to report (with reference to their families of origin) a "very rebellious child" and five times more likely to report someone got into the "wrong crowd" or had trouble with the police or school authorities than respondents in their 60s reported, you might say that's to be expected because the older adults report through a rosy lens on which memories of their early fami-ly life is etched, whereas younger adults in their 20s are still differentiat-ing themselves from their parents and exaggerate adolescent rebellion.

Such an interpretation is hard to sustain when we compare the same type of family trouble data reported for families of procreation for the same historical period. Here, it is not the *youngest* respondents who report a higher incidence of such troubles but *older* respondents who report in their role as parents, that is, precisely the cohorts we identified as A and B in Fig. 6.2.

To simplify data presentation, I show the results for only two items from the family troubles battery in Table 6.3: the percentage reporting a child was very rebellious, or someone in the family got into the "wrong crowd." The C pair, in which children were being reared in the 1950s, shows much lower reports on a rebellious child or on a family member in the "wrong crowd" than do the A and B pairs, in which children were adolescents in the 1970s and 1960s, respectively.

TABLE 6.3
Incidence of Selected Family Troubles in Family of Origin and Family
of Procreation by Age of Main Sample Respondents

Family referred to	Age of Respondent					
	19–30	31–40	41–50	51–60	61–70	71–92
% report a rebellious child						
Family of Origin	26.9	22.9	10.0	8.6	3.7	2.6
Family of Procreation	1.3	5.8	16.1	19.8	12.3	1.1
% report someone in "wrong crowd"						
Family of Origin	15.0	11.9	5.5	4.8	3.1	.9
Family of Procreation	5.1	4.5	12.8	17.8	12.2	–

Note: Pairs marked A were families with adolescent children in 1970s, B pairs were in the 1960s, C pairs in the 1950s.

My second illustration involves the dimension of affective closeness, a 7-point rating scale from very tense and strained to very close and intimate. Respondents not only rated their *current* relationship to parents but their relations to parents when they were 10, 16, and 25 years of age. Figure 6.3 shows the overall pattern, with the retrospective ratings for the earlier ages and current ratings for those in the several age groups. Figure 6.3 also provides an example of the differences I find when gender of parent and child is specified.

Several things can be noted in this figure. One, all four dyads show a decided dip in intimate relationships during adolescence followed by a steady shift to a high plateau of affective closeness over the years of early and middle adulthood. Second, the father–son relationship is the least apt to show high levels of intimacy in all four dyads at most points on the life course. And third, in childhood and adolescence it is the gender of the *parent* that matters, whereas in adulthood it is the gender of the *child* that matters: Mothers are closer to young sons and daughters than fathers are, whereas in adulthood, both mothers and fathers are closer to daughters than to sons. Once adult daughters form families of their own, they show more involvement with and greater emotional closeness to their parents than sons show after marriage.

Indeed, married men often have greater involvement with their wives' kin than their own, contributing to a maternal asymmetry in kin relations in adulthood that is also shown in the reports respondents gave on which side of the family they felt closest to while they were growing up: Maternal grandmothers and maternal aunts are cited *twice* as often as their counterparts on the paternal side of the family as the most "important," "admired," or "loved" relative, underlining the significance of women's role

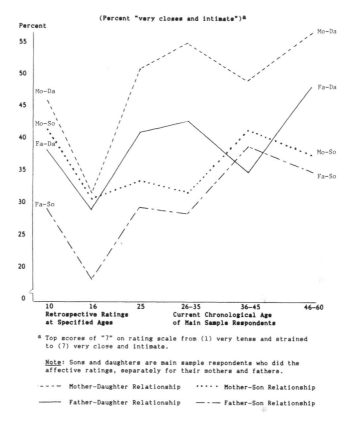

FIG. 6.3. Affective closeness of main sample respondents to parents by phase of the life course and gender of parent and child

as mothers in serving as *affective monitors* for their children's access to and feelings toward kin. This pattern has also been noted in research on the aftermath of divorce when predominantly women hold child custody, but our data suggest the maternal asymmetry is not unique to marital break-down, as some students of the consequences of divorce have argued (Cher-lin & Furstenberg, 1986).

A life-course analyst, sensitive to change in historical era, might ask if the adolescent dip in parent–child intimacy is more in evidence when adolescence occurs in a socially turbulent historical era than in a calm one. Figure 6.4 reveals a test of this proposition, showing a far more marked dip in intimacy with parents for those who were adolescents in the more recent period (1966–1975) than for those who were adolescents in the 1940s and early 1950s.

Note, too, that there were no differences between these two cohorts of adolescents at either the earlier age (10) or the later age (25), suggesting no preselection in strained relations in adolescence nor aftermath of troubled adolescent relations in early adulthood. There is considerable resiliency to the parent–child relationship, and many more significant events in the subsequent lives of both generations, for the past to have overriding influences upon contemporary intergenerational relationships. This should not be overdrawn, however, for other analysis shows that many family of origin characteristics (e.g., level of maternal affection) have *direct* effects on current closeness and help patterns, *net* of current needs, availability, and shared values.

My general point in offering these illustrations is to suggest that cross-sectional surveys can address questions important to life-course analysis. If you overcome the prejudice against retrospective data, seek data from two informants when your focus is on interpersonal relationships, and explicitly explore potential cohort effects in age-related patterns, the results may be of equal interest to both psychologists and sociologists who share a life-course perspective.

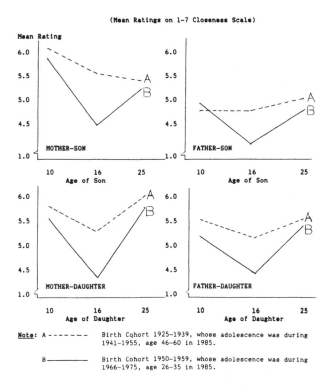

FIG. 6.4. Affective closeness of main sample respondents and their parents: Cohorts whose adolescence was in 1941–1955 vs. 1966–1975

SUBJECTIVE DIMENSIONS OF AGE

My next dip into the Boston data is to illustrate what may be called a phenomenology of age and aging. They also provide a somewhat damp-ening counter to the "optimism" about human plasticity life-course analysts cheerfully espouse. My interest was to explore how adults feel subjective-ly about their phase in the life course and to relate this to other predicta-ble age-related factors. To do this, I asked not only for chronological age but for *subjective age* — "What age do you feel like most of the time?" — and for *desired age* — "If you could be any age you wanted to be right now, what age would that be?" Respondents were also asked to assess their present life circumstances in a slightly larger time frame by describing the last five years of their life, with five response categories varying from the "very best years" to "the very worst years" of their lives.

Figure 6.5 provides some preliminary results to explore. The graph shows the percent who viewed the past 5 years in the most positive light, either as "the very best" or "among the best years" of their lives. The top graph in Fig 6.5 shows the pattern by gender and age, the bottom by health

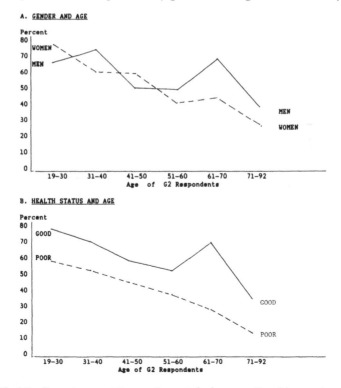

FIG. 6.5. Percent say past 5 years "among the best years" or "the very best years" of life, by gender, health status, and age

status and age. Both men and women show an overall steady decline over the life course in the proportion who view the recent period of their lives in a positive light, women more sharply than men. Men in fact show two upturns or inflections: those in their 30s and those in their 60s, with a slump in middle age. The condition of their health clearly contributes to but does not explain the downward life-course pattern in positive evaluation, though again, there is a temporary upturn among those in their 60s who enjoy good or excellent health.

Why do men and women show a different life-course profile, and why is there a slump in the 50s and an upturn in the 60s among those with top self-ratings on health? One might speculate that men in the middle years are reflecting a "life cycle squeeze," pressed financially by the costs of child rearing that the transition into their 60s assuages (Oppenheimer, 1974, 1982). Or related to this, there might be a cohort effect because those in their 50s have had on average 3.5 children, whereas those in their 40s show a much lower family size (2.7) as do those in their 60s (2.8). Perhaps the pattern calling for explanation is the upturn among men in their 60s: Are they indicating that retirement is a joy, that they are pleased to be released from the pressures of work and the expenses of late child rearing? Or are there gender-related mortality factors involved? If men show deterioration of health at an earlier stage of life than women, and more of them die in their 50s, then the men who survive into their 60s might be in better physical and psychological health and feel good about their own survival and phase of life.

Two additional pieces of information help to narrow the interpretive possibilities. First, let us explore the impact of sheer marital status on the

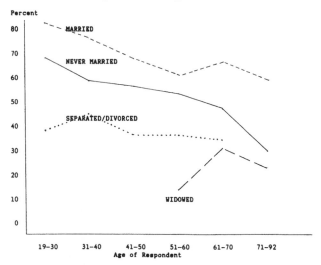

FIG. 6.6 Percent say past 5 years "the very best" or "among the very best" years of their life, by marital status and age

evaluations respondents have given us. Figure 6.6 shows one of the most interesting patterns I have found in this dataset. The group with the *highest positive* assessments are *young married adults*; the group with the *lowest positive* assessment are *widowed adults in their 50s,* perhaps reflecting an "off-time" loss that takes a higher toll than the death of a partner at a more "expected" time of life. Second, at every phase of the life course, the lack of a partner reduces the level of positive assessment, the contrast being greatest among the young who have separated or divorced compared to those who are married. Those who have never married, although more positive in outlook than those who experienced the rupture of a relationship through divorce or death, at no point show as high a level of life stage satisfaction as those who are married. Past middle age, adults are apt to lose a spouse, hence widowhood contributes to the sharp downturn in life phase satisfaction among the elderly.

What then of the health status of men compared to women in the middle years? Figure 6.7 supports the notion that men experience health declines at earlier ages: More men than women report poor health in their 40s and 50s, whereas the reverse holds from the 60s on, in part no doubt as the result of earlier deaths among men.

We can take one last step in this analysis by comparing men in their 50s with men in their 60s if we regress a variety of factors we have suggested or demonstrated to have an effect on judgments of the past 5 years: marital status, health condition, retired or not, family size, and *drive,* a variable that I have not discussed as yet. This is my closest approximation to a physiological, age-related personal trait. It was derived from a

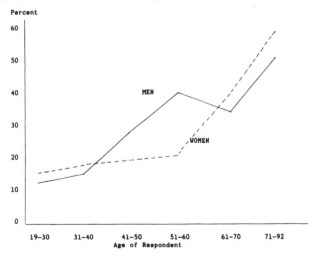

[a] "Poor" Health = bottom quartile on 10-point self-rating
of current state of health.

FIG. 6.7. Percent in "poor" health[a] by age and gender

battery of personal trait self-ratings designed to capture maturational change: 6-point self-ratings on the extent to which respondents viewed themselves as "energetic," "hard working," and "easily aroused sexually." Chronological age and health status are very significant determinants of drive ratings, net of each other, supporting the idea that the index taps maturational change but with some degree of individual variability.

Table 6.4 shows the results of this regression exercise, with separate equations for men in their 50s and their 60s. These data suggest that retirement and family size were false interpretations of the upturn in positive evaluation men in their 60s gave. The primary significant determinants of the life-phase satisfaction ratings are being married and a high drive level among men in their 50s: for men in their 60s, they are being married and enjoying good health.

Other analyses, not reported here, showed that men undergo a sharper decline in drive ratings in the middle years than women do. Further, I asked respondents to rate themselves not only today but also "10 years ago." This permitted a comparison of the *retrospective* ratings made by adults in one age group with *current* ratings given by those 10 years younger, from which we can gauge the probable extent of accuracy in retrospective ratings. Typically, adults in the later years have an exaggerated notion of the extent to which they have changed over the previous 10 years; this is particularly the case for older men, who report much higher ratings for themselves 10 years earlier on energy level and ease of sexual arousal than men 10 years their junior report. Hence, what the regression analysis results suggest is the particular sensitivity of men to drive reduction when they are in their 50s, whereas it is the state of their health that matters more when they enter their 60s.

TABLE 6.4
Regression on Best/Worst Years Assessment[a] of Past 5 Years
(Standardized Beta Coefficients)

Predictor Variables	Men in their 50s	Men in their 60s
Married[b]	.355***	.299***
Drive[c]	.247*	.168
Health Status (High = Excellent)	.130	.260*
Retired[b]	.025	−.068
Family size	−.026	−.024
R^2 =	.214***	.265***

Note: [a]High = Very best years; Low = Very worst years.
      [b]Dummy variables: Married = 1, all others = 0; Retired = 1, all others = 0.
      [c]Three-item index based on self-ratings on "energetic," "hard-working," and "easily aroused sexually."
   *$p < .05$
  **$p < .01$
 ***$p < .001$

Despite the relative success of our efforts to discount some possible factors to explain the age-related decline in positive life phase assessment, there remains a large unexplained residual. Elderly adults may be more acutely conscious of the dwindling years ahead of them than the more optimistic social scientists of the life-course like to anticipate. There is no escape from impending death in the real world of the elderly; hence an alternative, engaging in wishful thinking, may take its place. Let me illustrate this point with the contrast shown among actual chronological age, subjective age, and desired age, as these vary along the life course for men and women. Figure 6.8 shows the mean chronological age of men and women, together with their mean subjective age and desired age across the life course.

For the most part, adults tell us that they feel younger than they are but would like to be younger still. Second, the gap between *actual* and *desired* age increases over the life course, and does so somewhat more for men than for women. But note, too, that we see here something of the same, now familiar tendency among men in their 50s: On average, they feel *older* than they actually are as they do in their 20s as well. I read this

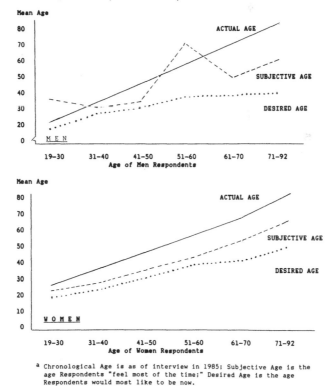

a Chronological Age is as of interview in 1985; Subjective Age is the age Respondents "feel most of the time;" Desired Age is the age Respondents would most like to be now.

FIG. 6.8. Mean chronological age, subjective age, and desired age[a] by phase of the life course and gender

as some support for Valerie Oppenheimer's finding (1982) of two strong
life cycle squeezes among men: in their 20s when they face a gap between
earnings and family formation needs and again in their 50s when most
have "plateaued" in earnings while family needs are still increasing during the late adolescence of children. This may be particularly acute for
today's middle-aged cohort of men, many of whom did not anticipate rising rates of college attendance, related expenses, and high youth unemployment rates. Our analysis of personal income over the life course lends
further support to this interpretation. The personal earnings "peak" of
men respondents at all levels of educational attainment is in their 40s.
Hence men in their 50s who still have dependent children to support,
may well experience added strain in meeting their obligations. Note too
that the personal earnings peak in a man's 40s is not particular to our
1985 Boston sample; we found the same profile in national sample data
(NORC surveys for 1984 and 1974).

Table 6.5 brings together several threads of the analysis, which I suggest illustrates the conjoint contribution of biology, psychology, and sociology to our understanding of adult development and aging. The
dependent variable involved is an age-dissatisfaction index that I com-

TABLE 6.5
**Regression on Age Dissatisfaction[a] (Married respondents
in Main Sample) (Standardized Beta Coefficients)**

Predictor Variables	Beta
Bio/psychological	
Current age	.491***
Affect balance[b]	−.105***
Drive[c]	−.081*
Health self-rating High = Exellent	.025
Family	
Marital happiness	.065*
Number of children	.001
Social Status	
Gender[d]	−.059*
Education	−.058*
Total family income	−.025
R^2 =	.325***
(N = 728)	

[a]Age dissatisfaction = Number of years younger respondents wish to be than they are. High
score = Number of years younger wish to be. Low score = Accept current age.
[b]Bradburn Affect Balance Scale (+5 to −5), where +5 means all positive affect, −5 means
all negative affect, and 0 means equal positive and negative affect.
[c]Drive index based on self-ratings on "energetic," "hardworking," and "easily aroused
sexually."
[d]Dummy variable, 1 = Female, 0 = Male.
 *$p<.05$
 ***$p<.001$

puted by subtracting desired age from chronological age. Hence, a high score on the index is an indication of the extent to which adults wish to be younger than they are, whereas a low score represents acceptance of current age (together with the very few respondents who wish to be older than they are chronologically). Included in the equation are a set of *biosocial* variables — current age, affect balance, drive, and health status; two *family* indicators — marital happiness and family size; and a third set of *status* characteristics — gender, income, and education.

As seen in Table 6.5, at least one variable is a significant predictor of age dissatisfaction from each of the three clusters: net of each other, those who wish to be much younger than they are tend to be older adults; those who report feeling more negative affect than positive affect recently; those with low drive, low educational attainment, male, and unhappily married.

CONCLUSION

Life-course analysts can do nothing about the dwindling number of years left in life for the elderly, little to change educational attainment, little to re-stoke energy and sexual arousal, little to improve marital happiness or to avert disease or death. But what little we can do through marital and sexual counseling, adult education, physical fitness programs, education in death and dying, more meaningful leisure time pursuits, and a minimization of the difference in life chances of men and women, we may be obliged to do or to recommend to policymakers.

For my part, however, I think it premature to propose such policy recommendations, just as I consider it premature to propose any one paradigm that links social structure to adult development and aging. There is still too much for us in life-course research to do in the various domains of human development of interest to us. But I hope my analysis and examples project four things:

1. My conviction that we can link sociological concern for specific status and structural variables with individual affect, self-assessment, and social interaction, while retaining a sensitivity to cohort and historical factors.

2. One need not apologize for using cross-sectional surveys rather than existing national data sets or "tag ons" to longitudinal studies, because these latter data sources rarely permit empirical explanations, whereas a creative analytic use of cross-sectional data can go a considerable distance from simple description to significant, demonstrated interpretation.

3. Explanations grounded in empirical evidence drawn from the study of contemporary lives are preferable to statistical portraits of cohorts, no matter how extensive and generalizable the latter are.

4. An optimism that efforts in life-course research can and will become interdisciplinary, not so much through collaboration and syntheses across the disciplines of biology, psychology, and sociology but through an increase in the number of researchers whose own minds comfortably embrace concepts and measures from these three feeder disciplines to the life-course perspective.

ACKNOWLEDGMENT

This chapter is revised from a paper prepared for the Conference on Social Structure and the Psychological Aging Processes at the Gerontology Center, Pennsylvania State University, October 20–21, 1986. Research reported in this chapter was supported by the National Institute on Aging under Grant R01 AG04263.

REFERENCES

Adams, B. N. (1968). *Kinship in an urban setting*. Chicago: Markham.
Adams, B. N. (1970). "Isolation, function, and beyond: American kinship in the 1960s." *Journal of Marriage and the Family, 32*, 575–597.
Bengtson, V. L., & Dannefer, D. (1986, April). *Families, work and aging: Implications of disordered cohort flow for the 21st century*. Paper presented at the Conference on Health in Aging: Sociological Issues and Policy, Albany, NY.
Bengtson, V. L., Mangen, D. J., & Landry, P. H. (1984). The multi-generation family: Concepts and findings. In V. Garms-Homolova, E. M. Hoerning, & D. Schaeffer (Eds.), *Intergenerational relationships* (pp. 63–79). New York: C. J. Hogrefe.
Bengtson, V. L., & Robertson, J. F. (1985). *Grandparenthood*. Beverly Hills, CA: Sage.
Carey, M. L. (1981). Occupational employment growth through 1990. In U.S. Department of Labor, Bureau of Labor Statistics (Ed.), *Monthly Labor Review* (Vol. 104, No. 8). Washington, DC: Government Printing Office.
Cherlin, A. J., & Furstenberg, F. F. (1986). *The new american grandparent: A place in the family, a life apart*. New York: Basic Books.
Collins, R. (1986, September 1). *A micro-macro theory of creativity in intellectual careers*. Paper presented at the meeting of the American Sociological Association, New York.
Dannefer, D. (1984). Adult development and social theory. *American Sociological Review, 49*(1), 100–116.
Easterlin, R. (1980). *Birth and fortune*. New York: Basic Books.
Elder, G. H., Jr. (1974). *Children of the Great Depression*. Chicago: University of Chicago Press.
Elder, G. H., Jr. (1982). Historical experience in the later years. In T. K. Hareven (Ed.), *Patterns of aging* (pp. 75–107). New York: Guilford Press.
Elder, G. H., Jr., Liker, J. K., & Jaworski, B. J. (1984). Hard times in women's lives: Historical influences from the 1930s to old age in postwar America. In K. McCluskey & H. Reese

(Eds.), *Life-span developmental psychology: Historical and cohort effects*. New York: Academic Press.

Elder, G. H., Jr., & Rockwell, R. C. (1978). Economic depression and postwar opportunity: A study of life patterns and health. In R. A. Simmons (Ed.), *Research on community and mental health* (pp. 249–303). Greenwich, CT: JAI.

Featherman, D. L. (1983). The life-span perspective in social science research. In P. B. Baltes & O. G. Brim, Jr. (Eds.), *Life-span development and behavior* (Vol. 5, pp. 1–57). New York: Academic Press.

Featherman, D. L. (1986). Biography, society, and history: Individual development as a population process. In A. B. Sørensen, F. E. Weinert, & L. R. Sherrod (Eds.), *Human development and the life course: Multidisciplinary perspectives* (pp. 99–152). Hillsdale, NJ: Lawrence Erlbaum Associates.

Featherman, D. L., Hogan, D. P., & Sørensen, A. B. (1984). Entry into adulthood: Profiles of young men in the 1950s. In P. B. Baltes & O. G. Brim, Jr. (Eds.) *Life-span development and behavior* (Vol. 6, pp. 160–203). New York: Academic Press.

Featherman, D. L., & Lerner, R. M. (1985). Ontogenesis and sociogenesis. *American Sociological Review, 50*(5), 659–676.

Featherman, D. L., & Sørensen, A. B. (1983). Societal transformations in Norway and change in the life course transition to adulthood. *Acta Sociologica, 26*(2), 105–126.

Fogel, R. W., Hatfield, E., Kiesler, S. B., & Shanas, E. (Eds.) (1981). *Aging: Stability and Change in the Family*. New York: Academic Press.

Geertz, C. (1972). Deep play: Notes on the Balinese cockfight. *Daedalus, 101*, 1–37.

Hagestad, G. O. (1982a, Winter). Divorce: The family ripple effect. *Generations: The Journal of the Western Gerontological Society*, pp. 24–31.

Hagestad, G. O. (1982b). Parent and child: Generations in the family. In T. M. Field, A. Huston, H. C. Quay, L. Troll, & G. E. Finley (Eds.), *Review of human development* (pp. 485–499). New York: Wiley.

Hagestad, G. O. (1986). The family: Women and grandparents as kinkeepers. In A. Pifer & L. Bronte (Eds.), *The aging society* (pp. 141–160). New York: Norton.

Hagestad, G. O., & Smyer, M. A. (1982). Dissolving long-term relationships: Patterns of divorce in middle age. In S. Duck (Ed.), *Dissolving personal relationships* (pp. 155–187). London: Academic Press.

Hareven, T. K. (1981). Historical changes in the timing of family transitions. In R. W. Fogel, E. Hatfield, S. B. Kiesler, & E. Shanas (Eds.), *Aging: stability and change in the family* (pp. 143–165). New York: Academic Press.

Hareven, T. K. (1982). *Aging and life course transitions: An interdisciplinary perspective*. New York: Guilford.

Hareven, T. K. & Adams, K. J. (Eds.) (1982). *Aging and life course transitions: An interdisciplinary perspective*. New York: Guilford Press.

Hogan, D. P. (1980). The transition to adulthood as a career contingency. *American Sociological Review, 45*, 261–276.

Hogan, D. P. (1981). *Transitions and social change: The early lives of American men*. New York: Academic Press.

Kiesler, S. B., Morgan, J. N., & Oppenheimer, V. K. (Eds.). (1981). *Aging: Social change*. New York: Academic Press.

Jackson, J. S. (1979). *National survey of black Americans*. University of Michigan, Institute for Social Research, Ann Arbor.

Jackson, J. S., & Hatchett, S. J. (1986). Intergenerational research: methodological considerations. In N. Datan, A. L. Greene, & H. W. Reese (Eds.), *Life-span developmental psychology: Intergenerational relations* (pp. 51–76). Hillsdale, NJ: Lawrence Erlbaum Associates.

Kohn, M. L., & Schooler, C. (1983). *Work and personality: An inquiry into the impact of social stratification*. Norwood, NJ: Ablex.

Lerner, R. M. (1984). *On the nature of human plasticity*. New York: Cambridge University Press.

Liker, J. K., & Elder, G. H., Jr. (1983) Economic hardship and marital relations in the 1930s.

American Sociological Review, 48, 343–359.

Litwak, E. (1960a). Occupational mobility and extended family cohesion. *American Sociological Review, 25,* 9–21.

Litwak, E. (1960b). Geographical mobility and extended family cohesion. *American Sociological Review, 25,* 385–394.

Litwak, E. (1969). Primary group structures and their functions: Kin, neighbors, and friends. *American Sociological Review, 34,* 465–481.

McGaugh, J. L., & Kiesler, S. B. (Eds.). (1981). *Aging: Biology and behavior.* New York: Academic Press.

Mangen, D. J., Bengtson, V. L., & Landry, P. H., Jr. (1988) *Measurement of intergenerational relations.* Newbury Park, CA: Sage Publications.

Mangen, D. J., & Peterson, W. A. (Eds.). (1982). *Research instruments in social gerontology. Vol. 1: Clinical and social psychology.* Minneapolis: University of Minnesota Press.

Mangen, D. J., & Peterson, W. A. (Eds.). (1983). *Research instruments in social gerontology. Vol. 2: Social roles and social participation.* Minneapolis: University of Minnesota Press.

Mangen, D. J., & Peterson, W. A. (Eds.). (1984). *Research instruments in social gerontology. Vol. 3: Health, program evaluation, & demography.* Minneapolis: University of Minnesota Press.

Markides, K. S., Bolt, J. S., & Ray, L. A. (1986, July). Sources of helping and intergenerational solidarity: A three-generation study of Mexican-Americans. *Journal of Gerontology, 41,* 506–511.

Meyer, J. W. (1986). The self and the life course: Institutionalization and its effects. In A. Sørensen, F. Weinert, & L. Sherrod (Eds.), *Human development and the life course: Multidisciplinary perspectives* (pp. 199–216). Hillsdale, NJ: Lawrence Erlbaum Associates.

Modell, J. W., Furstenberg, F. F., & Hershberg, T. (1978). The timing of marriage in the transition to adulthood: Continuity and change. *American Journal of Sociology, 84,* 120–150.

Modell, J. W., & Hareven, T. K. (1978). Transitions: Patterns of timing. In T. K. Hareven (Ed.), *Transitions: The family and the life course in historical perspective* (pp. 245–270). New York: Academic Press.

Neugarten, B. L. (1985). Interpretive social science and research on aging. In A. S. Rossi (Ed.), *Gender and the life course* (pp. 291–300). New York: Aldine.

Oppenheimer, V. K. (1974). The life cycle squeeze: The interaction of men's occupational and family life cycles. *Demography, 11*(2), 227–245.

Oppenheimer, V. K. (1982). *Work and the family: A study in social demography.* New York: Academic Press.

Reiss, I. L. (1986). A sociological journey into sexuality. *Journal of Marriage and the Family, 48*(2), 233–242.

Shanas, E. (1980). Older people and their families: The new pioneers. *Journal of Marriage and the Family, 42*(1), 9–15.

Shanas, E., Townsend, P., Wedderburn, D., Friis, H., Milhoj, P. & Stehouwer, J. (1968). *Old people in three industrial societies.* New York & London: Atherton and Routledge Kegan Paul.

Sherrod, L. R., & Brim, O. G., Jr. (1986). Epilogue: Retrospective and prospective views of life-course research on human development. In A. B. Sørensen, F. E. Weinert, & L. R. Sherrod (Eds.), *Human development and the life course* (pp. 557–580). Hillsdale, NJ: Lawrence Erlbaum Associates.

Sørensen, A. B., Weinert, F. E., & Sherrod, L. R. (Eds.). (1986). *Human development and the life course: Multidisciplinary perspectives.* Hillsdale, NJ: Lawrence Erlbaum Associates.

Sussman, M. B., & Burchinal, L. (1962). Kin family network: Unheralded structure in current conceptualizations of family functioning. *Marriage and Family Living, 24,* 231–240.

Taylor, R. J. (1986). *The extended family as a source of support to elderly Blacks.* Unpublished paper, University of Michigan, Institute for Social Research, Ann Arbor.

Winsborough, H. H. (1979). Changes in the transition to adulthood. In M. W. Riley (Ed.), *Aging from birth to death: Interdisciplinary perspectives* (pp. 137–152). Boulder, CO: Westview Press.

Social Structure and Interpersonal Relations:
A Discussion of Alice Rossi's Chapter

James S. House
Department of Sociology and
Survey Research Center
University of Michigan

When I first read Alice Rossi's chapter, I was struck that she had artfully written what she wanted to write but may have bypassed some issues with which the organizers had hoped she would deal under the topic of social structure and interpersonal relations. As I thought about and sketched out my remarks, I was worried that what I had to say was even more loosely connected to her chapter than it was to her topic. After listening to yesterday's discussions I decided, however, that we had both stuck relatively closely to our assigned tasks and need not apologize unduly for our transgressions.

We are all indebted to Alice Rossi for an enjoyable and stimulating chapter that, if I do not spoil things, provides a marvelous, upbeat ending for this book on aging. I am personally indebted to her for writing a chapter that allows me to follow almost perfectly the prescription that Tim Salthouse gave us yesterday for the role of discussant: I can find much to praise, some things to qualify, a way to talk about my own current research interests, and a basis for ending on an optimistic note.

Specifically, I wish to do three things. First, stimulated by the beginning of Alice Rossi's chapter, I offer some praise and some qualification of her comments on current theoretical and methodological trends in life-course research. Second, I similarly praise and qualify what she tells us about her current research. Finally, I make some comments on aspects of the topic that Alice Rossi was assigned — social structure and interpersonal relations — but addressed only partially.

THEORY AND METHODS
IN LIFE-COURSE RESEARCH

My initial impression of the first section of Alice Rossi's chapter was that it was somewhat peevish. This may have stemmed in part from her choice of the Panel Study of Income Dynamics (PSID) as an example in her critique of life-course research. To question the value of the PSID in the parts I come from is akin to debunking mother and apple pie. However, after reflecting on her comments and doing a little of what she had done — reading recent literature on life-course sociology and life span psychology and their intersections — I became quite sympathetic to her comments and concerns.

Many problems she identifies in current approaches to the study of the life course — excessive and sometimes premature preoccupation with formalistic theory, with disciplinary concerns and orientations, and with secondary analysis of large and often longitudinal public-use samples via complex multivariate statistical methods — are manifestations of more general problems in sociology, psychology, and the social sciences, which contribute to the malaise some currently perceive in these fields as well as in life-span and life-course research (e.g., Collins, 1986). Too often our research agenda is determined by predispositions to defend or extend disciplinary turf, to be prematurely advanced in theory, to be methodologically au courant, or to use large extant data bases, rather than by a concern to describe, understand, explain, and predict fundamentally important and problematic social or psychological phenomena.

As a social psychologist, many of the concerns that Alice Rossi advocates seem natural and appropriate to me. The human or social sciences must ultimately be grounded in the study of the life and lives of *individual* human beings as they are affected by, and affect, both macrosocial and microbiological structures and processes. This is especially true of the study of aging and human development. It is a biopsychosocial phenomenon that must inherently be studied from an interdisciplinary, not just multidisciplinary, perspective. And by focusing these diverse disciplines on a common problem or phenomenon, the study of aging and human development has the potential to help the social sciences transcend some of their current malaise and problems.

In such work, we must avoid being excessively guided and indeed blinded by any particular concept or method. The description and analysis of cohorts, Rossi suggests, is central to study of the life course but may have become excessively so. Too often documentation of a "cohort effect" is seen as the end of life-course analysis rather than just its beginning. As Rossi argues, our task is not simply to document or describe cohort differences but to explain them or even to explain them away.

Cohort effects are one type of contextual effects, and the analysis of cohort effects is subject to all the caveats we associate with analyses of context effects. Before attributing effects to cohorts, we need to be sure that the observed data are not explained solely by the composition of cohorts. Before we attribute a cohort effect to a particular cohort attribute, such as size, we need to rule out effects of other "contextual variables." Under such rigorous scrutiny, even very intriguing and plausible propositions about cohort effects, such as much of Easterlin's (1980) theory about the effects of cohort size, often fail to be confirmed.

Similarly, before we say we have a cohort effect, such as Elder (1974) proposed regarding the Great Depression, we need to clarify whether the effects of growing up in the Depression, which Elder has artfully elucidated, are simply effects of parental income and job loss on children that occur in all places and times, or are they special effects of the experience of parental income and job loss in the Depression. In all cases, our goal is not to do cohort analysis or show cohort effects but to understand variations in human lives with age and the passage of time.

On the side of methods and data, too, the key is to have our methods and data dictated by substantive concerns rather than vice versa. Archival data are not inherently to be preferred to new data, nor longitudinal to cross-sectional data, nor LISREL and event history analysis to simpler methods. It depends on what we know and what we want to learn at any given point. All this said, and it repeatedly needs to be said, Rossi's comments ought not lead us to throw the baby out with the bath water. That is, we must also remember that much of the ultimate understanding we seek to achieve about the phenomena of aging and human development simply cannot be achieved without sophisticated longitudinal and multivariate analyses. This perhaps can best be illustrated with reference to some issues Rossi addresses in her presentation of her own research.

ROSSI'S THREE-GENERATIONAL STUDY

Rossi's exciting and innovative Boston three-generational study overcomes many problems she insightfully identifies in existing three-generational research. The interpersonal relationship issues she wishes to address clearly could not be addressed with existing national longitudinal data sets (e.g., CPS, NLS, PSID) that focus on economic and demographic matters. Thus, her study is a clear example of why and how we continue to need ingenious new research designs and data collections.

Rossi shows how such cross-sectional data can be used creatively to address issues of aging and historical change. Still many inferences she wishes to draw remain uncertain and problematic in the absence of longitudinal data. Specifically, she seeks to attribute observed variations in both parents' and childrens' reports of the turbulence of adolescence to cohort differences in the historical period or context in which individuals passed through adolescence. Clearly, the differences she observes cannot be attributed simply to age or aging. It is less clear to me, however, that they may not be attributable, at least in part, to changes in the perception of past events with time regardless of age. That is, we may simply choose not to, or be less able to, recall negative rather than positive aspects of the past as time goes on. Thus, in her Table 6.3, negative reports about family of origin decline monotonically with age (or time since adolescence), as do reports for the family of procreation once parents are beyond childrearing ages (i.e., 51 and up). Parents in their 20s and 30s have usually not yet fully experienced the trials and tribulations of adolescent children.

In summary, it is not that I find her explanation implausible or even less plausible than a time-decay explanation. Indeed I hope her explanation is right. It is simply that we cannot definitively choose between these explanations in the absence of longitudinal data that allow us to see whether individuals' perceptions of adolescence change over time as they age, or rather vary by cohort but once established remain constant as cohorts age.

Rossi's fascinating data on changing perceptions of the quality of life (or what were the best years of life) *with age* are, as she indicates, subject to a wide range of interpretations. Are these aging effects, cohort effects, or effects of selective mortality? Or again does the past simply look better as we get further from it? Such questions can only in the end be answered with longitudinal data. How much do a variety of factors—such as gender, marital stress, health—account for these changes. These questions are answerable with more complex multivariate statistical techniques. Rossi cannot do longitudinal analysis, but she can do complex multivariate analysis and begins to do so. By separating her sample by sex and age for these analyses, however, she fails to do the analyses necessary to explain the fascinating age and sex interaction she has discovered.

Rossi's data on her Boston sample's perceptions of the best years of life and their desired and subjective ages are also made more interesting and problematic when put in the context of national sample data, which used somewhat different measures and showed life and job satisfaction curvilinearly related to age—with the peaks in later middle age—and psychological distress highest among younger people (Campbell, 1981; Veroff, Douvan, & Kulka, 1981). Perhaps it is as Will Rogers once said: "Things aren't as good as they used to be, and they never were." Youth often looks like the prime of life, except when you're in the midst of it.

In summary, I would argue that Alice Rossi's study shows the need for and utility of both descriptive analysis of carefully designed, focused, cross-sectional studies, and complex multivariate analysis of national sample longitudinal studies. The greatest gains will come from the appropriate use of each in conjunction with the other.

SOCIAL STRUCTURE AND INTERPERSONAL RELATIONS

Let me close with a few comments on Alice Rossi's assigned topic of social structure and interpersonal relations. Her chapter is relevant to the topic in important ways but also ranges rather far afield from it. I feel a need to refocus our attention on the problem of social structure and interpersonal relations, not only because Tim Salthouse informed me that a good discussant should talk about his or her or her own area of research interest but also because interpersonal relations have been shown to be significant determinants of both quality and quantity or longevity of human life.

As you all are probably aware, the study of social relationships, especially in relation to health, has become something of a growth industry in the last decade. Whether termed social integration, social networks, or most commonly social support, a higher quantity and/or quality of social relationships have been shown to reduce morbidity and mortality, lessen exposure to psychosocial stress and other health hazards, and buffer the impact of stress on health. Although the results of individual studies are open to alternative interpretations, the patterns of results are remarkably consistent from diverse types of studies: laboratory experimental studies of animals as well as humans, cross-sectional and retrospective field studies of human populations, and a growing number of longitudinal or prospective field studies as well (e.g., House, 1981, 1986).

Although considerable effort has been devoted to studying social integration, networks, and supports as *independent, intervening*, and *moderating* variables that may affect social stress or health or the relation between stress and health, almost no attention has been paid to social relationships, networks, and supports as *dependent* variables. That is, in our haste to document their health consequences, we have neglected to analyze the causes or determinants of social relationships, networks, and supports. This omission is a source of practical as well as scientific concern. If we wish to modify or enhance the levels and types of social integration, networks, and supports in any population as a means of increasing quality or quantity of life, we must understand the forces that determine such social relationships. These forces must be both social and psychological in origins, but in my view the highest priority is to understand the social structural determinants of social relationships, networks, and supports because these have been most neglected, even though they offer very powerful potential avenues for modifying the quantity and quality of social relationships, networks, and supports in our society.

Existing evidence is very limited on this issue, because most studies of the association of interpersonal relations with stress and/or health have been done in samples that are small and often limited to a particular organization, community, or population of persons experiencing a particular stress or health problem. Variation in the social structural positions of people is very limited in these samples. What evidence we have (cf. House, 1987) suggests that people are disadvantaged in terms of social relationships, networks, or supports if they are absolutely or relatively low in socioeconomic status or power; living in more urban areas; isolated from forming relationships by forces such as widowhood, divorce, or simply aging; or in contact with men more than women (which Rossi's data on the closeness of mothers to both sons and daughters and later of daughters to fathers and mothers once again confirms).

A concern with the social structural determinants of the quality and quantity of relationships, especially with the kin relationships and parent–child relationships on which Alice Rossi's work is focusing, seems especially appropriate at this time both for the general population and particularly for the elderly population. Evidence from surveys of mental health in Americans in 1957 and 1976, performed by my colleagues Gurin, Veroff, Douvan, Feld, and Kulka at the University of Michigan Institute for Social Research, indicate that the *prevalence* of significant informal social relationships, networks, and supports has been declining over the last quarter century while the tendency of people to call on informal sources of support in dealing with personal problems has increased. In the 1970s, American adults were less likely to be married, more likely to be childless, more likely to be living alone, less likely to belong to voluntary organizations, and less likely to visit informally with others compared to adults in the 1950s. Yet people were much more likely in the 1970s than in the 1950s to report talking to nonprofessionals in an effort to deal with problems and crises (Veroff et al., 1981).

Alice Rossi, Dave Featherman, and others have noted that as we move into the 21st century our elderly population will be growing; however older individuals will be increasingly without either spouse or children, who are the major sources of support for most people in dealing with problems of old age. Again the demand for social relationships, networks, and supports appears to be increasing as the supply is dwindling. If we are to counteract this growing discrepancy between the need for and the availability of social relationships and supports in an aging society, we need to understand much better than we do now the social structural and psychological determinants of the quantity and quality of social relationships and supports people experience over the life course.

REFERENCES

Campbell, A. (1981). *Sense of well-being in America: Recent patterns and trends.* New York: McGraw-Hill.

Collins, R. (1986). Is 1980s sociology in the doldrums? *American Journal of Sociology, 91,* 1336–1355.

Easterlin, R. A. (1980). *Birth and fortune: The impact of numbers on personal welfare.* New York: Basic Books.

Elder, G. H., Jr. (1974). *Children of the Great Depression.* Chicago: University of Chicago Press.

House, J. S. (1981). *Work stress and social support.* Reading, MA: Addison-Wesley.

House, J. S. (1986). Social support, and the quality and quantity of life. In F. M. Andrews (Ed.), *Research on the quality of life* (pp. 254–269). Ann Arbor: University of Michigan, Institute for Social Research Monograph Series.

House, J. S. (1987). Structures and sentiments of social support. *Sociological Forum, 2*(1), 135–146.

Veroff, J., Douvan E., & Kulka, R. A. (1981). *The inner American: A self-portrait from 1957 to 1976.* New York: Basic Books.

Afterword

Carmi Schooler
National Institute of Mental Health

In her introductory remarks, Matilda Riley puts forward two challenges to those writing about the relationship between psychological aging processes and social structures. The first is to forego the realm of abstract and general statements and to get down to particulars by specifying the actual connections that exist between these psychological and sociological realms. The second is to recognize that the relationship between psychological aging and social structure is one of dialectical interdependence in which each is both a cause and a consequence of the other. In reviewing the contents of this volume, I believe that we authors have generally met her challenge. Each chapter delineates specific empirical linkages between social structure and psychological aging. Many examine how social structural conditions affect the nature of psychological aging. Some even show how different demographic and psychological patterns of aging may affect social structures.

Despite these real accomplishments, my rereading of the chapters revealed another equally profound dialectic—one between the authors and their discussants. Each chapter is subjected to trenchant and challenging criticism. This has not happened because the authors of the chapters are particularly dense or the discussants unusually acute. Rather, I believe that the sharpness of the criticism reflects the state of the field. Although we know enough about the interconnection of social structures and psychological aging to come to specific empirical and theoretical conclusions, we do now know enough to make it possible to do so without leaving ourselves open to serious questions about both the exact nature of the facts and their scientific and practical implications.

The limitations of any single author's knowledge or perspective should not be surprising given the large number of disciplines, facts, and

245

paradigms that seem to be relevant to an examination of the intercon-
nections of social structure and psychological aging. Thus, Aitchely takes
a demographic approach. He explores how various demographic trends
may alter the social system in ways that may affect psychological aging
and concludes that "the size, composition, and distribution of the population are important dimensions of the sociocultural context within which
adult development takes place." Although generally accepting the tenor
of this conclusion and many of his more specific points, Myers and Featherman, both of his discussants, have reservations about some of his "sweeping generalizations." Featherman, like several other discussants, presents
an alternate approach to the problems of the chapter he is reviewing. He
uses a "developmentalist population–person" paradigm based on three
key ideas: (a) individuals' behaviors affect not only their own development
but also that of others; (b) individuals do not just passively accept structural constraints but affect their own and others' destinies; and (c) behaviors that are comparatively adaptive at one life stage may not be so later.

   Willis' chapter centers on the questions that life-span psychologists have
raised about the nature of cohort differences. She provides evidence that
cohort effects vary for different mental abilities and that the characterization of cohort-related change involving a positive linear trend is much
too simplistic. In his critique, Salthouse uses the findings of Willis' own
cognitive training research to shed light on the mechanisms underlying
cohort and other social-environmental effects on cognition at various life
stages.

   In his comments on the Willis chapter, Glaser argues that studies of
age and cohort differences in cognitive competence "must accord equal
importance to knowledge as a generating source of cognitive processes
as had been previously accorded to the 'pure processes' of memory, induction, spatial visualization, and so forth." Based on this belief, he sketches
a set of dimensions of knowledge-derived competence. He sees the study
of such dimensions as a necessary complement to the psychometrically
based studies of aging and cohort patterns described by Willis.

   Lawton, taking a general ecological approach, provides a model of how
the older person's functioning is maintained at optimal levels by particular uses of the environmental context. He concludes that, although both
environmental docility and environmental proactivity (the individual's active attempt to change the environment) may lead to psychological well-
being and enhanced competence, only proactivity shapes the environment.
Thus, when proactivity is exercised in a range that maintains at least a
minimal level of congruence between person and environment, it
represents a unique pathway toward growth. In critiquing this view, Weiss
raises a series of questions reflecting an evolutionary genetic approach,
whereas Bronfenbrenner's comments reflect a social ecological one.

   In my own chapter, I try to indicate some lessons that social and cognitive science might learn from each other, particularly those that would be useful for understanding the relationship between social structure and cognitive functioning over the life course. In doing so, I focus on problems connected to two senses of the term *generalization*. One problem is how questions of sampling affect the legitimacy of the scientific generalization of the results of cognitive experiments. The second is the neglected importance for social theorists of the mechanisms underlying the psychological generalizations that individuals make in "carrying the lessons" of one situation to another. Both problems lead to questions of how environmental factors determined by social structure, particularly those related to environmental complexity, affect the individual's cognitive functioning. In his critique, Abeles shows the relevance of a large body of theoretical and empirical work that I had neglected to take into consideration — Berlyne's on the positive reinforcing qualities of environmental stimulation.

Keating's critique of my chapter implies that, if anything, I understate the importance of cognitive socialization. He presents a "poststructuralist" theoretical and research agenda and sees it as following from the many findings indicating "that cognitive structures are neither given nor unfolding but are inherently inseparable from the physical and social system in which the organism develops." Agreeing that the nature of generalization is one key issue in the study of cognitive functioning, he also provides a different and challenging tripartite categorization of types of generalization: largely algorithmic generalization involving some form of automaticity that occurs within a well-identified knowledge base; generalization through the use of analogy; generalization across previously different knowledge systems through the search for and discovery of common principles.

Lachman, in examining the antecedents and consequences of stable and changing personalities during the aging process, generally takes the perspective of personality psychology. Her central message is that in examining the relationship between social structure and personality, "it is necessary to consider both the objective aspects of the social structure and the person's subjective interpretations in tandem."

Her discussants raise quite opposite objections. Basing her comments on the object relations theory of psychoanalytic self-psychology, Whitbourne maintains that when in early childhood "the core identity is formed, it becomes an underpinning of the individual's personality that is relatively impermeable to social structure or to any other experiences." Kohn begins his critique by noting that most studies seriously understate the stability of personality because they do not take into account correlated errors in repeated measurement of the same dimensions of personality. However, in contrast to both Lachman and Whitbourne, he argues that "social structure can explain not only change but also stability or maintainance of personality." It is in part because job conditions, which tend to be stable, affect many facets of personality that personality is stable. He also disagrees with Lachman in that he views social structure as mattering for personality primarily because it directly affects the proximate conditions of life. People learn from their experiences and generalize the lessons learned in one realm of life to others. Kohn maintains that it is through such learning processes, rather than through subjective reactions or face to face interactions, that social structure has its effects.

In the last chapter, Rossi describes a series of interesting results coming from her three-generational study of gender, aging, and intergenerational relations. In examing how historical circumstances, on the one hand, and gender on the other, affect intergenerational closeness and strain, she finds, among other things, that "rearing adolescents in the 'troubling' 1960s and 1970s created problems in families of a different order than did rearing adolescents in the 'calmer' era of the 1950s." She also provides compelling evidence that in predicting the closeness between parents and children "in childhood and adolescence it is the gender of the parent that matters, while in adulthood it is the gender of the child that matters: Mothers are closer to young sons and daughters than fathers are, while in adulthood, parents are closer to daughters than to sons." Rossi believes her results validate the use of carefully crafted cross-sectional surveys rather than existing national data sets or "tag ons" to longitudinal studies conducted for other purposes. In commenting on Rossi's chapter, House notes that although Rossi's work demonstrates the usefulness of descriptive analyses of carefully designed and focused cross-sectional studies, many questions raised by her data can, in fact, only be answered by complex multivariate analyses of national sample longitudinal studies of the type she decries.

Such a brief review of the points made by the authors and their discussants perforce leaves out much of merit and much worth disputing on each side. Each reader will, of course, come to somewhat different conclusions about who is right about what points. What is clear is that we do know something about the nature of the relationship between social structure and the psychological aging process, but not enough to stop reasonably informed people from disagreeing. The true worth of this book will be in the fertility of the synthesis of the ongoing dialectic between author and discussant reached in the minds of its readers — particularly in the minds of those who turn their insights into research that helps us understand the relationship between social structure and psychological functioning in human lives.

Author Index

Numbers in *italic* indicate complete
bibliographical information

A

Abeles, R.P., 95, *111*, 149–153, *153*, 247
Abramson, L. Y., 183, *186*
Adams, B. N., 215, *234*
Adams, K. J., 212, *235*
Alderton, D. L., 132, *146*
Allport, G., 169
Anastasi, A., 168, *186*
Anderson, J. R., 136–139, 143, *145*
Apatow, K., 179, *188*
Arenberg, D., 193, *198*
Atchley, R.C., 11–32, *32*, 35–39, 41, 42, 44, 45, 49, 53, *54*, 246
Antonucci, T. C., 51, *54*

B

Bachevalier, J., 136, *146*
Baltes, M. M., 51, *54*, 74, *76*, 178, *186*
Baltes, P. B., 3, *9*, 43, *54*, 95, 107, *11*, 175, *186*
Bandura, A., 48, *54*, 60, *76*, 169, 182, *186*
Barker, R. G., 62, *76*
Barr, R. A., 139, *145*
Barter, J., 73, 77
Barton, E. M., 74, *76*, 178, 182, *186*
Beck, P., 74, 77
Bengtson, V. L., 171, 172, *186*, 212–214, 217, *234, 236*
Berg, C., 103, *111*

Berlyne, D. E., 71, *76*, 152, *153*, 247
Berry, J. W., 143, *145*
Blank, T. O., 184, *186*
Block, J., 169, *186*
Bloom, D. F., 21, *33*
Blumstein, P., 49, *54*
Bollas, C., 194, *198*
Bolt, J. S., 217, *236*
Bowers, K. S., 167, *186*
Bradburn, N., 73, *76*
Bransford, J. D., 116, *120*
Brim, O. G., Jr., 181, *186*, 209, *236*
Broca, P., 143, *145*
Bronfenbrenner, U., 3, *9*, 85–92, *92, 93*, 160, *164*, 246
Brown, A. L., 116, 117, *120*
Brownbridge, G., 73, 77
Bryan, W. L., 133, *145*
Buehler, C., 171
Burchinal, L., 215, *236*
Butler, R., 171, *186*
Bultena, G. L., 17, *33*, 74, *76*
Bumpass, L. L., 47, 53, *54*
Busch-Rossnagel, N. A., 46, *55*

C

Cain, M., 52, *54*
Campbell, A., 58, *76*, 240, *243*
Campione, J. C., 116, *120*
Caplan, L. J., 139, 145

L

Lachman, M. E., 167–186, *187*, 191, 192, 194,
        197, 199, 200, 202, 247, 248
Lago, D., 74, *76*
Lair, T. J., 8, *9*
Lamb, M. E., 194, *198*
Landry, P. H., Jr., 217, *236*
Langer, E. J., 51, *55*, 75, *76*, 77, 180, *187*
Lanius, U. F., 58, 77
Larkin, J. H., 133, *146*
Lawton, M. P., 57–76, 77, 80, 84–92, 246
Lerner, R. M., 42, 45, 46, 52, *55*, 209, 212, *235*
Lesthaeghe, R., 48, *55*
LeVine, R. A., 176, *187*
Levinson, D. J., 174, 176, *187*
Lieberman, M. A., 65, 77
Liker, J. K., 211, *234*, *235*
Lipsitt, L. P., 175, *186*
Litwak, E., 215, *236*
Livson, F., 73, 77, 170, *188*
Lohman, D. F., 134, *146*
Longino, C. F., Jr., 17, *33*, 74, 77
Looft, W. R., 171, *187*
Lorence, J., 177, *188*
Luria, A. R., 143, *146*, *147*
Lynch, K., 58, 77

M

Maas, H. S., 170, *188*
MacLean, D. J., 156, 159, 161, *165*
Madsen, K. B., 71, *76*
Magnusson, D., 167, *188*
Malamut, B., 136, *146*
Mangen, D. J., 216, 217, *236*
Manis, F. R., 162, *165*
Mann, C. H., 195, *198*
Mannheim, K., 45, *55*, 129, *146*
Manton, K. G., 28, *33*
Markides, K. S., 217, *236*
Markman, E. M., 116, *120*
Markus, H., 194, 195, *198*
Martin, J. B., 167, *188*
Marx, K., 129, *146*
Marshall, V. W., 51, *55*
Maslow, A., 169
Matarazzo, R. G., 169, *188*
Mauss, M., 140, *145*
May, R., 169

McArthur, L., 184, *187*
McArthur, L. Z., 179, *188*
McClelland, J. L., 137, *146*
McClelland, K. A., 74, 77
McCrae, R. R., 73, *76*, 172, *186*, 193, *198*
McDermott, J., 133, *146*
McGaugh, J. L., 209, *235*
McGuinness, D., 70, 71, 77
McLanahan, S. S., 47, 50, *55*
Means, B., 161, *164*
Merleau-Ponty, M., 157, *165*
Merton, R., 129, 140, *146*
Meyer, J. W., 208, *236*
Milhoj, P., 216, *236*
Miller, J., 204, *205*
Miller, K., 162, *165*
Miller, K. A., 130, 140, *146*
Miller, K. F., 134, *147*
Miller, S. J., 21, *32*
Mischel, W., 167, 169, 178, *188*
Mishkin, M., 136, *146*
Modell, J. W., 212, *236*
Morgan, J. N., 209, *235*
Morrison, F. J., 162, *165*
Mortimer, J. T., 177, *188*
Moss, H. A., 170, *187*, 192, *198*
Mott, P. E., 12, 15, *33*
Mueller, W., 151, *153*
Murray, H., 60, 63, 77, 173, 175, 179, *187*, 202,
        205
Myers, G., 28, *33*, 35–39, 246

N

Nahemow, L., 63, 67, 68, 77
Neisser, U., 70, 71, 77, 157, 160, *165*
Nesselroade, J. R., 3, 6, *9*, 95, *111*, 159, *164*
Neugarten, B. L., 19, 20, *33*, 73, 77, 150, *153*,
        170–172, *188*, 211, 217, *236*
Newell, A., 116, *120*
Nisbett, R. E., 133–135, 139, *145*, *146*
Norman, D. A., 143, *146*

O

Oliver, L. M., 133, *145*
Olshansky, S. J., 28, *33*
Olson, D. R., 161, *165*

Subject Index

A

Aborigines, 143

Acquisition and maintenance of cognitive ability, the role of social indicators, 107–109

Activation, 70

Activities of daily living, competence and, 59–60

Activity theory, 170–171

Adaptation level, 67

Adaptive goals,
of the aging individual, 81–82
of the population, 82–83

Adaptive reciprocal activity, developmental trajectories and, 89

Adaptiveness of humans, 80–83

Adding generations to the family, 31–31

Adolescent turbulence, 223–224, 239–240

Adult children and aging, 51–52

Adult children, influence on elderly parents, 90

Adult development as evolution, 12

Adult development of the baby boomers, 28–29

Adult development perspective, 12

Adult development,
changes in the American population, 47–50
demographic influences on, 11–13

expansionist viewpoint, 43–45
population analysis, 45–46
population process and, 47–50
social structures and, 2
societal transformations and, 47–50

Adult education, 14

Adult intellectual development, 3–7

Adult personality development, psychoanalytic theory, 193–194

Adult psychological development, demographics and, 35

Adulthood,
changes in the American population, 47–50
stability and change in personality, 169–170

Affective closeness, gender and age differences, 224

Affective self-regulation, 60–61, 72

Age
as a component of social structure, 150–151
at birth of first child, cohort changes in, 6–7
at marriage, cohort changes in, 6–7

Age differences
in attributions, 184–185
in control beliefs, 182

Age discrimination in employment, poverty in old age, 26